MW01051720

"Dr. LaMar minces no word. ~~ ~~~~~ ~~~~~ ~~~ ~~~~~ ~~~~~~ of many intimate family situations. This account of transcenders who rise above the disparity of the human predicament of unthinkable beginnings is important reading. It is a book highly worthy of personal study and will make an excellent textbook for group and class discussion."

Reverend Doctor William D. Mercer,
United Methodist Church Minister

"This timely and important book addresses the impact of poverty and/or the lack of family support for the growing and developing individual. The author presents, through clear and detailed examples, the fact that some individuals, herein called 'transcenders,' have (in spite of the distressing and destructive pressures put upon them) managed to actualize their potential and experience a meaningful, successful life."

Cereta Perry, PhD, Professor Emeritus, Humanistic Psychology,
Center for Humanistic Studies, Detroit, MI

"The author shares years of research and clinical experience in her investigation of persons who have successfully emerged from dysfunctional families. Through personally told stories, Dr. LaMar outlines complicated and painful journeys undertaken by 'transcenders.' Persons in mental health professions or self-help groups will find this book a valuable resource."

Jacqueline K. Wilson, MSW, ACSW, Community Services Director,
Training and Treatment Innovations, Inc.

"In her comprehensive and highly readable book, Donna LaMar leads us from the dark beginnings of transcenders, through their self-realizations, and onto their courageous journeys to healthy adulthoods. Illustrated with vivid, often painful, and finally rewarding accounts from a multitude of transcenders interviewed in the author's thirty years of research, her book tackles an enormously difficult and elevating subject: the victims of abuse who exceed their difficult origins to forge stable lives. It is a book of horrific beginnings and astonishing happy endings, framed in a cogent and thoughtful academic exposition. It is highly likely that people who never thought of themselves as transcenders will find themselves in the pages of this book. Readers will find blessed relief from the morass of psychological books on problems with no ending and barest direction for meek survival—the subjects of this book are companions. Indeed, LaMar's book is more than a text on a psychological phenomenon—it is a celebration of lives that, but for sheer strength and courage of the individuals, could have been destroyed.

Lynn VanDine Howard, Freelance Writer

"Dr. LaMar presents the transcender topic in easy reading and powerful words. I am a counselor in a school and can use the techniques and interventions given by transcenders with my students. I learned a great deal, and my students as well as myself will benefit from the information. Surprisingly I found myself among the transcenders and felt for the first time not alone in my struggle to be."

A School Counselor and Fellow Transcender

"This book is a comprehensive approach to a difficult problem—how do you heal and grow after being abused and neglected? Dr. LaMar's book covers the subject thoroughly and gives many techniques shared by transcenders that are life lines. It is one of the most helpful books I have read in a long time."

A Substance Abuse Counselor

"Donna LaMar presents this book in a way that everyone can benefit from. The book is informative, and Donna is compassionate as well as passionate about the subject area. She is amazingly insightful, knowledgeable, and combines her intellect as well as her intuition. I have taken another step in my own growth and have learned at a deeper level what it means to help another person get through their emotional pain."

A Registered Nurse and Fellow Transcender

"This is a masterful grasp of this complex topic. Dr. LaMar presents a genuine, accessible, honest approach which works to touch the inner place of one's self and soul. She has incredible experience, and I found the information presented not only helpful, but hopeful. If Marie Did It, So Can I! is extremely helpful and useful. It addresses issues that are relevant for today's society and circumstances. Depression is on the rise in all socio-economic levels and walks of life. What a great opportunity for healing and growing."

A Social Worker

"This book is very enlightening and helpful and can be used in everyday living. It contains educational, insightful, tangible techniques which are very authentic and usable. The author's passion and understanding of the subject has brought to life a very important topic which is presented in a very realistic way. The book contains outstanding handling of a complex insightful subject. I will apply the information immediately."

A Youth Worker

IF MARIE DID IT, SO CAN I!

HOW TO SURVIVE, HEAL AND TRANSCEND ABUSE AND NEGLECT

Donna F. LaMar, PhD

SECOND EDITION
REVISED

LIVING FARM PRESS

DONNA LAMAR'S–IF MARIE DID IT, SO CAN I!
*HOW TO SURVIVE, HEAL AND TRANSCEND ABUSE
AND NEGLECT*

Living Farm Press
623 E. Main St.
Fremont, Michigan 49412 USA
books@livingfarm.org

Edition ISBNs
Hardcover (*Transcending Turmoil*) 978-0-306-44127-1

Softcover
First edition 1992. Second revised edition 2009

Library of Congress Cataloging-in-Publication Data

Transcending Turmoil: survivors of dysfunctional families
    Donna F. LaMar.

p. cm "Insight Books." Includes bibliographical references and index.

    ISBN 978-0-306-44127-1

    1. Adult children of dysfunctional families.   2. Adjustment
(Psychology)   3. Problem families.   I. Title [DNLM:
1. Adaptation, Psychological. 2. Child of Impaired Parents-
psychology.   3. Family-psychology. BF 335
L215t]RC455.4.F3L35 1922 158'.1–dc20 DNLM/DLC
For Library of Congress   92-3216
                                                              CIP

DEDICATION

To all transcenders—
For their courage to be

About the picture on the cover

On the spine of this book are Donna and one of The Farm's St. Bernards, Luke. Luke loves people and would rather be with them than have special treats. Luke, as well as two previous Saints—Heidi and Pluto—work to help people heal and grow. He has been known to sit on people's laps (can you imagine a hundred and fifty pound dog sitting on you?!) He started out working as a therapy dog at the age of six weeks. He especially loves when buses drive up to spend the day at The Farm. He can't greet and love everyone fast enough! Pluto (2nd) has just joined The Farm and is learning from Luke how to be a therapy dog. Pluto came to us from St. Bernard Rescue.

Luke helps to oversee The Farm's sampling of farm animals. The Farm is committed to "Heritage animals," which are our American farm animals that helped settle the United States and now are in danger of becoming extinct. Our sampling of Heritage animals includes a Miniature donkey, Dexter steer, Cayuga ducks, Rhode Island Red chickens, and Jacob sheep. Luke also patrols the woods to keep our animals safe. For more information, look up Heritage animals in resources such as the *American Livestock Breed Conservancy.*

Preface to the Revised Edition

Marie survived and overcame horrific abuse and neglect. I often have wondered how she even stayed alive. While growing up, she decided to be different than her family both as a child and as an adult. Her healthier life didn't just happen; she worked hard. Marie teaches us that through determination and hard work we can survive, transcend and heal from severe trauma. Marie, because of her past and integrity, became a licensed psychologist to make a difference in other victims' lives. All of us who come from an abusive childhood can make a difference in ourselves, others and the world by doing what Marie did.

As the world's problems continue, it is becoming more evident we "regular, grassroots people" have to do something positive to change it and make a difference like Marie has. I strongly believe that each one of us can create a better world by healing and growing from traumas we have experienced in our lives. If I heal, I gain insight, wisdom, and understanding that affect not only me but also have the potential to create ripples of healing and growing that go into the world. If I heal, my ripples go out and can touch you; your ripples then go out and touch others. My ripples join yours, which join others, and so forth. Eventually the world is covered in healing, growth, integrity, and love ripples. Eventually the world begins to change because enough people have done their healing work and are sending out healthy ripples instead of anger, hurt, vengeance, and dysfunction. We are then adding to the world in a healthy, integrated way where all people are valued. In this way, we can each help our hurting world. If each person makes the decision to heal and grow, can you imagine what the world might be like?! I believe it would change for the better. I also believe healing for our world will come not from governments or politicians but from us, regular, grassroots people who care enough to make a difference. Each one of us can make a difference one life at a time!

If Marie Did It, So Can I! is a revised edition of *Transcending Turmoil,* published in 1992. In the years between the first edition and this revision, I have found the material to be constant and true. There continue to be many individuals who not only survive but overcome trauma in our world today. These are transcenders who have worked hard to overcome and go beyond the dysfunction of their original families. I have continued to interview more transcenders since the first book was published and have added their information to this book. In addition, I have revised chapter five so that it is easier to understand. Philosophical groundings do not have to be as challenging as they were in the first edition.

It is my ultimate hope and prayer that the information in this book will help people to heal and grow from traumas, realize what an incredible feat they have accomplished, feel less separate, and teach that each one of us can help this world one life at a time. This book can also be a help for those professionals who work with survivors to help them rise above their dysfunctional patterns. We are all in this life together, and together we can change the world one life at a time!

I would like to hear from you how the information shared by transcenders has helped you or those you work with. I welcome comments and questions. Please contact me through our Website at www.livingfarm.org or by calling (231) 924-2401. You can also email me at donna@ livingfarm.org.

Donna LaMar

Foreword

From a Therapist

During my many years as a therapist, I have been privileged to be trusted by my clients who have shared their stories with me. Many of these people who have sought out therapy seem to be successful, highly functioning individuals leading happy, fulfilling lives. Inwardly, they are suffering, often silently, with feelings of anxiety, depression, and confusion. Additionally, they have thoughts of worthlessness, loneliness, and insecurity, and they don't understand why. They also do not take credit for all they have achieved. Instead, they attribute their accomplishments to circumstances, chance, or something else outside themselves—anything but their own will, persistence, and intuition. They discount themselves, minimizing their ability to survive in a world where it seems everything was against them. Nothing was easy about their lives while they were growing up.

Time and time again I have been impressed and awed by the strength and undying spirit of my clients. I have often wondered aloud: 'How did you do it? How did you not only survive but thrive in spite of your history? What was the secret spark that stayed alive and caused you not to give up or give in and allowed you to overcome poverty, abuse, and neglect? How did you maintain your independence and honesty, your sensitivity, and your ability to give and receive love?'

The answers usually start with 'I don't know.' After we explore the course of their childhoods, experiences, and family histories, we are able to understand where they have come from. We invariably determine they possess several important attributes or ingredients that have accounted for their survival and ultimate transcendence of their chaotic childhoods. There is a common thread that runs through their stories and weaves a remarkable pattern. Their journey of self-discovery in therapy leads them to self-love and creates a greater understanding of their strength and innate wisdom. This reduces their inner struggle, and then the inside matches the outside.

Many enlightening books have been written recently that explore codependency and dysfunctional families. They help us understand why we suffer, how we were affected by our families, and how we sabotage our own lives. My friend and colleague Donna LaMar has taken up the challenge to explore, in depth, the phenomenon of transcendence, an adaptation that goes beyond survival. Dr. LaMar seeks to understand the individual who soars beyond the limits of the dysfunctional family and breaks through the barriers into the realm of the exceptional. She has made it her quest to explore the secret place inside these exceptional people where the true self is kept safely tucked away, nurtured and protected from the destructive forces of emotional, physical, or sexual abuse, poverty, and neglect. *If Marie Did It, So Can I!* is an important book that examines how and why transcenders manage to stay healthy in an unhealthy environment. It is a book about life, about love. This is a book that celebrates and affirms the human spirit. Read and be aware of the survivor, no, the transcender in each of us. Thank you, Donna, for helping to answer my question, 'How did you do it?'

Diann Braun, M.A., Therapist and Administrator, Center for Realistic Living, Troy, Michigan

From a Transcender

Dr. LaMar offers understanding, insight, and hope to those of us who have grown up in dysfunctional families. In reading this book I found a roadmap that explained where I have been as well as the direction necessary for me to arrive at my destination, that of a healthy human being in touch with all of my feelings.

This book is the first opportunity I have had to look objectively into the lives of other transcenders and realize that I am not alone. Those of us who bear the scars of abuse speak a common language: shame. After finishing this book, however, I felt a sense of pride about what we accomplished, often against great odds.

The author's commitment and dedication to those of us on the journey of recovery come through with great sensitivity and sincerity. She tells it like it is. My tears flowed freely as she took me back into the pain and loneliness. And yet there is an awareness in Dr. LaMar's words of the determination and the strength that each of us showed as we found direction for our own lives.

For anyone who has grown up in a dysfunctional family or is close to someone who has, Dr. LaMar opens the doors to an understanding of the hard work involved in the healing process. She challenges and encourages each of us to become all we are capable of being, to take in the warmth and love from the light at the end of the tunnel that we so richly deserve.

Marie

With Gratitude

First Edition

It is with deep gratitude and love that I thank the many individuals who contributed and labored with me in the creation of both the original book and its revision. These individuals gave me caring support, encouragement, energy, time, and prayers over the many years of preparation. The journey has been full of challenges, inspiration, and love. This manuscript is the essence of our journey together.

First, I thank all the transcenders who have shared their journeys with me. They offered their stories, their struggles, their pain and joy, as well as their being. I was touched deeply by these many individuals, and they often enhanced my own personal healing and growth process.

To my family goes some of my deepest appreciation. Without their understanding of not having a "regular mother" this book may never have been. Also, I thank my parents, Don and Athena Nelson, for their continued love during the process. A special thanks goes to my father, Don Nelson, for his continued faith and unbelievable patience in convincing me that my teachers had been wrong when they said I couldn't write.

There are many who lovingly contributed by editing, typing, listening, sharing ideas, and running my children to activities so I could write. They include Barbara David, Diann Braun, and Betsy Laney. Members of my doctoral committee who helped clarify the research and its essences include Dr. Clark Moustakas, Drs. Cereta Perry, Patricia

Rourke, Steve Nett, Colleen McNally, Frank Campbell, and Larry Schmidt. I thank all these individuals for providing a special lifeline.

A different kind of lifeline was provided by my "barn people," with whom I ride. They helped reduce my stress by providing support, caring, fun, and a place to re-create my energies. A few of them are Deborah Butler, Bob and Carol Kerr, Chuck and Jackie Wilson, and Heddy Waggoner.

I express deep thanks to my two powerful prayer partners, Sue Miller and Dorothy Pongranz. In the darkest hours, these individuals brought light. I also thank the staff at the Center for Realistic Living for their constant support and encouragement. I always found love and unfailing belief in what I could accomplish. (Note: Sadly, this clinic no longer is in existence.)

Revised Edition

A huge thank-you goes to Betsy Laney for the many ways and many hours, days, and weeks she contributed to this revision. Betsy edited, read, reread, reedited, gave valuable feedback, and prayed. Without whose courage and steadfast commitment this book may not have been possible. My thanks and deep appreciation to Pastor Rob Henderson for his prayers, support, and encouragement. Deep gratitude goes to the many other people who prayed for me and this book and continue to do so. And a final thank you goes to the Marble family, who allowed me to use a wonderful cottage in Canada by Lake Superior, where I began this revision. All these people and others contributed their abilities to help this book take another step forward. Each of these people in their own special way has had a part in helping transcenders heal from past abuse and neglect.

                                          Donna LaMar

Information Qualification Statement/Disclaimer

The information in this book is based on over thirty years of qualitative phenomenological, formal, and informal research as a Ph.D. psychologist in the area of the transcender, a person who overcomes and rises above the trauma of abuse and neglect. Other information that is not "common knowledge" is noted and referenced as it occurs in the book. Most of the bibliography represents material that was part of the development of this book, with the addition of some recent references. The profession of psychology continues to grow, and there are many valuable books now available in this field if you are interested in further exploration.

This book is designed to provide information that came from research about transcending abuse and neglect, not to replace the need for a psychotherapist or counselor. *If Marie Did It, So Can I!* is not intended to replace other reading material but to complement, amplify, and supplement the reader's knowledge base along with other texts. It is assumed readers will continue to explore and learn according to their own needs and concerns. I urge readers to study all available information and learn all they can to help them on their journey of healing and growth.

If Marie Did It, So Can I! is not a read and heal book, not a quick fix! Healing and growing is a journey that requires many forms of help—books, therapists, counselors, groups, etc. Plan to invest in yourself with time and effort as well as money. It will not happen overnight or because you read one book. Know that you are worth the time, effort, and money.

Every effort has been taken to make this book, based on my research, as complete and accurate as possible; however, this book should not be taken as the ultimate source in this area. Its purpose is to educate and add to the pool of knowledge already in the world. The author and Living Farm Press shall have neither liability nor responsibility to any person or entity with respect to any loss or damage caused, or alleged to have been caused, directly or indirectly, by the information contained in this book.

The individuals mentioned in this book have given me permission to tell their stories in the hope of helping others. The information they contributed as co-researchers is from their life experiences and struggles to heal and grow. They offer what it was like for them to grow up and transcend their dysfunctional families. Due to the need for confidentiality, the names of coresearchers, as well as any other identifying information, have been changed. Coresearchers chose their own pseudonyms for this book. These changes did not in any way change the data of the research.

Donna LaMar

Table of Contents

Biography

Donna F. LaMar, Ph.D.

Donna LaMar has a deep compassion for those who are suffering from the effects of abuse and neglect. Her research about the transcender began early in her career and grew into a passion to understand the phenomenon of transcending abuse. How do we overcome and grow? How do transcenders create a different life? Donna's work spans over thirty years of research during which she coined the term *transcender* as related to these extraordinary people.

She is one of the cofounders of The Farm: Where Living Things Grow, Inc. The Farm is a nonprofit organization for youth and families that uses ecotherapy (plants, animals, and nature) as well as traditional ways to help people of all ages heal and grow. She is presently the director of The Farm and helps guide its programs and development.

Dr. LaMar or "Donna" as we know her, has been the clinical director and co-owner/partner of two psychological clinics. She has invested her life's savings into *The Farm Where Living Things Grow Inc.* and reaffirms her commitment to those who wish to heal and transcend at the beginning of each day.

During the course of her career, Donna has become an expert in the evaluation and treatment of trauma, depression, anxiety, post-adoption syndrome, abuse and neglect in youth, adults and families of all ages and ethnicity. She has repeatedly helped individuals to help themselves teaching her patients to transcend, heal, and grow from abuse and neglect. She is a woman of deep faith and spirituality who gains strength by living her faith without projecting her beliefs unto others. She has additional training in play, regression and animal assisted therapies. She is also a master gardner and an experienced animal handler who shares her abilities with her patients by bringing them together with heritage animals and nature on a 10 acre facility, *The Farm's Nature Center*. Here is where the most fundamental part of her teaching is presented as her patients learn to transcend and heal as well as learn to respect other autonomous creatures such as Saint Bernards, cattle, sheep, chickens, roosters, and ducks while absorbing natures beauty.

Donna is continuing her phenomenological and heuristic research with the transcender with a focus on issues that still remain, which she calls "leftovers," after healing from the abuse and neglect.

Donna has two biological and four "adopted" children as well as seven grandchildren, who enjoy visiting The Farm. She enjoys gardening, taking care of animals, and doing things that help others heal and grow. Donna presents conferences and workshops throughout the country.

To Contact Donna:
www.livingfarm.org
(231) 924-2401
press@livingfarm.org

Introduction

My introduction to transcenders was startling. I was around twenty years old, in college, and engaged to Richard. My discovery, fascination, and to understand the transcender's phenomenon was powerful and has lasted for decades. Little did I know that my first visit with Richard's family would be the beginning of a lifelong journey of investigation and discovery.

Richard, my first fiancé, was kind, generous, loving, responsible, and emotionally stable. I was young and naive. When Richard invited me to meet his family, I was excited and a bit afraid. I was sure he must have a wonderful family who loved and adored him. I believed they would be kind, generous, responsible, and stable just like he was. I had no idea they could be anything but the warm and loving family I had pictured. I just knew they supported and treated each other with dignity and respect.

Richard tried hard to tell me about them before the visit, but I was so sure about his family that I could not hear what he was saying. It was not until after the visit that I recalled his saying things like, "Donna, my family is different. My dad gets real angry. My mother is not a good housekeeper. My sister is not well and has not been for a long time."

Prior to the visit I decided that Richard was just nervous about my meeting his family. I wish I had heard what he was saying. The day of our visit arrived. I was anxious, nervous, and excited. I wanted to make a good impression. What if his family didn't like me? What if I made a social goof and insulted someone? I desperately needed and wanted to get along with them; after all, they were Richard's family!

We drove up to the house and I was surprised to find the outside untended and dirty. Inside was worse—unkempt, dirty, and smelly. This was only the beginning!

Once I was inside, Richard's mother invited me to sit down in the living room. As I started to sit on a three-person couch, four other people tried to sit there with me at the same time, including Richard's mother. She actually sat on me! Comical, in a way, it was my next insight into his family. I soon learned there was literally little space for any individual here.

I had eagerly looked forward to sharing with Richard's family and had fantasized hearing stories about Richard's growing up. However, I rapidly learned that people in his family did not share. Instead, they talked exclusively about themselves in loud voices and tried to dominate all conversations. Communication was done by put-downs and/or excessive demands. Their voices were harsh and imposing. Individuals were told, "Move, I want to sit there! Get me that! Can't you do anything right?"

When I asked one person a question, everyone tried to answer. When I was asked a question, no one bothered to listen for an answer, not even the person who had asked the question. There was a sense of desperation and few smiles. They were desperate for attention, any attention.

I was shocked and confused. I had only one thought: Get out now. Yet I wanted so much to get along with my future in-laws. For Richard's sake, I forced myself to smile, talk, and listen. As I did, I was bombarded by individuals demanding that I accept and give—give and keep giving.

I was totally dismayed when I heard how the different family members lived. Their energy seemed to be used only to exist, to get through the day. Richard's family members appeared to take little responsibility for their lives and had few life goals. One wanted to retire at age seventeen;

another had been in and out of the state hospital; two others were on public assistance; and still another was abusing drugs. All of this was in direct contrast to Richard's drive to succeed and grow.

I felt repulsed and empty. I had never witnessed such chaos, neglect, and emotional deprivation. I had expected to find a warm, loving family. Instead, I found an emotionally destructive, draining family who crumbled my false belief that all loving, responsible individuals come from loving, responsible families. Nothing was further from the truth. Nothing!

Although I still wanted to get along with Richard's family, I found my behavior changing toward them. I began avoiding eye contact, hoping that by doing so there would be fewer demands. I stopped asking questions, and I began giving one-word answers to their questions hoping they would leave me alone. Nothing worked and, actually, the demands increased. It did not seem to matter to them how I felt. It just mattered what I could give. The more I withdrew, the more they seemed to force themselves on me. I felt drained. It seemed nothing I could do was enough; perhaps nothing I could ever do would be enough. My stomach contracted into a knot. I was losing me in the destruction and chaos. I knew I had to leave soon in order to find me again.

Finally, after seemingly endless hours, we left. As we drove home, I slowly began to recover from the emotional shock and to find myself again, but I was confused. I began to compare Richard with his family. My questioning began: How could Richard have come from this family? How had he grown up to be the person he was now? Those questions were the beginning of over twenty years of formal and informal research.

What I had painfully discovered that day of the visit was the amazing phenomenon known as transcending. Those who transcend are individuals who grow up in difficult, painful, destructive families and emerge with a meaningful productive way of life. These individuals, as children, somehow maintain a sense of self strong enough to with-stand the onslaught of abuse and neglect from their families.

We realize the truly amazing accomplishment of the transcenders when we look at the families from which they come. These children are frequently victims of phys-ical, emotional, verbal, and sexual abuse, and/or neglect from within their own families. They endure betrayal, abandonment, loneliness, and at times, terror. These painful, destructive families cause intense pain and lone-liness. Families like this are called dysfunctional. They do not supply the protection and nurturance necessary for a child's healthy developing personality or sense of self.

Transcenders are neither magical nor invulnerable. They are children who work hard to raise themselves. They work hard to create resiliency. From a core deep in-side, transcenders make important decisions that protect, nurture, and guide them through the difficult, painful fam-ily years. These decisions, or turning points, are valuable commitments used for the individual's survival and future, and these commitments appear to last a lifetime.

Through the strength of these commitments made in childhood, transcenders pull away from their families and preserve a precious part of their inner self. This part, even if quite small, is not touched by the abuse and neglect of the dysfunctional family but is held in reserve and used to nur-ture, protect, and guide the transcender through the years ahead. Often, this is done at a young age. Transcenders de-velop and use remarkable techniques to sustain the inner self until they can leave their families and create their own world. They do this for not weeks, months, or years, but for decades.

Once free of the family, transcenders work hard to rid themselves of the no longer needed emotional and behav-ioral patterns they used to survive their families. They also work to develop themselves in a growing, authentic direc-tion. They seek to heal by grieving all that has happened to them as well as reclaiming their original authentic self with all the talents and abilities that may have been prevented from developing by growing up in their destructive families. Transcenders are not content to simply exist. They risk, work hard, and push for changes in their development and personal growth. They successfully overcome huge obstacles in spite of their backgrounds.

This description by a transcender relates the process well:

"Transcending a destructive family is like living within prison walls while expending constant energy trying to recapture and maintain that sense of self, that natural state of freedom and purity one has when one is born. Although there is a feeling of being trapped by the extreme limitations and boundaries established, whether this be poverty, negative family values, harsh criticism and/or punishment, or miserable, gloomy, and nonstimulating environments, somehow there is an inner knowing, or sense, that I will be okay, that I can overcome these barriers. I will push ahead and survive."

For over thirty years I have observed and admired transcenders. I started by calling these people survivors; however, this name did not adequately describe the phenomenal process these individuals were living. Thanks to a friend, *survivor* was changed to *transcender.* Through these years my passion to know and understand led me to explore their processes through university research, private professional clinics, as well as in everyday life. During my many years of research, I interviewed transcenders, ministers, teachers, and mental health professionals seeking an understanding of the phenomenon.

Formally, in 1984, I finished a comprehensive phenomenological research project at the doctoral level on what I then still called the survivor. I asked questions such as, "How did you survive? What did others do for you? What helped? What did you do in the abusive times? During the lonely times?"

My many years as a psychotherapist working with children, families, and many transcenders have added to my depth of understanding of the process. Throughout the years, transcenders have touched me deeply. I am appreciative of them everywhere. Their courage to be is truly heroic. I am grateful to the transcenders who shared their stories for this book. Their names and some of the details have been changed to protect their identities; however, the research has not been affected.

Even though this book had its origin in a disillusioning visit, from it came wonderful knowledge. Too often in the mental health field, we have focused on what is wrong with people and how they become mentally ill. The focus of this book is on how individuals create productive lives in spite of destructive families. How they change pain and devastation to healing and hope. This book is a wellness model.

We have many different organizations/areas that help individuals recover and heal from abuse: Adult Children of Alcoholics, Codependents Anonymous, Alcoholics Anonymous, Gamblers Anonymous, Over Eaters Anonymous, and the list goes on. These groups often are considered separate, believing one type of abuse is different from another. There may be different focuses, but the healing and growing process is the same. Abuse is abuse. Neglect is neglect. Adult children are adult children, no matter what the abuse or dysfunction. It's all damaging!

The information presented here is intended to enhance your understanding of the ability to grow in spite of tremendous odds. Please take and use what fits for you. Add to it. If you wish, write or e-mail me about your healing and growing process. This will help unite our knowledge to help others.

It is my ultimate hope and prayer that the information in this book will help individuals heal and grow from past trauma, feel less separate, and learn that we can help one another. This, in turn, will help us remember we are human and need to share, support, and give to our world. We are in this life together, and we can change this world one life at time!

Donna LaMar

CHAPTER 1

Transcenders and the Dysfunctional Family

I believe that as human beings we come into this world to love and be loved and that we have within us everything we need to accomplish this. We have many talents, facets, and abilities ready to be developed. With these abilities we can offer love, and in return, we can be loved by others through their abilities. When sent out into the world, these assets create ripples that offer healing and growth to others. We also come into the world with handicaps and challenges, such as learning disabilities, physical handicaps, or personality and genetic traits. These challenging traits sometimes make it difficult for us to get along in our world and fulfill this "love command." For example, a child can be supersensitive or strong willed, which may keep people away. This may make it more difficult for that child to make friends. Whatever we come with, our abilities and disabilities comprise our "original package," the one we use to relate to and make our way in the world. Even as early as the moment of birth, we are ready to grow, move, develop, learn, and relate using this package.

This love directive can become confused, sidetracked, complicated, infringed upon, and destroyed, or it can be enhanced and developed, depending upon our life experiences and how we personally view them. *Life experiences* are made up of relationships and situations in which we are involved as children and adults, that is, what happens to us in life. These experiences include family, work, leisure, religion, health, and the like. Children are especially vulnerable to early life experiences because of their great need for protection and nurturing. How children develop their abilities, their personalities, and their views of themselves largely depends on how they are treated and what happens to them in their growing years. Children raised with violence are often violent. Children raised with neglect are often negligent however, transcenders are different.

Who Are Transcenders?

Transcenders are individuals who in spite of growing up in difficult, painful family environments are able to emerge and pursue meaningful, productive lives. Somehow, these individuals as children maintain a sense of self strong enough to withstand the onslaught of abuse and neglect from their families.

The accomplishments of transcenders are truly amazing when we look at the families they have survived. Individuals in these families may have been physically, emotionally, verbally, and sexually abused and/or neglected in varying degrees. They are often betrayed and abandoned. Such abusive families inflict intense pain and loneliness on their victims.

The majority of life experiences for transcenders in childhood are experiences that are damaging to the healthy growth and development of children. Their families do not provide the nurturing, stability, or protection needed to sustain physical and emotional health, let alone to develop abilities, personalities, and potentialities. One's *potentiality* includes the many areas of abilities that are not yet developed but have the possibility of being developed. Often these families interfere with and damage the inner guiding forces the child needs for healthy growth and development.

Dysfunctional Family Systems

The field of psychology terms this type of family a *dysfunctional family*. In a dysfunctional family, the pattern or system of relating and communicating is painful, abusive, damaging, and difficult.

A *family system* is the way individuals relate to each other and the outside world, as well as how the family members interrelate. Every functional family has a unique system that works to help its members relate within the family as well as outside of it.

In a family system, all individuals are connected. If one individual changes, the rest of the family is affected. An example of how a system works is seen in a mobile. What happens when you pull or touch one part of a mobile? The whole thing moves. What happens in a family when Mom gets sick? When Dad leaves? When Sister goes to college? In each case, the entire system moves and shifts. One person moving or changing causes another person to shift, and not always in a healthy, productive manner. In a dysfunctional family, if an individual grows and becomes healthier, other family members may not only try to block the growth but may actually sabotage it. That is why it is so very difficult to change while still living with the family.

Abuse and/or Neglect within Dysfunctional Families

In a dysfunctional family, there is often physical, verbal, emotional, ritual, and/or sexual abuse and/or neglect. It can range from severe to subtle in intensity, from constant to rarely in occurrence, and from minutes to weeks or years in duration. The abuse may be so severe that the individual can be in danger of dying or losing his or her inner self and becoming mentally ill. Or the abuse may be so subtle that it is extremely difficult to identify what has happened to the individual.

There can also be many different types and variations of abuse in the same family, from mild ridicule to severe acting out. Abuse may be directed at all the children, or at just one child. In its subtle forms, the abuse and neglect interfere with the child's growth and are hard to recognize because the family looks and functions relatively "normal." The more severe forms are so devastating I have often wondered how the individual could still be physically and emotionally alive. Whether mild or severe, abusive and neglectful behavior interferes with and damages the child's ability to develop and grow normally.

An example of mild abuse/neglect is a family that insists the children be perfect and pretend feelings do not exist—that is, denies them. Children from this type of family may grow up unaware of who they are because a "perfect" person does not exist. They don't know that perfection does not exist anywhere, so they judge themselves as wrong and bad. Their real, or authentic, self (original package) is actually hidden and never developed within the family. This kind of abuse translates to a young mind as: "Do not be yourself. You are not okay. Be what your parents want you to be—perfect," which depends on whatever *those* parent's definition of "perfect" is at that particular point in time.

The individual then goes through life attempting to be perfect, which is actually unauthentic. Often, individuals with this background do not know what is wrong with them, but are tense, depressed, angry, and have little sense of their own worth. They have no idea their family damaged them, and they may even believe they have a perfect, wonderful family. Their goal is to be that perfect person they believe will please their parents and who will win them love and acceptance. As long as they work to maintain this perfect, but false identity, they have little chance to develop their authentic abilities, talents, personalities, and potentialities. This type of life is painful and damaging to their original package.

An example of severe, painful abuse is physical violence toward children. Children who are physically abused work especially hard not to disturb the individual who does the abusing. Often they don't know what they have done to deserve to be punished. They may believe they legitimately brought on the abuse because the abusing parent tells them it is "all their fault." For example, "If you had done the dishes right, I wouldn't have to hit you!"

What the children don't know (and can't because they are children) is that Mommy's and Daddy's anger is out of control, and they are looking for any reason to strike out. This anger is not rational. For example, rational families do not beat up children for wiping a dish wrong. Healthy parents teach children how to perform a task and allow for the imperfection of growing children. In abusive/neglectful families, children learn to be very careful about what they say and do. They learn that surviving is their priority. Again, the result of severe abuse, like that of subtle abuse, is the hiding of the authentic self, along with undeveloped abilities, which leads to fewer healthy ripples in the world.

Transcenders Somehow Maintain Who They Are

Every transcender has a unique story that includes a painful and difficult childhood. However, transcenders are different than children who later in life become abusive, neglectful, or mentally ill like their parents. While they may end up having some personality traits similar to their family's (which they can change), they are different and work hard to be different.

Transcenders do not go under or give up. Somehow, they manage to maintain some contact with their original package. Somehow they are able to envision a more authentic world with love or, as one transcender puts it, "the way it should be." They work not only to maintain themselves in a difficult, painful environment; they are also able to develop some of their authenticity in the face of violent and crazy life experiences.

This does not mean transcenders as children avoid the pain and craziness of the family. Instead, transcenders survive the experiences with scars and grow in spite of them or, as we shall see in Chapter 3, because of them. This book is about this incredible phenomenon. Who are these transcenders? Are they perfect beings? Invincible? Invulnerable? Super-healthy geniuses? Resilient? Actually, transcenders are varied and can be found in every walk of life: wealthy or poor, traditional or modern, liberal or conservative, professional or blue collar, religious or nonreligious, permissive or rigid. The list goes on. Transcenders are different from each other in appearance, behavior, and personality. They may be athletic, studious, withdrawn, or outgoing. But, they share one uniqueness: a dynamic ability to raise themselves in a dysfunctional family and to grow into adults who create meaningful, productive lives.

Transcending Is a Process

As you read this book, please remember that transcending a dysfunctional family is a *process,* a process of surviving and then healing and growing. A process is everything that can't be put in a wheelbarrow. A product is something that can be put in a wheelbarrow—things like a hammer, doll, art creation, and even a building—if the wheelbarrow is big enough! Examples of a process would be surviving, learning, healing, growing, and loving. A process unfolds from within us, takes its own time and direction, and has a life of its own. A process usually has vague beginning and ending points. Occasionally, a process ends with a product. For example, at the end of my doctoral-level education I had a research paper, a product called a dissertation, but the education itself was a process.

A transcender's process is a struggle to survive conflicts and feelings of pain and loneliness emotionally as well as to survive abuse and neglect physically. Transcenders have two ultimate goals: to get out of the family with all its abuse, neglect, chaos, and pain and to create a more nurturing, loving, safe world. In spite of tremendous odds, they accomplish this goal. They create safety, structure, goals, authenticity, fun, and love. Transcenders create this world for themselves by working hard to overcome struggles, conflicts, problems, obstacles, and scars left over from childhood as they heal and go forward.

I have watched in amazement the process of transcenders. It is a process that takes years of concerted effort and courage. To understand the process, we need to take an in-depth look at what transcenders have overcome: their own personal dysfunctional family existence. In the rest of this chapter, I will share five stories about transcenders and their dysfunctional families to give you an understanding of the variety of their backgrounds. These stories are not exclusive or inclusive. Every transcender has a unique family story, and each individual member of that family has a unique perception of his or her experiences in the family. This unique perception of the family is very important, as will be seen in Chapters 3 and 5. Each family has its own secrets, its own particular type of pain, and its own history. Each history is important to the person who is struggling to understand and recover from it. In Chapter 2, I will describe general characteristics of dysfunctional families.

Five Transcenders' Stories

The stories of Marie, Paul, Chris, Steve, and Tiffany follow. I ask you to put yourselves in their place, feel their pain, and imagine what their childhoods were like. Some of you will have little problem doing this because you are, or have been, in their place.

Marie

Marie is the only child of a schizophrenic mother and an alcoholic father who were both ritually abusive. Schizophrenia is a severe mental disorder that often causes people to live a dark, delusional existence. It is characterized by disorganized speech and behavior, delusions, and hallucinations. The person with schizophrenia often has very little, if any, contact with reality, and the personality continues to break down over time. Medication is usually needed to maintain even a limited contact with the environment. Marie's parents' conditions were severe and untreated and were allowed to run rampant. Normal functioning for them was limited or nonexistent except in public. Abusive functioning was the norm at home.

Marie's descriptions of her childhood are beyond belief. During intensive therapy, Marie remembered tortures by her parents from early in her life.

"My mother would give me ice water enemas which would cause horrible stomach cramps. She would force me to satisfy her sexually (she was bisexual) and then would punish me for being a 'bad girl.' At times she would tie me to a tree for several days and nights or lock me inside a coffin-like box with only small holes for air to get in. Frequently these punishments were for things she had done herself (wetting the bed while sexually excited, vomiting on the floor, etc.). After being locked in the box for long periods of time and not being able to hold my urine any longer, I would have an accident and urinate in the box. I then dreaded being let out of the box because I knew that punishment would follow. She would become furious at seeing my wet clothes, and her eyes would glow like pieces of coal as she would defecate and then smear my face with her feces.

"Once she tried to sew up my vagina because she was mad at a man and wouldn't allow him to have sex with me. (I was about 10 at the time.) I often passed out from the pain (physical and emotional), which would only make her angrier and more violent with her tortures. My mother and father both demanded that I satisfy them sexually (either individually, or both at the same time) as well as anyone else they decided could use me. Beds are still terrifying for me.

"My father was just as cruel as my mother. He used me sexually at his convenience and tried to kill me many times. He would bring home little kittens and puppies for me and would tell me that if I was good enough the animals would be allowed to live and I could keep them for my own pets, but if I was bad, the animals would have to die. I was never good enough, and to this day I can see and hear those pitiful little animals as he killed them while I was forced to watch, all the time being told that they had to die because I was a bad girl. No matter how hard I tried, I was never a good girl by my parents' sick standards.

"My parents were also both into satanic worship. They sacrificed animals and I had to help bury the bodies. I know it sounds so unreal, so awful, and it was. It was so horrible and terrifying that I had a hard time believing it myself when the memories first began to return.

"At times, as I got older, when I tried to tell other relatives or teachers what was happening, my parents had already set the scene. They had convinced everyone that I was a liar and had severe emotional problems. When dealing with other people, my parents presented the façade of the perfect warm, caring, loving couple who went to church. How often I was told how lucky I was to have parents like this. It is no wonder that when I did try to confide in anyone they did not believe me and would tell my parents what I had said and, once again, I would be severely punished. It did not take long for me to learn that no one could be trusted.

"I felt total relief when each of my parents died. I was accused by one of my relatives of being responsible for killing my mother in a car accident. I wasn't even driving the car!"

One of the ways Marie survived was to block out the memories until years after her parents died. Then, after years of intensive psychotherapy, she was able to allow herself to remember her past. Marie's experience is the most severe and abusive I have encountered as a therapist. Often as I listened to Marie, I would wonder how she physically stayed alive, let alone sane, in her obviously severely dysfunctional family. The above experiences are only some of the horrors she lived through. In spite of the tortures from infancy into adolescence, she is a respected member of the community, has raised three children, and holds a full-time job.

Chris

Chris has been the scapegoat in his family. That is, anything and everything that went wrong in the family or sometimes in life was blamed on him including accidents, behavior, feelings, thoughts, and even family history. Sometimes a certain child is picked because of sex, position in the family, or resemblances to someone the parents don't like, or sometimes it is because his or her parents are having a hard time, and this child came when any child would have been too much. Here is Chris's story.

"I was born a scapegoat. I was the middle of three children, and I was blamed for everything. I think I was blamed even before I was born. It felt as if I could do nothing right and they all hated me. They hated me if I tried; they hated me if I didn't try. They hated me no matter what.

"I have an image of myself at about age three that describes my childhood: I am looking toward my mother and older sister and I'm trying to get some attention. I reach out my arms and then they turn and walk away, completely ignoring me. I then turn away from them and find a place to hide and cry.

"I never understood it. Never! Why me? Why? Was I odd looking? Did I hate them? I guess, at a real deep level, I suspected it was not really me. That's what helped keep me going. After being in therapy for a while, I came to know that it was really them.

"My mother used to go into these rages. I tried real hard, as a kid, to avoid her when she was in those moods, but she could shift so fast from okay to monster and I'd get caught. When she would catch me, I'd have to get my dad's belt, go into the bathroom with her, strip to nothing, and be beaten until I had welts. This occurred until I was in my late teens. Here I was, either a little kid and had to bring her a belt bigger than I was, or a teenager big enough to beat her. It was all real crazy.

"I remember one time the family planned to go see *Around the World in Eighty Days.* I was so excited. But, my mother got in one of her moods and found something I had done wrong. She locked me in my room while the rest of the family went to the movies. I can remember looking out the window and watching them go, it was so painful. Other times, she would make me kneel down on the old fashioned heating grates on the floor for hours or she would lock me in my room and not feed me for a day. Dad just let all of this happen. He never stopped her, never. He just watched like it was okay to do this to me.

"My brother and sister would also join in and ridicule me when they were in a bad mood or something had gone wrong in their lives. I was never included in play and never included in family affairs. Even now, the family will exchange Christmas presents with everyone but me. In the past, I sent presents to them which they either never acknowledged or criticized. It's crazy, really crazy. Recently, when my father died, my brother and sister cleaned out his stuff. I was not told and was not offered anything from his possessions. Everyone else got something.

"It never stops. Now, even my nieces and nephews are part of it. They believe I'm to blame for their problems even though I rarely even see them or are part of their lives.

"One time, when I was 17 and still in high school, my mother threw all my stuff out on the driveway—she did this regularly—and told me to leave. It was February, and I had to sleep in my car, go to school, and then go to work. I was so cold and hungry. Finally, I asked to come back home, and she let me come back. Again, my dad did nothing. I don't know which was worse, her direct abuse or his total neglect and nonaction. I know all I ever wanted from my family was to be loved and for them to accept my love. I was always rejected and so was my love."

In later years, Chris wrote this:

Cradle Pains
Cherry red splashes on velvet baby skin—
The fury of your Hell had landed.

Tiny soft arms ending in virgin baby hands—
They hold tight the dead weight of empty air.

They open, they close,
A lullaby tune of whimper and moans
Sung not too loud
By a broken heart that's two days old.

Steve

Steve is the oldest of ten children. He lived in extreme poverty with his parents. He describes his story this way.

"All I can remember is how poor we were. There was never enough to eat and only a few clothes and rarely shoes. When I was about four years old, I was taken to live with my grandparents. I was so lucky to live with them for a couple of years because they could provide better than my parents could. At least with them I had food, shelter, and clothing. When I lived with my parents we barely existed.

"It was awful when I had to go back and live with my parents again. I was about nine, and once again I found myself scraping for enough food to live on. I can remember being so hungry that I was weak and couldn't go to school. On rare occasions, when I had enough energy to go to school, I didn't have clothes or shoes to wear. Most of the time, however, I was too weak from hunger to go, let alone concentrate. Once I got there I can remember so much pain from the hunger and the cold and no one to help us. My parents did almost nothing. My father eventually abandoned us. I can remember everything about growing up. I never want to forget what it was like.

"The worst part was the neglect. There was no love, no sharing, no caring, no nothing—just neglect. My parents were just sort of there in a world of their own. They would have all sorts of men and women over and never knew we were around. It was awful.

"Being the oldest, I was totally responsible for my brothers and sisters. I was responsible for trying to get food as well as firewood for the family. For firewood, I'd have to walk into the woods a long way. If I got lucky and found some wood, we would quickly build a fire and kneel so close to the heat our legs would burn and turn black because we were so cold. Sometimes for food I'd go to a neighbor's house, and they would give me the scraps from the table to take home for us to eat. I'm not talking about good scraps. I'm talking about just the stuff left on the dishes after you eat. It was bad, so bad.

"I knew it was not right but I didn't know why. I tried to take care of my brothers and sisters, but at times they would turn on me and ridicule me for trying to help or for not helping enough. I think I was the target because I was the substitute mother. I hated it. We were just all hurting so badly.

"At the end, I watched my mother die of cancer. I was sixteen then. All of us were farmed out to relatives or orphanages. I was lucky and went to live with my grandparents again. I had it a little better there.

"My grandmother, however, was an alcoholic by then and drank up my grandfather's wages. Money was again nonexistent, but at least I ate, had clothes, and could go to school. I still had a load to carry because my grandmother was so out of it. I had to run the house and do all the errands. I don't remember any love or caring there then, but I at least did not have the heavy responsibility of my brothers and sisters like I had when we lived with my parents. I knew early that learning was important, and I never wanted to go back to what it was like with my parents."

Steve graduated from high school and went on to earn a bachelor of science degree in health.

Paul

Other types of dysfunctional families create other kinds of emotional chaos, as in Paul's case. Here is his story.

"There was little money in our house, and there was always tension and stress. Dad was an attorney and struggled in our early years to establish his practice. Mom worked for him at home while trying to run the house and raise five children. I was the middle child and was lost in the chaos. Mom gave everything I wanted to the other kids. For example, I wanted to take dancing lessons; my sister got them. I wanted to be in sports; my brother did it. Everything, just everything I wanted, was given to others. I was never driven anywhere for any activities or helped in any way. It's like I didn't exist.

"I remember the chaos the most—chaos, stress, neglect, severe ridicule, and at times, verbal and physical abuse. My mother was gutless and abusive; my father was absent and critical. I was forced to go to a church school, which I hated, and begged to be allowed to go to public school. My younger brother and sister got to go to public school while I was forced to stay in church school. I could never figure out the reason and tried to be perfect. It just felt real crazy.

"There was always fighting and screaming at our house. Either the kitchen wasn't clean enough, a bed was not made right, or something was not perfect. If this was the case, I would then be spanked or beaten, but I rarely ever knew what I had done or not done. I would be beaten again if Mom felt I needed it or if Mom wasn't done getting her anger out.

"The worst part for me was never having a niche for me at home. I never fit. I was always wrong, bad, and ignored. I really was lost in my family unless I was blamed for something and being punished. One time, when I was about 12 or 13, we were going up north for a fishing vacation in Canada. The family got everything ready the night before and left it by the front door. I got up early and packed everything in the car before anybody else got up. After breakfast we went out and got in the car and started down the driveway. My father stopped the car and said he had to check the trunk. He got out and opened the trunk, looked inside and said, 'How could you possibly pack it like that?' He began to take every article out of the trunk and repack it. I remember how that really made me feel like a piece of shit. I sat in the car and cried and cried. I would get so angry when he would get angry with me and when he would just criticize me and be all over me. I felt so bad about myself."

Paul is now in a career transition, which he finds very difficult. This transition has thrown him back into some old patterns. However, he put himself back into therapy and is working through these difficulties. He is confident that he will work through the transition and the feelings the transition triggered. Paul is single and was successful in his previous career.

Tiffany

The last transcender's story is Tiffany's. Her story is a little different because the dysfunction was so subtle. The damage is just as harmful as with more severe dysfunction. It still causes chaos because the person feels abused and not "all right" but can't pinpoint why. The person from this type of background may feel "crazy" but does not know why. The reasons usually come out after a long, hard, sorting-out process in therapy. Here is Tiffany's story.

"My family was male dominated and strict. My father was a professional, and my mother stayed home and took care of everything and everyone. Dad was rarely home because he worked so much and later became an alcoholic. I was the only girl among four brothers. Traditional in my family meant the men as well as boys were the superior breed. They were to be taken care of, waited on, and watched over. My father and my brothers ruled the roost. Whatever they wanted they got. In so many ways I was discounted because I was a girl, and this constantly chipped away at my self-esteem. Girls had to do women's work—dust, cook, and wash dishes—even though I really enjoyed working on gardening and other projects. The chaos for me, which I came to understand after working hard in therapy, was being the only girl who was wanted for playing the role of a girl and not for who I was as a person. I tried very hard to please my parents and be the good girl who would someday become the good little housewife and continue taking care of the men in her life. The tragedy was that because this was not really me, I felt discounted and not wanted.

"In addition to all this, I was expected to be perfect, act perfect, buy perfect products, speak perfectly, accomplish the perfect goals, feel nothing, and above all, be a totally successful intellect. To make a mistake was to be ridiculed and severely criticized about it by my brothers forever. Even the friends I picked had to look and act perfectly or I'd be criticized after they went home. In time, I learned not to bring anyone home.

"I never felt accepted or loved because my parents loved my brothers and an image of a good girl. My brothers made sure I was kept in my place with ridicule, criticism, and threats of physical violence. I was never okay, but they never really got to know me.

"Eventually, I went into a deep depression as a teen and went underground. That is, part of me functioned at one level and tried to be the good girl. At the same time, I held my real self underneath and hidden from others. I became totally isolated and alone. I was told not to share any family situations with anyone because of the rule 'Don't hang your dirty laundry out for the neighbors to see.'

"At an early age I was expected to be independent and not rely on anyone for anything. At the same time, we were strictly controlled and not allowed to do much of anything other than be home with the family. I never could gain support or another perspective to help me with the pain I experienced in the family. I had to be mature beyond my years so I could figure out how to raise myself. On top of all this, I was also expected to be my mother's mother, and felt I had to take care of her. She was 'a rager'—yelling and screaming and appeared to be out of control.

"The real crazies were that my family looked and acted typical—wonderful and loving with perfect, wonderful children. God, no wonder I felt crazy! I lived between the world of 'I have a perfect family, yet, I am abused and neglected.' Later, after a lot of therapy, I discovered that my mother had beaten me physically and I had put these memories in a memory block."

Tiffany is a successful professional and mother. She struggles at times when life experiences trigger past memories and feelings, but as she says, "I am different from my parents, and I intend to stay that way."

Summary

Children in dysfunctional families do not get the nurturing or the protection they need to grow and develop into healthy, productive adults. At times, like Steve, the family is at a physical survival level. At other times, there is a lack of affirmation and validation (a confirming and sorting out of feelings, thoughts, and growing process), as seen in Tiffany's family. A wide range of abuse and neglect is seen in all the families. Often the children do not count and are only seen as being a number or to service others. Usually, no adult spends any length of quality time with the children to teach them how to get along in the world. This teaching is crucial to healthy emotional development and includes helping children set limits, to follow an established value system, to feel loved, and to develop their original package.

If the most basic of needs, such as food, shelter, clothing, and emotional nurturing, are not met, children grow up extremely needy and dependent on others for life resources. Too often, children in these families may become aggressive, withdrawn, depressed, lethargic, or emotionally ill and dysfunctional in other ways like their parents. They may even become afraid that existing in the world is so difficult they withdraw or commit suicide. Too often, these children develop character disorders; that is, they lack conscience, morals, and values, and they retain little or nothing of their original package. Our jails and prisons are full of them. None of these patterns are healthy or desirable. The cost of the damage is great to them and society. For the children who survive and transcend, their accomplishment is great in comparison!

CHAPTER 2

Dysfunctional Family Characteristics

What do transcenders overcome? Particular interactional and family systems have been identified as characteristics of dysfunctional families. These characteristics will provide a basic understanding of the manner in which dysfunctional families communicate, function, deal with pain, and relate to the world. Each family is unique and may have one or many of these characteristics, which range in severity from mild to severe. These characteristics are learned and passed down from one generation to another and usually send out unhealthy ripples. As you read, please keep in mind that the children who survive and overcome a number of these obstacles and manage to create a world that leads to healthier functioning. There are two areas of these characteristics: interactional and family systems.[1]

Interactional Characteristics

The term *interactional characteristics* refers to how individuals in a family relate and communicate with each other. Different families may have all, some, or none of these characteristics, depending on the amount of dysfunction within the family. These characteristics include:

1. *Nonexistent or poor interactions.* Some families don't interact. That is, they do not communicate on any level. The parents may ignore or neglect the children, and the children may become more like objects than human beings. Some families actually stay in silence

19

most of the time. Others may yell and scream about everything and at everyone with little basis in reality. If there is no healthy interaction, there is no shared interest and no chance for the children to gain emotional support. If there is a lot of yelling, there is also tension, stress, and conflict. None of these patterns, nor any combination of these patterns, brings about any meaningful communication.

2. *Nonexistent or little sharing and/or feedback.* This means children receive little or no confirmation (affirmation or validation) of who they are as persons. They do not gain needed information essential for development. Receiving feedback through sharing is the process children normally use to set up their identities and personalities with healthy limits, values, morals and abilities. If feedback is not available, children seek out information from television, the street, or other negative sources. For example, the child will need to answer questions such as: What am I capable of? What are my special talents? What things can't I do in my world? What things will get me into trouble? How do I handle being angry?

   Without a significant caring adult sharing and giving feedback, children can become other-oriented (taking care of others and trusting others to lead them in their lives) to the point of losing themselves, having no connection to anyone, becoming delinquent, withdrawing, or underachieving. At times, they can become so attached to anyone who will give them direction that they will put up with abuse for the attention. The individuals often become very good at reading others' facial expressions and vocal intonations to pick up cues about to how to act.

3. *Isolation of the individual.* Many children who grow up in a dysfunctional family experience isolation and

intense loneliness. The isolation may be created in many ways: the family's saying they don't trust anyone; children not being allowed to play with other children (concern that they might tell the family secrets); children choosing isolation as a form of protection from embarrassment and the onslaught of the abuse; or perhaps, the children's being seen as objects or just numbers and receiving little attention. In any case, there is usually little, if any attempt to help the children out of the loneliness or relate to them in any meaningful way.

4. *Denial of problems, feelings, and thoughts.* Some families pretend that everything is great and there are no problems. They may even believe their children are the most wonderful, well-adjusted children in the world. Yet, underneath this perfect picture are problems that may include perfectionism, ridicule, denial of feelings, and abuse. An example is a family with an alcoholic parent in which the family members pretend everything is wonderful in spite of Mom's or Dad's drinking up the weekly grocery money or abusing family members. It amounts to pretending there is no "elephant in the living room" when there really is. Everyone then pretends, adjusts, and goes around the elephant and all that goes with it.

5. *Distorted or "unreal" feelings.* Individuals in dysfunctional families often warp, or distort, their feelings. Because they are very important for growth, feelings can become a major problem when they are not valued. Individuals can act out feelings in distorted ways due to emotional illness, inability to deal with the world, or generational learning (patterns of handling feelings that are passed on from one generation to the next). For example, I may feel afraid to cross the street, but instead of dealing with the fear and then

taking precautions for safety, I totally lose control, scream, or become angry with another person because I fear that if I cross the street I will get hurt or die. Anger is another example of a feeling that is greatly distorted. Anger is a normal, important feeling that tells us something is wrong in our life. It needs to be expressed appropriately, not inappropriately in ways such as hurting yourself, hurting something alive, or damaging property. Anger is a normal feeling and needs to be felt; however, my being angry does not allow me to beat on a person or animal.

6. *Failure to meet individual needs.* One of the basic tasks of a family is to support each other and to provide a way for each member's needs to be met. Human beings all need food, shelter, and clothing for physical survival. We also need emotional support and nurturing to develop our original package. In dysfunctional families, parents or other adults are unable to meet these needs in themselves, let alone in others. Many of them came from dysfunctional families themselves. Because the children are unable to have their needs met, they become the next generation of needy, dependent, isolated, and hurting dysfunctional people.This cycle continues through the generations until someone, such as the transcender, stops the cycle of abuse and neglect.

Characteristics of Family Systems

As mentioned in Chapter 1, how the family as a whole functions and interacts is known as a *family system.* Family systems have specific characteristics that are the rules governing each person in relation to others and the world. Dysfunctional family characteristics include:

1. No clear boundaries. In healthy families there are distinct, clear boundaries between individuals. A boundary is an unseen line where "you" begin and "I" end. There is not only physical space, such as one's bedroom or clothing, but also psychological space, which includes one's feelings, thoughts, and responsibilities.

In a dysfunctional family, these boundaries or limits may be weak or nonexistent. For example, one parent may make one of the children responsible for that parent's anger. The child may be blamed for making the parent angry, or the child may be required to act out the parent's anger. In either case, the boundaries are enmeshed and entangled, and children get lost in the entanglement.

The accompanying diagram may help you understand boundaries.

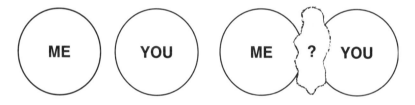

If boundaries are poor, individuals may not know who they are and whose feelings belong to whom. This symbiotic state is natural for the infant, but the child must develop into a more independent and separate state, which usually starts around the age of two. The two-year-old stage of temper tantrums, as well as the teenager's rebellion, is all about separating and setting up boundaries. Poor boundaries encourage poor self-concepts. Without a personal boundary, saying no is not only difficult but painful because it is like saying no to oneself. The individual cannot distinguish between his or her needs and feelings and those of others.

2. No clear values. How we function in our world depends on the values, beliefs, and morals that we have decided are important. These are traditionally passed down through families and transmitted to the children through examples in the process of daily living. If values, beliefs, and morals are not clear or are nonexistent, children suffer. They suffer from the lack of direction and guidance necessary to grow and develop in a healthy manner. Without values, beliefs, and morals, the sense of right and wrong can be lost or never developed. For example, if parents use lying as a way to get along in the world and do not enforce consequences for their children for lying, the children may also learn and use this pattern of getting along in the world. This impacts others in society through crime.

3. Expecting children to be adults before their time. I have often heard people say things like "I raised myself"; "I had to be mature beyond my years"; or "I was my mother's mother." These individuals are saying they had to supply the support and guidance needed for their own growth and development—support that should have come from their parents. These children learn early that they have to rely on themselves for the knowledge and wisdom needed to make it in their world. This process requires constantly thinking ahead and figuring out how to handle something because no one will be there who is capable to teach or help. It requires a "knowing before you know" living. Children are not developmentally ready to do this and often succumb to the dysfunction in the family.

Perhaps a child is required to run the household and watch over younger children while the parents neglect the children's needs and/or act like children themselves. Steve's situation is an extreme example. In his family, he was required to supply food and fuel for the family because of his parents' lack of responsibility. This can also happen when the parents are alcoholic or codependent. No matter how it happens or for what reason, the child can be robbed of needed support for growth and development and, in fact, robbed of a whole childhood.

4. Problems of the couple are acted out through the children. In some dysfunctional families, the parents take little or no responsibility for their feelings or for the problems in their relationships. Instead, they dump the responsibility on their children. The children are expected to feel, act out, and handle these feelings and problems for their parents. After all, it is more acceptable to have an acting-out child than an acting-out adult. Sometimes, the parents may look wonderful but have one or more children who are delinquent, underachieving, sexually promiscuous, lying, or abusing drugs. In some families, these children are responding to their parents' feelings, problems, and expectations. This undercurrent may not be shared with the outside world. While outwardly everything may look fine, the real atmosphere is frequently one of conflict and tension.

The job of the children in this type of family is to act out and divert attention from the parents' feelings and problems and refocus the attention on themselves. This distracting system relieves pressures, tensions, and conflicts not only between parents but also between other family members. It works to keep the entire family in a state of balance, or equilibrium. This unhealthy balanced state enables the family to continue to function in the world, looking okay.

5. Nonexistent or poor support for individuals. Dysfunctional family systems don't usually support or help individuals to develop and grow. Individuals may not even feel they're noticed. I have often heard "I was only a number"; "No one knew I was alive"; "They really didn't care about me"; and "All I was good for was to be their slave." If an individual child works to develop his or her unique talents and abilities, there is usually little support or acknowledgment. Some family members may sabotage that child or even use the child as a scapegoat. For example, the parents may not attend the child's sports events, activities, or acknowledge academic achievement. Some children continue to strive under these circumstances, while others may give up and become lost in the system.

6. Rigid family structures that do not change with the individual's needs. The structure of a dysfunctional family may be so set and rigid no one can move. That is, rigid limits, rules, and roles in the family keep individuals trapped. For instance, the parents may make one child a substitute mother for the family, so there is no escape from that role, no matter what the child needs. This child then feels trapped, controlled, and isolated, and growth is stifled. Limits in a healthy family move and grow as individuals' needs change, especially in children. If you think about the things you needed as an infant and those you needed as a teenager, you will get some idea of how limits and structures must be flexible and change to support growth. Rigidity works to keep everyone controlled, limited, and deindividualized.

7. Family secrets are kept and played out in feelings and behavior. I once worked with a child who, when emotionally hurt, would cover up the hurt and make it a secret hidden deep inside of her. The secret and its pain, however, caused the child's behavior to change because it took energy to keep the pain hidden and because feelings intensify when not appropriately expressed. When the hurt had no release, and it festered, grew, and intensified creating tension that had to be released. She would go from a sweet child to an aggressive, out-of-control child in a matter of minutes.

Family secrets, or skeletons in the closet, as some people call them, function in the same way causing tension, anxiety, and shame. Secrets affect all members of the family through feelings, thoughts, behaviors, and stress. The more secrets, or the larger and more serious the secrets, the more acting out and shame in the family. This acting out may take the form of aggression or withdrawal depending upon the individuals and the family system that has been developed over generations. Secrets are often handed down from one generation to another.

8. *Secrets that create shame.* Part of having family secrets is the underlying feeling of shame. Family members have a deep fear that people will find out about the secret(s), and the individual will be considered the guilty party. Each member guards the secret as if he or she actually did the awful deed even though it may be generations old. The individual takes on the responsibility of the shame and feels as if he or she should be punished for causing the family's social ruin. This shame creates embarrassment, depression, and feelings of fear that "someone will find out." The damage to self-esteem of such shame is intense and deep. Individual family members feel they are the shame.

Even the deep feeling of shame becomes a secret to keep hidden. There may be an intense fear that once the secret was found out, everyone would know that the individual (not just the family) is not okay, and this becomes another secret to keep hidden. This shame can be acted out through aggression, withdrawal, and denial. One person put it this way: "I just knew my family was not okay, but I had to keep the secret hidden. If I didn't—well, the thought was so awful I believed I would die and my family would be destroyed."

9. *Myths surround the family to "protect" secrets from discovery.* This characteristic goes hand-in-hand with the previous two, secrets and shame. To protect and keep the secrets hidden from the world, myths (or lies) are created about the secrets. These myths can be passed down from one generation to the next for decades, or they can be created in the immediate family, depending on the need. For example, if my mom is a heavy drinker, irresponsible, and an embarrassment to the family, I may tell others that Mom

is sick and can't do much. My siblings and I take over the household responsibilities and raise ourselves. We, as a family, try to project an image that says we are okay or, better yet, that we are wonderful and everything is terrific. The outside world doesn't suspect the truth, and no individual within the family is free to tell the truth. The fear and shame keep the secrets and myths in place. For children, this causes poor self-esteem, poor or no sense of boundaries, and unbelievable confusion between fantasy and reality. If Dad is great and everything is wonderful, why does Dad beat up Mom, and why does she pretend she is happy? This type of thinking twists any developing sense of logic.

10. Blame, guilt, and shame are used to handle family problems. Dysfunctional families use blame, guilt, and shame to shift responsibility from the person to whom it belongs to someone else. For example, if I can blame my spouse for all (or most) of my failures, feelings, and problems, then I don't have to struggle, suffer, feel pain, or be responsible for my feelings or actions. My spouse then feels guilty and, underneath the shame, continues in the relationship to keep everything in control. Basically, if I can blame you and make you feel guilty and ashamed, then I'm okay myself.

The scapegoat in a family is the most extreme example. Everything that goes wrong in the family is blamed on one person, so the rest of the family is okay. All the yelling, abuse, and punishments are aimed at this one person, and in turn, the family's tensions are relieved. The family, as well as the scapegoat, may truly believe the scapegoat is responsible for all the bad that occurs. This is one of the most difficult roles from which to recover.

11. Different types of abuse and neglect. Physical, emotional, verbal, ritual, sexual, and drug and alcohol abuse, as well as neglect, commonly occur in dysfunctional families. Abuse and neglect occur in different forms depending on the individuals in the family. Typically, neglect and abuse are out-of-control, inappropriately expressed feelings such as anger, jealousy, and sadness. Abuse and neglect are also used by dysfunctional adults in an attempt to relieve their own tension, deal with problems, and punish in inappropriate ways.

12. Imbalance of power. Often in dysfunctional families, certain individuals control all of the family's power—every individual's as well as the family's. This is an imbalance. In a balanced family, each individual has his or her own personal power, and the family works together in a cooperative, noncontrolling way. In an imbalanced family, the father may run the house and whatever he says goes. It doesn't matter if Mom or the children have needs. All that matters is what Dad thinks or wants. The entire family system is then developed to take care of Dad and give Dad what he wants, or Dad may act out by punishing or abusing. Another example of an out-of-balance family is when there is a pecking order. Dad picks on and makes demands of Mom; Mom makes demands of her son; Son makes demands of his sister, and so on. In these families, individuals learn very early that they do not count and are not important. No one feels good and everyone loses!

13. Profound disorder of family responsibilities. Dysfunctional families often deal with responsibilities very poorly, including physical work around the house, caring for the children, and being responsible for one's emotions and behaviors. These families range from total permissiveness to being so rigid that no one can begin to meet the demands. In both extremes, children become lost. In an extreme example, one family member is assigned the role of family caretaker. As one person put it, "I always worked hard to clean the entire house all the time. My family yelled at me constantly saying I didn't do enough and I was lazy. I actually believed them until a friend told me I did more than anyone else in the family and that was the reason I was always tired. I was so caught up in it I really thought I was lazy."

Summary

The above characteristics are important to keep in mind as we further explore the world of the transcender. These characteristics provide the background for understanding just what the transcenders have lived with in their daily lives and what they have overcome. Transcenders work to find ways to grow, develop, protect, and nurture themselves in spite of the dysfunction. Out of the pain and dysfunction, transcenders create a turning-point decision—a decision to be different and *not* to be like their families. This decision is the pivotal point of surviving and transcending.

CHAPTER 3

Decisions: The Turning Point

How do you grow up in a dysfunctional family, cope with intense stress throughout your childhood, and raise yourself because no parent is really available? How do you do all this and not become severely emotionally impaired? When asked these questions, transcenders respond matter-of-factly, "I did what I had to do. Doesn't everyone do what I did? I'm no different than anyone else."

Transcenders, though, are different. They are different from siblings who grow up in the same family or in similar family situations and become severely emotionally ill, extremely dependent, or delinquent. They are also different from emotionally healthy children who grow up in a loving, nurturing family. They make a strong decision and choose to be different.

What transcenders accomplish in the face of great obstacles is nothing short of miraculous. Their incredible process begins by feeling intense pain and loneliness that leads to a monumental *turning-point decision:* to emotionally divorce themselves from their family of origin, take responsibility for their lives, and raise themselves to be different from their family. This turning-point decision appears to continue and to be reaffirmed throughout the transcender's life.

Pain and Loneliness

Transcenders suffer emotionally as well as physically from the many kinds of abuse that can occur in a dysfunctional family—physical, verbal, emotional, ritual, and sexual—as well as neglect. These abuses include assaults to the spirit as well as to the body, and they cause unbelievable pain. Experiences of agonizing pain and loneliness are described again and again by transcenders.

The pain, whatever its cause, is a chronic condition of growing up for the transcender and continues well into adulthood. Transcenders describe physical pain from beatings as sharp, acute, and temporary. They also describe the never-ending pain from unmet emotional needs. Transcenders relate constant pain from the lack of support and struggle for identity. They feel embarrassment, betrayal, and abandonment. They agonize over being deceived, not belonging anywhere to anyone, and fearing the uncertainty in their world. They relate the worst pain as a gnawing, aching, ever-present emptiness. This pain is heavy, depressing, and chronic.

Loneliness is another part of the transcenders' experience of suffering. They describe the loneliness of being-in-the-world with no one to turn to for help or support. (Being-in-the-world is the individual's unique way of relating to his or her world; see Chapter 5.) They feel no one cares, no one regards them as special, and no one accepts or loves them. Transcenders also express feelings of alienation from themselves and others and a strong sense that they can rely only on themselves. At times, they feel alienated from God. Their loneliness is like the pain—a constant ache, a deep inner emptiness.

Incredibly, it is from this suffering—the suffering of chronic, intense, deep pain—that life comes. It is this pain and loneliness that gives birth to the positive, motivating force that grounds transcenders and enables them to change their lives. They make their turning-point decision. Their pain moves them out of their families into more growth-directed channels. Their intense suffering forces them to realize they do not want to live as their families do. It focuses them on a goal of having a world without this kind of pain. Psychologically, the suffering triggers a shift in the transcender's internal frame of reference. (The *internal frame of reference* is the individual's view of the world. This includes thoughts, beliefs, and feelings. This view helps determine how we function in the world and what decisions we make. For example, if I believe the world is wonderful and exciting, I will choose a different path than if I would if I believe the world is a terrible, fearful place to live; see Chapter 5.)

In the following descriptions, Marie, Chris, Steve, Paul, and Tiffany share some of their experiences of pain and loneliness.

Marie

"I grew up in a family where there was no way to win. I was never good enough to win my parents' approval. As a child, my only goal was to be good enough to be loved by my parents. With each baby animal my father would bring home, I prayed I would be good enough so it wouldn't have to be killed because I was a bad girl. Each time, with childlike faith, I believed my dad. Each time, with satanic madness, he tortured them and killed them while making me watch. The pain was horrible, and I felt so alone and so guilty because I couldn't save any of them. They all died.

"Except for school I was kept isolated from children all through my childhood, and I was only allowed to be with other adults when my parents wanted to use me sexually. They tortured me with hopes of having friends. For example, my parents would tell me I was going to have a birthday party. I would anxiously wait for the big day to arrive, standing at the door, full of excitement, waiting and waiting for the first guest to arrive. But no one ever came! I thought no one came to my party because I was a bad girl. But the real reason no one came was because no one was ever invited. For years I thought it was because I was a bad girl and not good enough to celebrate my birthday. I can never remember being wished a happy birthday by my parents. That was a day neither of them wanted to remember. I felt responsible for making them unhappy by being born.

"During the times I was being tortured by my parents, I felt loneliness beyond any description. I learned to retreat into myself in order to escape the pain. At times, I would be tied up in a chair and would watch the hands on the clock move ever so slowly, hour after hour. I would be punished if I wet myself because I couldn't hold the urine any longer and no one would untie me. The fact that I would wet my pants was proof of what a bad girl I was. How I hated that clock. I always hung on to the belief that, if I could just last a little longer someone would come and untie me. (Crying out for help brought more punishment.) No one ever came, unless it was with a belt or a whip.

"Verbal communications in our house were almost nonexistent. My mother would go for weeks without speaking a word to me, and I would have to anticipate what she wanted of me or from me. If I didn't anticipate correctly, I would again be severely punished. I longed to talk to anyone, about anything. This was never possible in our house because I would be punished for 'using up my words.'

"I was terrified when I went to school because I had never played with other children. My mother added to the terror by telling me each morning as I left for school that one day she was going to decide she was sick and tired of taking care of me and leave forever while I was at school, and I would never see her again. I was so terrified she might go away while I was at school and I would be all alone. It's no wonder I vomited every morning before I went to school until I was in the fourth grade.

"An A was the only acceptable grade on a test, paper, or report card. When I did make an A, however, I was punished for calling attention to myself. Once, a teacher wrote my parents a note telling them how well behaved I was in class and how he wished he had more students like me. (Unfortunately, this teacher didn't realize that I was too good, and that something was wrong.) I'll never forget the explosion when my parents read the teacher's note. I was supposed to be a good student and never have to be corrected by my teachers. Here was a letter confirming that I was being a good student, but were my parents pleased? I was severely beaten for again calling attention to myself. The funny thing is I knew what my parents' reaction would be when the teacher wrote the note. In fact, I begged him not to, but he said that good behavior deserved to be rewarded. Little did he know what kind of reward I would receive. Truly, I grew up in a home where there was no way to win."

Chris

The scapegoat of a family experiences pain and loneliness not only from growing up in a dysfunctional family but also from being blamed for all the problems in the family. Chris describes his pain and loneliness this way.

"They hated me. I kept trying and trying to get along, to do something right—something that would make me okay and accepted. Nothing worked. Nothing ever worked. I was always on the outside looking in, hoping. The pain—God, the pain! I was so anxious. I thought at times I was going to just die because the feelings were so intense.

"The pain and tension would overwhelm me. There were times when I couldn't function, and I would just go to my room or a place in the park and sit there. I wouldn't think, feel, or anything. I'd sit in a stupor just trying to stop the pain. Other times, I just kept going because it hurt too much not to. The pain of the beatings was awful but not half as bad as the loneliness and the emotional pain from being isolated in the family. That pain lasted forever. It was like an empty black void where my pain accumulated. My family just kept pouring more and more pain and suffering into it. One of the ways they did this was to play emotional games. They would pretend that I could be part of the family. I would get so excited to finally be a part, to belong, but at the last minute they would change their minds and reject me. They would invite me to a movie or to go visit relatives with them, but at the last minute they'd always find I had done 'something bad' and had to be punished by not being allowed to go with them. It really hurt. I was tricked so many times. I felt like an unacceptable awful kid who could not be given to because everyone knew I was awful, bad, and not worth anything. I was so alone, so incredibly alone. There was no one there to fill the void, to tell me I was okay or that the problem was not me but the craziness of the family. There was no one. I remember always being cold, hungry, and left out. I was never okay in my family."

Steve

Steve, who lived in poverty and took care of his brothers and sisters, experienced a combination of physical and emotional pain. The feelings included isolation and being overburdened with responsibility. He describes it this way.

"It was just terrible. The pain and loneliness was awful, just awful. I can still feel the pain on my legs from trying to get close enough to the fire to get a little warmth and how horribly cold the rest of me was. I will never forget that no one helped us except for table scraps from the neighbors. We were always so hungry. No one should have to live like that, so hungry and so weak—too weak to go to school.

"Later, when I was able to go to school, I never looked okay. The other kids, including my brothers and sisters, would make fun of me. I was always made fun of. I was awkward, weak, dirty, and hungry. They'd call me retarded and dumb, and I believed it. I would study for hours and hours and get so frustrated I'd beat my head on the table saying, 'Why can't I do this? I must be dumb like they say!'

"But there was so much physical and emotional pain that I didn't have room for academics. It was all taken up with pain and just trying to survive. I always felt so very, very alone. My parents were never there for anyone. They were only there physically. I realized there was nobody I could get close to. So I was lonely in the worst sense of the word. I think I felt so unbelievably alone for a lot of years. One of the worst things about being that alone for so long is you believe this must be the way it is or someone would have helped out and changed it for you. You begin to believe all life is like this, with all the pain and loneliness. At times you just lose hope."

Paul

Paul experienced a variety of abuses. What he remembers the most is the chaos and stress. Here are his words.

"Most of all, I remember the stress—the unending stress. There was always yelling and screaming. It seemed like I was always being beaten by my mother. I can remember not being able to sit down for three days after one of Mother's beatings. I was black and blue. It was the stress and the chaos that was the worst, though. The physical beatings, yeah, they hurt, but it was the pain from the constant turmoil and confusion that created the terrible never-ending pain.

"I never felt loved or accepted. Everyone else got to do what I wanted to do—public school, art lessons, dance class. I never knew what was wrong with me because 'me' was not okay. I really didn't know how to be anyone else. I couldn't be perfect because I couldn't get the rules right. And I couldn't get the rules right because they were always changing. I was lost in the chaos, which was like not having any ground to stand on. I didn't know who I was. I didn't know how to figure me out even though I tried, really tried. I didn't have anyone to adhere to in order to begin to figure it all out.

"My loneliness was like a deep, gnawing monster inside of me that kept eating up anything and everything that did get to that empty spot deep inside of me. That spot never got filled as a child, and it took me years to begin to fill it as an adult. No one should ever feel that empty."

Tiffany

Male-dominated roles often create isolation and loneliness. Perfection also creates a different pain—isolation from within oneself. Tiffany, being the only girl, was expected play a traditional role. That, combined with sibling abuse, made Tiffany feel alone and trapped. Her pain was deep and full of fear. Here are her words.

"Fear. All the fear. I was so afraid. The fear in my family was everywhere. I had a fear of not being safe, of not having enough to eat (my brothers would steal my food), of not getting enough love, of not being perfect, of being handicapped, of being criticized. I can't pinpoint the exact age I started being afraid, but it seems to have always been there—always. I desperately needed someone to guide me and teach me how to live, but no one was ever there for me. I was expected to be perfect even though there was no one to help me figure out and understand what perfect was. At times, I would hear deep inside of me: 'Please, I'm scared. Please help me. Tell me things; teach me things I should know. Hold me. Tell me it will be all right.'

"I didn't know how to grow up. I would tell myself to be a big girl, a good girl so Mommy and Daddy would love me. Part of the crazies for me was that I could never show I was afraid because that would mean I was not perfect. And here I was, not just afraid, but terrified! So, I tried to be perfect and hide my fears so that my parents and brothers would love me. One of the worst parts of growing up was knowing my parents really didn't want a girl unless she fit the traditional girl role—one who was prim and proper, took care of the males, who acted, felt, and thought like a good girl. They wanted a girl, but they didn't want me. I just didn't fit. Lord knows I tried, but I just couldn't do it.

"It was such a terrible waste, so sad. I remember having no one there for me—no one I could talk to or be the real me with. It seemed like every time I talked or tried to share something, I was criticized and made to feel wrong. I don't remember anyone ever trying to listen to me. I was so lonely, and the pain was so intense at times that it seemed intolerable. I was so depressed, at one point, that I read every one of John Steinbeck's books, which are horribly tragic. When I got to the last one, *The Red Pony*, I couldn't finish it when I realized the pony was going to die. That was the beginning of my turning point and knowing I'd never do this to me again!"

The Turning-Point Decision

Suffering is the core of the turning-point decision. Transcenders experience intense depression, anger, pain, and loneliness throughout childhood. At times, the suffering is so overwhelming they honestly believe they won't survive. Amazingly, it is out of coping with this intense suffering that the turning point emerges. It is from the individual's feeling the pain so deeply and so intensely that he or she comes to a point of knowing life is not supposed to be this way and begins to seek out a new direction. To the transcender, the turning point sounds like this: "This is not my family. I am not like them, and I don't belong here. Someday I will get out of here and create a world that is less abusive, neglectful, or in other ways hurtful to me. Someday I will be me and have a life I want. I will be different from my family for the rest of my life."

Transcenders' awareness of their turning point includes: (1) not being able to continue to go through the suffering; (2) feeling challenged by and attracted to alternate lifestyles; (3) wanting to maintain the "me" within themselves; and (4) realizing that they are in their world by themselves and it is up to them to make the best of it.

The turning point is an emotional divorce from the family of origin and the family's way of living. It involves a crucial shift from the pain and loneliness to goal-directed, productive living that radically alters the transcender's internal frame of reference. This alteration eventually includes a feeling of liking and loving oneself as well as feeling good about oneself. It is as if a miracle happens that begins to change the person's view of him- or herself.

What transcenders decide in this divorce is to make it in spite of family problems, obstacles, and handicaps. The decision is so powerful it becomes the pivotal point—the motivating force not only for survival but also for transcending and guiding the rest of their lives. The power of this decision supports, grounds, and helps sustain them throughout childhood and beyond. The turning point is a powerful leap into the future. It is the essence of survival. It says "I will make it!" Without this decision, transcenders would not make it.

How is the turning-point decision made? Sometimes one crisis brings the turning-point decision into focus; sometimes it is a series of crises over a period of years. However it occurs, transcenders often feel forced to accept the painful reality of their families, to reflect on themselves, and to realize their families will never be capable of giving them the love and acceptance they so desperately need. This is an agonizing decision to make, and it is not done overnight. Sometimes it takes years. Sometimes individuals struggle with it into adulthood. At times, it has to be reevaluated as an adult, especially if the family continues to act out. Transcenders watch, feel, think, and finally have to decide to emotionally divorce and pull away from their family because they believe they will not survive otherwise.

The cost is great. It often means emotionally divorcing themselves from the little, if any, closeness they may have had in the family and maintaining a state of independence long before they as children, are developmentally ready to do so. It also means taking care of their own physical and emotional needs and being wise and mature far beyond their chronological years.

Transcenders are not superhuman, invincible, invulnerable, immune to pain, or both with resiliency. The major difference between the transcender and the child who succumbs to the family's dysfunction is the turning-point decision. Instead of becoming dysfunctional and/or impaired like their families, transcenders choose to find ways through the struggle and transcend. It is a concerted, difficult decision. They work to be different from their families and divorce themselves emotionally while they still have to live physically within the family. They seek out what they need elsewhere and develop their inner self. This means reaching out to others for support, guidance, and information on how to live in the world differently from their own family. At the same time, they cope with tremendous stress at home by using survival skills. Through survival skills, transcenders work to create meaning out of chaos, nurturing out of barrenness, and protection in the face of violence.

The turning-point decision occurs at different ages for different individuals. For some, it seems to occur in early childhood, whereas for others it occurs in the late teens or adulthood. The most common age mentioned by transcenders in my research and professional experience is ten to thirteen years. The time of the decision is *not* important. What is important is that the decision is made and healing and growth occur.

What follows are examples of turning points.

Marie

"I am not able to identify the particular time of my turning-point decision when I decided to be different. I know it was at a very early age before I could identify my emotions. Actually, there were probably several turning points, each one stronger, more determined than the one before. I suppose the real turning point was when I internally rebelled against my world and said, 'No, I will not be like these people. I will be different. I will make other choices for myself.' It was a definite conscious awareness. I decided that I may be from the mud but never of the mud. Deep inside myself I knew I would rise above this insanity. I knew there was a better way, a different way, and I just had to make different choices than my parents had made in their lives.

"To make these different choices, I had to weigh and measure actions, behaviors, and values in order to determine what was real and worth keeping. At the same time, I had to decide what to discard, reject, or remove myself from. Basically, I had to be my own parent—a terrifying way of life for a small child and for a teenager. I just remember so many things in my life that did not feel right.

"I don't remember the first time I was sexually abused or subject to sexual encounters no child should have knowledge of. I do remember it did not feel right and I did not want to be there. I grew up knowing that I could never let anyone know what my family was really like. My mother always told me that if anyone found out how bad I really was, I would be put up for adoption. As crazy and abusive as she was, I was terrified of her leaving me.

"During therapy, I remembered being with my parents in a department store. They were walking just behind me and then all of a sudden, they were gone, hiding from me. I remember so well the terror of looking for feet that I recognized so I could find my parents again. I didn't dare act lost or cry. After all, I had been a bad girl. At the time, I really thought I was such a bad person I deserved this kind of treatment and abuse. And yet, at other times during sexual abuse, I would cover my eyes or try to put my fingers in my ears in an attempt to block the sights and sounds from a world in which I knew I did not belong. No, I can't say there was any real one turning point but rather an accumulation of turning-point decisions to not ever be like my mother and never have to do those horrible things again. That has truly sustained me and been my focus for life."

Chris

"I became determined again and again and again, like a mindset, to take care of me in spite of my family. I simply did what I had to do until I could get out of there. For example, I can remember this mindset being part of me when I was very young. I came home from school when I was four and I said to my mother that I didn't need to walk to school with anybody. I mean even at four years old and school a mile away, I had this goal. So I don't know. I even think that it can be prenatal. I sensed that I would have to tune out the world until I got out of that family in order to not be like them.

"Sometimes I'd get angry and say over and over to myself, 'I'll show you. I'm not going to be like you guys, because I'm not. Life doesn't have to be this way.'"

Steve

"I remember deciding that I would never live in poverty again with the neglect, hunger, cold, and no parent. I never wanted to go back. That's what kept me going. It was my drive, my energy for working, getting ahead, and moving forward. Nothing could ever be as bad as that. Nothing! I won't let it.

"It was fear, but also a commitment to myself to keep moving forward and not to stay in a spot where I just kept rehashing my life over and over again and become like my parents. I never wanted to do that. I knew I couldn't be that poor again. Oh, it was so awful. I wanted to keep moving forward and to never, never repeat how I grew up. I wanted to be different, very different. I wanted to be different from my environment, different from my abandoning parents, different than all of it. I wanted to be me and whatever risks it would take, I'd take them. I never again wanted to put myself in a position of being cold, hungry or neglected."

Paul

"I was always scared shitless that I would be a fool like my father. I considered my father a fool, and he really was. That's harsh language, but his behavior was so strange that it was kind of like a buffoon's. I do imitations of people who are out of control. For example, people you meet in bars, people who are just squirrely and how their mind gets going and they talk about things that really don't make any sense at all, and yet, they don't know that. My father was always that way, so I grew up thinking that if you are yourself you will be a fool. So, I monitored everything that went on in my mind before I said a word because I was scared to death that I would say things like my father and I would come out sounding like a fool and not know it. I worked really hard not be like my father."

Tiffany

"It was from the pain, so much pain. I can still feel it. I was so alone and so afraid and yet I had to act so independent. I can still bring back the terror of it and my body shudders with it. I had become unbelievably, painfully shy, but out of this pain came my decision. I can remember the day of my decision. It was sunny and beautiful out, but all I could see was darkness, pain, and emptiness. I was reading Steinbeck's *The Red Pony* and had come to the place where the pony was going to die. I closed the book and I said, 'I'll never do this to me again, never. I'll never be this depressed and in this pain again.' I never have finished that book. I still have it as a reminder to me. I decided that someday, somehow, I'd be me in a world where I could be me and not have to hide. I'd be me no matter what it took. That's what it felt like, the real me was hidden because the real me was not okay.

"To exist, I functioned on two levels: one was the girl my family wanted that cooked, cleaned, helped my mother, got good grades, did what she was told, and took whatever my brothers dished out, and the other me—the creative, vital, authentic me—withdrew, fantasized, and was nurtured underground.

"It was this decision, to be me 'in the world,' that has continued to be my focus for life. It is a special, powerful promise I made to myself and one that I have rarely veered from. This promise meant that I emotionally divorced my family and looked in other directions for my life.

"I still use it when I become lost in the world of others. It helps, even now, when I have a hard decision to make. I ask myself, 'Is this how I want my world?' If the answer is yes, I go ahead because not to do it would mean going back to that suffering and losing me, and I couldn't ever do that again. Ever! Just the thought of it shoots a feeling of fear and pain through me with a scream. This promise is ab-solutely one of my most precious possessions.

"Somehow, deep inside of me, I was in touch with a kernel of truth—that part of me that was good, precious, and worth everything. It's this kernel that I protected and nurtured as much as possible. I cared for it and affirmed it. I kept the real me protected from the hurts of the family. It was tucked away, safe, waiting for its time to surface. It helped ease the pain."

More Turning Points

Tim

Tim transcended a family in which the parents were totally enmeshed and left little room for a growing child.

"My turning point was around my mother's hospital-ization for a hysterectomy. She had ovarian cancer. It was shortly after we moved to a new town, and I was just un-believably lonely. I had a real hard time making friends and I felt very out of it. I tried to be the teacher's pet and be smart. I found no support whatsoever at home. I was put out into the world of school, new friends, and strange town with no support from home.

"My father was zoned out. I can't remember much about him during that time even though it was just the two of us for two weeks while Mom was in the hospital. I do re-member him taking me to the hospital to visit her and then telling me I couldn't come in because I had to be fourteen to visit. I was only ten or eleven. I was really angry and hurt. I would take a small stepladder (my mother was on the first floor of the hospital), set it up, and wave to her from outside her window. One time I made a little snow-man for her.

"I think the symbolism of being outside the window in the cold, looking in, and seeing my parents in the warmth together hit me very hard. I was not really conscious of it, but I think after that time I checked out of my family. I had tried to be part of the family. I had tried to make them into my parents and kept banging on their doors. After a while, I did not bang on the doors anymore.

"I made the decision to divorce myself from the family. I really had left them. The situation was an exaggeration or magnification of what was really going on all that time in everyday life. It was a symbolic thing because my mother was always acting like a little girl. She was so de-pendent, almost like an invalid. Basically, she was flat on her back in the hospital, my father was administering to her emotionally, and there I was standing outside on the ladder in the snow.

"I felt a lot of sadness, hurt, and anger all mixed up. I wondered what it was about me that was so unlovable.

They were always in the warm, well-lighted room, and I was always out in the snow. I wondered what it was about me, and turned it on myself: Maybe it is not them; maybe it is me. And then again, I felt really helpless to do anything about it. God knows I was trying. I felt like a victim and was really helpless. There was nothing else I could do because I had tried everything there was to try. At that time in my life, there was nobody I could connect with, and so I began to seek what I needed elsewhere and divorced my family."

Bill

Bill grew up in an ethnic ghetto with an alcoholic father, and he had a deeply symbiotic relationship with his mother. In this type of relationship, the connection is so close that there is little separation between mother and child. Here is his turning-point process.

"Part of my moving away from the family occurred when I went to high school out of my old neighborhood. It was a parochial school. It was not an ethnic parochial school; people actually spoke English. They did not speak Polish or Italian but everyday common English in a school run by Irish nuns. There was a mixture of kids, and I was forced to adapt. I blossomed, and I became aware of other lifestyles, values, and attitudes that were different from mine. I met people who were sons of doctors, successful insurance men, and attorneys who did not drive ten-year-old clunkers but who bought this year's car this year. They were successful that way but were also successful emotionally. I saw real closeness between parents and sons. It was like I was in a different atmosphere in a different way.

"I started shifting away. My father and mother were no longer going to be how I measured life. My father was not capable of giving me guidance or direction, and he was always going to drink and be crazy. I also came to realize that I couldn't rely on my mother. I started pulling away from that kind of emotional relationship. I began to invest in other relationships and create my world."

Tom

Tom's turning-point decision was a shift to more positive messages rather than a major decision.

"No, I didn't make a conscious decision. I don't think I did. But I did make a kind of shift where I was looking for positive messages. I remember, especially in terms of girls, I felt very ugly and got real crazy about it. I was just acting out the message I got at home: a lot of criticism, a lot of nonverbal messages that I'm not much of a human being, nor was I very desirable as a human being. So, I just gave up girls altogether. And then I remembered hearing in my senior year a rumor that some girl wanted to date me. It just blew me away. I was so surprised. So, I did it. I dated the girl—someone I never thought would have been the least bit interested in me, and that was a real help. From there I continued to look for more positive messages."

Important Parts to Turning-Point Decisions

Transcenders create turning-point decisions as a result of an inward shift triggered by intense suffering. There are three important parts to the decision: (1) a separation from the family, emotionally and physically; (2) refusal to be like the family; and (3) a commitment to personal growth.

In the first part of the decision, transcenders realize there is a different, healthier way to live without so much pain, loneliness, and anger. Separating from, or "emotionally divorcing," the family often includes leaving emotionally, socially, and/or physically until transcenders are able to move out permanently. Transcenders come to a strong realization of the need to separate, and they detach in order to survive. They describe this part of the turning point as a strong will to live; an intense inner drive to go beyond or transcend the family, as well as determination to attain internal independence.

The second part of the decision is a refusal to be like the family. There is a realization that the family is wrong, painful, horrible, violent, or ignorant, as well as an awareness the transcender does not have to be like the family. This part helps maintain the separation by reminding transcenders of their intense fear of being like their families. They also describe the refusal as an inner drive to be much more than the family. This area requires an active, determined commitment to be different, which in turn maintains and encourages growth in other ways. For example, they feel forced to seek role models in other areas of their lives.

The third and last part of the turning point is a strong, long-lasting commitment to personal growth. This part of the turning-point decision seems to begin at the time of the decision. It includes: (1) a fear of ending up stuck like their family; (2) an awareness and search for their possible potentialities and talents; (3) the search for a way to make up for time and opportunities lost because of the family; and (4) the search for growth at all cost. To create growth, transcenders use their *will* (that part of us that focuses and helps us use all available resources; see Chapter 5) and seek other areas for developing competencies, overcoming anxieties, and finding needed, available resources. Their commitment to personal growth is a continuing, lifelong process.

One transcender describes it this way: "I feel very proud of what I am because I worked hard to be able to be here. It's a lot of hard work. I see people today who want to make changes overnight, and it doesn't work that way. It takes a long concerted effort. You have to work, work, work, and when you can't stand it, you work some more. Sometimes you just have to go to sleep.

"Many nights I just sat up reading books, trying to find something to hang on to. Somebody gave me a copy of *The World's Greatest Salesman,* and boy, there were nights I sat in the bedroom and just read the same chapter over and over again, just trying to hang on. I'd wake up the next morning and read it over and over again, just trying to make it through the day.

"Sometimes, I'd just go to bed at night and say, 'Go to sleep and you won't feel it.' And it helps. It's helped to deal with those things; to reach part of the potential that I have. I still have a long way to go yet, but I'm excited about the growth I have gained."

The Internal Shift of the Change

Transcenders create a remarkable internal shift. They change how they view their world, their families, and themselves. To do this, transcenders maintain a concerted effort over a long time — even years or decades. Some transcenders remember a very conscious decision, whereas others remember beginning to look for more positive messages in their world. No matter how the shift occurs, it is amazing that it can be maintained over years of dysfunctional family life.

Transcenders describe two processes in changing their internal frame of reference, each of which takes a huge effort to accomplish. The first is to create a more positive self-image and a better lifestyle. To accomplish these goals, transcenders struggle to overcome feelings of self-doubt, self-degradation, and a fear of life. They work to be accepted and to accept themselves as people (not objects or numbers in the family), to be independent, and to move away from the family. They find ways to help themselves through traumas, to be first-class citizens, to seek positive messages rather than criticism, to continue working to change their old internal frame of reference, and to create a new way of being. They protect themselves from the negative influences, and they work to gain the nurturing they desperately need. Often, as will be seen later, transcenders as adults put themselves in psychotherapy to help their healing and growing process.

They are persistent and stay focused on their goals. They refuse to give up. If they have feelings of wanting to give up, they usually feel a panic, and they will then regroup and keep going. They work hard not be like their family. If you want to trigger anger in transcenders, just tell them they are like their family!

The second process transcenders use in the struggle to change their internal frame of reference is a shift to a more a positive focus in their lives. Transcenders describe a dawning awareness of the world's beauty and goodness that kindles a sense of warmth. This connection inspires them to take control of their lives, to have the courage to move away from their dysfunctional families and to gain the strength needed to continue working "to make it." They begin to believe in, rely on, and be responsible for themselves.

Once they decide to be different from their families, their belief in themselves helps them to know there is something better and they are capable of creating it. This belief connects them to their potentialities, talents, goals, and hope. Often it provides an internal affirmation of themselves. In this process, their being-in-the-world (See Chapter 5) is in transition, and they apply the needed work, persistence, active willing, and a belief in themselves that sustains the effort through many years.

Summary

The process of creating the turning-point decision involves individuals' examining their lives and making a commitment to themselves for the future. In this way they become free from their family's control and free to seek what they need in other areas. Additionally, inward shifts become pivotal points in their lives. Transcenders work to create a more positive internal frame of reference relying upon their belief in themselves.

CHAPTER 4

Techniques of Transcending

How do transcenders get through the day while coping with the extreme stress from their family life? How do they create a new and different life for themselves? Where do they get needed information, protection, and nurturance to survive? This chapter details the everyday skills and techniques of survival and transcending that transcenders use to create a different lifestyle while managing and coping with extreme stress and trauma.

Survival depends on *actively* developing techniques that gain two very important supports: protection and nurturance for the body and the precious core—the authentic self. Often one technique offers both protection and nurturance. The more trauma, the more effort is needed. In the beginning, the skill level may not be adequate, but through determination, perseverance, and practice transcenders develop techniques strong enough to survive.

Protection is an absolute necessity because transcenders have to become less vulnerable to the dangers in their world. They need to escape, seek refuge, find safety, and defend themselves whenever possible. Protection techniques shield, curb, hinder, and at times stop the onslaught of injury and destruction.

Transcenders also have to develop techniques that gain nurturance. They seek out people, places, organizations, animals, plants, nature, and situations that offer assistance, support, revitalization, and learning. These, in turn, help the transcender maintain and develop the original package.

From these techniques, transcenders gain feelings of being gratified, bolstered, rescued, relieved, encouraged, and reinforced in their battle to survive. The nurturance and protection that transcenders obtain may not fill the emptiness or take away the pain, but it is enough to maintain the self and give hope for the future.

Eleven survival technique categories used by transcenders have been identified: (1) using inner personal resources, (2) using fantasy, (3) using available environmental resources, (4) transcending the family, (5) getting out and staying away, (6) developing a style of relating to others, (7) developing roles in the family, (8) seeking relationships with others, (9) developing competencies, (10) playing, and (11) developing spirituality. In the following examples, each category is illustrated by many different transcenders including ones we've already met in previous chapters. These categories demonstrate how transcenders use techniques to provide protection and nurturance limited only by their creativity. Techniques can also overlap; that is, they can belong in more than one category. While reading, please remember that some techniques protect, some nurture, and some do both. Take the time to feel what it must have been like to develop and use these techniques. Many of you, I am sure, can easily add to the list because you have lived it.

1. Using Inner Personal Resources

Inner resources include those abilities, talents, or skills that originate from within the person. Transcenders reach deep within and use what is available. Intuition, manipulation, withdrawal, reverse psychology, and being alone are a few examples of inner resources used by transcenders to deal with their assaultive world. Other examples include distancing from others, drawing close to others, feeling one's feelings fully, and choosing when to use a certain technique.

When transcenders must be at home, their inner resources function to preserve the self while their world is working to destroy it. Their deep commitment to the turning point, along with their strong will, helps them in this process. The following illustrations are examples of how transcenders use inner personal resources for protection, nurturance, or both. Inner resources are listed under seven different types: (1) affirming oneself, (2) reality-basing the abuse, (3) using intuition, (4) being alone or withdrawing, (5) yelling, (6) observing, and (7) others.

Affirming Oneself

Transcenders often have to affirm and support themselves. The following quotations describe some of the ways they do this.

"First, I had to immerse in myself and work on getting my self-image together. At times, I wondered if I was ever going to, but it was really necessary for me to invest in me, because there was not anyone else who was going to. It was an absolute necessity of survival."

"I really felt my mom gave my sister a lot more credit than she gave me. I have always felt she believed my sister was more intelligent and more attractive. In my own mind, I felt I was every bit as intelligent and as attractive as my sister. It was a knowing that supported me all through growing up."

Reality-Basing the Abuse

In dealing with the abuse, transcenders realize they are not to blame for the abuse and they did nothing wrong. Some transcenders express this to themselves. The following are some of their words.

"During the physical abuse, I remember many times crying, 'Why am I being hit? What am I being beat up for?' Because I didn't do anything wrong, it really bothered me. I'd get slapped in the face or get a lot of verbal abuse, which I hated. I was awfully mad about it. I would think, well, I was not wrong, they were wrong."

"I didn't have any cognitive awareness because it was not safe. I did think, 'Well, I didn't do anything that bad.' But I'd go pay the consequences and shut my mouth because something worse could happen. For example, my parents could say, 'Go clean that room again with a toothbrush because you didn't dust it well enough.'
"'That's insane!' I'd say to myself, 'What did I do wrong?' It's like looking for some sort of reasoning, except it was not there. There's a part of me that knew it didn't make sense—a positive core of me helping to sort out their crazy reality from mine, and that helped."

Using Intuition

Another inner resource is intuition, knowing something but not really knowing how we know it. Transcenders not only rely on this area, they develop it fully.

"I was given myriads and myriads of opportunities to develop my intuition and my handling of emotionally difficult situations. For example, I can remember thinking, 'If I say such and such, okay. However, if I say this, boy, they're going to get mad.' I would work and figure this all out. I also had to learn to manipulate my brother because he was stronger and he'd tear up all my comic books. I tried psychology on him—some reverse psychology—and

I found out it worked, it really worked! My brother didn't tear up my comic books."

"When my dad was drunk," he would have DTs (delirium tremens which is a form of alcoholic psychosis), and I was smart enough to handle them. For example, I'd be in the bedroom and he'd say, 'Get the snake that's on the wall.' He was hallucinating. I'd think, 'Dad, I can't. Where in the hell is the snake?' I knew there was no snake there. I was trying to sort out what was real and what was not. There was a real battle going on in me. But I was smart enough to say, 'Yeah, Dad, I got it. It's not there anymore.' I had to go with the system to survive.

"Another time, Dad put his head in the stove and I was scared. I think I said something like, 'Daddy, you don't want to be with the devil.' That snapped him out of it and helped him not to die. It's like I could go into his craziness. I could understand what he was doing, and if he was dead he was going to be with the devil."

Being Alone or Withdrawing

Transcenders find being alone and withdrawing into themselves very comforting and nurturing. During these times, they do not have to be on guard and can relax and be themselves.

"I think being alone, being in a world of my own that was not connected to the bunch of crazy acting-out people in my world, helped the most. It was not too real as far as a normal reality because I had to create my own, but it was safer and saner than what was in the family."

"There was a difference between my outer and inner world that goes back to daydreaming and my withdrawal into reading. Yeah, because in the reading and the daydreaming, I could be in a world that was my own creation and not somebody else's. These were the seeds of my survivorship. I used to say to myself, 'I'll be what you want me to be, but when I'm not around you, when I'm among my friends or by myself, when I choose to, there are some things you cannot take away from me. You can't take away my daydreaming. You can't take away my fantasies, and you can't take away what reading means to me as long as I am a very fantastic student academically.'

"They would actually refer to me that way. They'd say, 'He's studying,' or 'He's forgetful because he's reading his book.' And they'd leave me alone."

"I would get so angry and when my father would get mad at me. He would just criticize and be all over me. I felt so bad about myself. I would go off by myself and just close everything off. I would hear my mother say I was just going into my shell, and then I'd just go blank. I heard the words but didn't feel anything. The only way to protect myself from my father was to shut him off and shut out the words so I couldn't hear what he said. I couldn't fight him. I would then just go off somewhere."

"I stopped sharing me because it hurt too much to put me out there with my family criticizing, smashing, and making me wrong all the time. So I literally went underground. One part of me functioned on the surface and the other, the real me, was underground, protected, and away from the people that could hurt it. It was like escaping inside of myself."

Yelling

Yelling serves as a release for built-up emotions. When releasing any emotion, it is important to remember to release it appropriately. The rules are: (1) you can't hurt yourself; (2) you can't hurt others or something alive; and (3) you can't damage property you don't want to damage. Here's how yelling worked for some transcenders.

"When things got real bad around the house and the pain had built up inside of me to the point of being more than I could handle, I'd explode by yelling, screaming, and throwing things around. I'd have a major temper tantrum! It felt so good to release all that stuff. At times, I felt I could go on screaming forever. After the temper tantrum, I could go on again. It felt like a limit I was drawing inside of myself that screamed, 'That's enough. Back off.' And for a little while they did."

"I used my anger to keep people away, especially my family. I would yell, scream, throw things, and really pitch a fit. I did anything I believed would keep them away from me."

"I would yell, scream, run into my room and slam the door. I slammed it so many times the molding came off. My dad would threaten to take off my door if I did it one more time. I would. He never did."

Observing

Transcenders at times pull back and observe others intensely. From this, they learn many things, such as other ways to live and how to relate in their world.

"I watched and watched. In school, I may have been observing more than working and getting involved, but that's how I learned what to do and how to fit in. I needed to observe in order to know what normal was, because all I knew at home were crazies. Finally, I quit watching and began to act, to be a part of life. I got involved."

"Watching and listening. I was shy so I watched and observed. I learned what life could be like. I listened to relatives who would just let me hang around. My relatives did not know I was being abused."

Others

Techniques are limited only by the creativity of the person involved. Many variations are possible. Included often are art, music, mying, manipulation, stealing, and so forth.

"There was always a difference between my outer self and the inner, real me. I would screen all incoming stuff and decide if I was going to let it go deeper to the real me. If it was not okay—that is, not matching what I thought I needed or wanted—I rejected it. I had to be very strong willed. If it was something I needed, I would allow it in, and I would use it to nurture myself. I wasn't always successful in keeping the pain away, but it helped."

"My brother and I always had a strong German pride that kept us together. When we first arrived at the farm and wanted to discuss something but didn't want our foster parents to know, we would speak in German. They were Italian and didn't understand what we were talking about. It gave us privacy and a sense of family."

2. Using Fantasy

Fantasy is one of the inner resource techniques and is important enough to be put in its own category. In fantasy transcenders give themselves what they do not or cannot have in reality. It's almost like having the real thing. Through fantasy, transcenders create another, different life. For example, in fantasy, they can be powerful enough to overcome abusive parents or to have everyone love and take care of them. They can be in demand, liked, confident, pain-free, and even playful like a regular kid. Fantasy offers escape when escape is impossible, relief from the trauma when trauma is everywhere, and hope for the future when there is none. Fantasy can even help set goals for the future.

"I daydreamed a lot. Fantasizing really helped me survive because I could be in another world—a world of my very own—and have things the way I wanted them. I controlled this world, and I decided who and what happened in it. I felt relief and power over the insanity that was in my family. I can remember also setting goals back then that I am still working on today."

"Through pretending, I dealt with my world and experienced my feelings. For example, if I was really upset or scared about something that was going to happen, I'd pretend how I wanted to handle the situation. I'd act it out in my imagination and try many different solutions. At the same time, I would experience and release all my feelings about it that were not safe to do so at the time. It was such a good release for my feelings, and it helped me get ready for what was going to happen. I also did this with things that had already happened that I was still upset about and wished I could change."

"I lived in a dream world. I even had fantasies when I was five years old about having a better life. I wanted to be the king of England, and I fantasized about it all the time. I read *The Prince and the Pauper*, where the two kids change places. I said to my mother, 'How come you did away with my twin?' She said, 'What are you talking about? You are my kid.'

"I wanted to be knighted, to be the English heir. Actually, my mother's heritage goes back to Scotland, to the Ross Clan. The Earl of Ross became James I, King of England. So, my fantasy and dream for a better life was based in some reality."

"When I was in school I would pretend a lot. I would say, 'Oh, there are my friends. This teacher is a lovely person.' When I was in Boy Scouts, everyone was my friend, brother, and my scoutmaster was my dad. I found people and made believe they were my family, my real family, not the one I was stuck in. It felt so good and gave me such support."

"I would act out being a hero. I felt powerful and important. People noticed me as the hero. I had power that I did not have in the family. I also acted out my death. I'd even cry because I was sad for me. Even in my fantasy, no one cared. No one came to my funeral."

3. Using Available Environmental Resources

The third technique acknowledged by transcenders is using available environmental resources discovered or offered in their world. Transcenders view these offerings as opportunities to learn, grow, be revitalized, and develop areas of security and competencies. These resources include education, recreation, animals, plants, nature, organizations, situations, and other personal opportunities. Through these environmental opportunities, transcenders find support, caring, and encouragement. In addition, they become involved with available protection and nurturing resources.

"My growing up world was made up of sights, sounds, and smells of a multiracial and ethnic neighborhood. My senses were stimulated viscerally, visually, and tacitly so that my preparation in the world was indelibly imprinted. To see, to hear, to touch, to taste, to smell, to sense the tacit filled me with such stimuli and imagery I wanted to know more. I became an observer, a wanderer, and an explorer at an early age. I was an intensely curious child, and I got into difficulty at times for experimenting with household elements or wandering away from home without permission. The smells and tastes and sights and conversations of countless delicatessens, bakeries, ethnic markets, as well as the music of dozens of languages shall remain with me to the end of my days. I am able yet to recognize the sounds of a dozen or more languages even if I am not conversant in all of them."

"I had a wonderful seventeenth summer. I went to muscular dystrophy camp for the first time and really loved it. I felt really good about myself. I liked helping those kids because it made me feel really good inside. Also, five boys liked me. For the first time, I was liked and it was a very sharing, giving, good experience, and I loved it. I found out I could feel good by doing good. I got this wonderful reward that is very hard to get any place else."

"In the seventh grade, I began to live in convents to escape my father's violence. When one no longer wanted me (which happened for a variety of reasons), I found another. The nuns accepted me because they had no background from the other convent. I was clever and would find another place."

"I remember arriving at the farm for foster care as a big day in my life. It had a lot of exciting things for boys to do such as trapping, hunting, chasing rats, playing with the dog, and playing with the cats. There was all of nature with insects, wild animals, pheasant, and wild swamp birds of different kinds. The farming life had a powerful influence on me because it showed me that if I worked hard, even through I was not the smartest, I would succeed at something."

"Probably one of the most exciting things to me happened when I was thirteen years old. My aunt and uncle took me with them on vacation. We went to New England. I remember they had a Mustang—a brand new Mustang that had just come out in the 1960s. I remember riding in this Mustang all the way out East and seeing things like the *Mayflower*, Plymouth Rock, battleships, and Niagara Falls. I really enjoyed it, and it gave me a vision for the future."

"Nurtured by nature, that's how I survived. I grew up around lakes and woods, and I spent every chance I could in them. It offered me safety, a way to be, and rest. Somehow nature revitalized me, energized me, and helped me regroup to keep going. Somehow things were lighter and less intense. I still love being in the woods."

4. Transcending the Family

Transcendence is a technique that enables an individual to rise above and go beyond the immediate situation. In doing so, individuals consciously shift to and gain another perspective of themselves and their world. Their ability to transcend helps to overcome difficult and what seem at times to be insurmountable obstacles.

Relationships, activities, and fantasies, as well as other techniques, help transcenders rise above the family situation. For example, they use fantasy as a way to give themselves what they did not, or could not, have in reality, which is one type of transcendence. Using educational opportunities to see the world in a new way is another. Once a situation is transcended, they gain a heightened awareness of their situation and gain strength. They see more clearly how to create nurturance, protection, hope for the future, and goals for their lives. Above all, transcendence offers relief from the immediate situation.

"I struggled to invest in activities with new and different people. To compete, socialize, date, and to have an awareness that people outside my family saw and experienced differently than my family of origin. Without this different perspective I would not have sustained my will to survive."

"I used many things to transcend my family situation. I worked with clay, fantasized, read, prayed, and spent time alone. Basically, I did anything that shifted me out of my present world into a less tense, less vulnerable, more nurturing and warm place. At times, I'd 'leave' my world completely and fantasize I was in another. Other times, I'd be half in and half out of my family's world. That is, half of me was in the family activity and half was focused on the future. My fantasy world often contained my hopes and dreams for my future. I could actually feel what it would have been like to accomplish those goals. Now, in real life, as I actually do those things, I feel them for real."

"At times, I had to just leave the pain and get time to sort me from the family—sort of like rising above it so I would not be affected by it. It's as if I went to another level inside of me where I was detached from the pain—a place where I could think and feel clearer. I felt relief and a separation or distancing from my immediate situation. This was a major part of my survivor-hood."

5. Getting Out and Staying Away

A major technique used by transcenders is getting out and staying away when they have the freedom to do so. Transcenders physically leave their family any way possible, as often as they can, for as long as they can. They get out through activities, organizations, or by adopting other families. They go to churches, schools, convents, and neighbors' and friends' homes. They go for bike rides and walks. They go out with friends and significant others. They go to sanctuaries. At times, they gain competencies while getting out and connecting to others. Getting out and staying away are purposeful actions, they do not just happen.

By getting out, transcenders escape their home situations, release feelings, relax, and gain nurturance. They also refocus, spend time being their authentic selves, and gain a sense of freedom as well as safety. At times, the family gives the transcender the freedom to get out by being negligent or being unable to cope with the situation. For some parents, it is easier if the children are "out of their hair."

Other times, transcenders have controlling parents and leave by rebelling. In any case, getting out and staying away involves using safer available and accessible people and places. The final getting out and staying away occurs with the move out of the house into the adult world through marriage, work, military, or college.

"One time, my father tore the basement to pieces coming after me and beating on me. I didn't fight back. I just ran out of the house and headed for a field and lay there for a long, long time just trying to figure out what I was going to do next with my life. Eventually, I started walking back home."

"I just adopted this other family as mine. I used to spend all my weekends there during most of high school, which enabled me to leave home emotionally and definitely physically. I was about fifteen or sixteen. As I look back on it, it was a great adaptation because if I had gone any other route I would have landed up in juvenile court and probably in a home somewhere. This way, I was able to get away from my home, which was a dynamite keg ready to explode. It finally did explode a couple of times with my dad and me."

"I spent lots and lots of time with a close friend of mine who was also a survivor. We drove around town together and helped each other survive. Tom and I found each other basically to hang onto. We put thousands and thousands of miles on his car, driving around town, doing nothing but staying away from our respective families. Round and round and round—we were such experts on that town. We probably put 200,000 miles on his car, literally. That was part of surviving—getting out and staying out."

"I left home quite often, especially when I was feeling anxious or lonely. I got out in the evening when I played for dances and got away in the summer in college by playing at resorts all summer. I was very involved in school activities. Thank God, because I was able to stay away from home as long as possible and connect to really nice people. That's how I maintained my sanity."

"There is something about adventuring or exploring that I have always liked. I like to travel, and I like to venture out into the world and explore. I think that has been my theme from day one. The running away was venturing out into the world. It's sort of like there was nothing at home so let's go see what's out there in the world."

"I was just very distraught over all the stuff that was going on at home, and frankly I avoided going home. It was lonely, but I preferred it over going home because it was just that old tension again. It was just the pits, and I avoided it as much as possible. There was nothing I could do about it, so why subject myself to that?"

"I was always on the go, always running. My sister stayed at home more, and she got worse. I kept at it. I went to places that were crazy but sane, that is, the same thing as my family because even the nuns couldn't talk and they'd walk around the halls with their heads down. At least they weren't acting out violently. I knew that I would come and scrub the floor today or buff the chapel with the big buffer machine or wherever I'd be working. In the ninth grade, I lived there and joined the order. It was more or less like going away to school, wanting to become a nun someday. I left home in the ninth grade—actually, I left way before that."

"If I had not gotten married, I would probably have run away from home. I couldn't stand living there, but I was afraid to leave because my parents would have come and dragged me back, no matter where I went. So, I got engaged. I knew that the only way to get out of my parents' clutches was to get married. My husband was the first to ask, so he got me."

Sanctuaries

In the category of getting out and staying away we find the sanctuary. This is any special place that a transcender uses to get away from the family. Sanctuaries offer protection from the family and nurturance for the self. Above all, these special places offer a chance just to be, where transcenders can escape their homes, release feelings, relax, gain nurturance, and in general, regroup within themselves. The sanctuary is a safe, accessible, available place to go when the world closes in.

"I loved the out-of-doors with the sun and woods. That has always been my sanctuary—warm, sunny, on walks, bike rides. I relaxed with the warmth, comfort, and good smells. Most of all, it was comfortable and safe. I could pray, cry, and let it all out. It was my special place to be just me."

"I had a special place in our basement. When I felt like I had absolutely had it with the stuff going on in my family, I would crawl in the space and stay until I could face the world again. For some reason, my family never realized I was there or just didn't care. I would spend a long time there, thinking, feeling, being alone, and being lonely. It was my special sanctuary, a place to be just me. There was part of me, however, that wished someone would have noticed I was gone and come and asked me what was wrong. I wish someone would have tried to talk to me about it. No one ever came."

"I used to get away as often as I could—go anywhere. I did have one special place—my sanctuary. It was near the lake, and I'd spend hours there. I would be alone, and it was peaceful and calm, and there would be no fighting or criticizing."

6. Relating to Others

Many transcenders develop a style of relating to others that helps them gain protection and nurturance. A style of relat-

ing is a way of communicating with others, a way of being with the world outside the family. It is not usually the same as a role in the family, although at times it may be. Among these styles are being rebellious, shy, witty, entertaining, or even playing dumb. Styles of relating can fend off negative influences, keep people at a distance, bring people close, and help reaffirm the sense of self. Often, transcenders hope that someone will take the time to discover the intense hurt that is causing their style of relating. The following illustrates how styles help children survive.

"I was totally out of it. I mean, I played dumb to the point of being labeled retarded in the second grade. I was smart to do it because it wiped out all that was going on in my family." (This was taken from a doctoral candidate.)

"My school friends lived nearby. I visited them, and their parents liked me. I received affection from my friends as well as from their parents by being a witty, entertaining child. In return, my friends offered applause and encouragement."

"My ability to tune out was amazing. I realize that I didn't relate in my family. Instead, I shut down, avoided, and stayed aloof when I was at home and related when I was among my friends. When I had to be home, I would study, eat dinner, watch TV, listen to the radio, and at times even read the newspaper, all at the same time. I don't know how I did it, but it sure kept my family away because I was not available to anyone for anything. I didn't even hear my name if someone called me. I only tuned in the things that were important to me, which were usually outside of my family."

"At times, I kept myself together by making promises to myself. For example, 'You have your day. I will get you. You will pay. It's not going to be very subtle or very tricky.'

"I remember one of my aunts, when she was disciplining me, said, 'As long as you're in this house you're going to obey this rule. You're going to do this and do this.' And I'd say, 'No, I'm not. No, I'm not. Who do you think you are? You can't make me do that.' She'd say to me, 'Look, you are an eight-year-old, and you will not be that bold with me. You're so bold.' I'd sit there and I'd say, 'Sure.' Here I am this little brat. It gave me a security inside of myself by fending off the oppression."

"I was a real character. I was labeled the class cynic under my high-school picture. As a matter of fact, I organized a group that seceded from their own class. We had our own float in the homecoming parade. That was my style. I was not willing to conform to anything without a fight. I think all the crazy things I was doing—getting erratic grades, skipping school—were kind of intellectual rebellion. For example, a friend and I were going to do a survey of sexual activities at school for psychology class. The board of education went crazy and I was suspended for a day. But things like that would just get under my skin. In my gym class, there were teachers who were more authoritarian and ran the thing like the military. I gave them holy hell in various ways. I was very bright so I figured out real creative ways to screw them, and enjoyed it immensely. I would get in trouble and sometimes get caught. But that was the fun part, getting caught and sticking my tongue out at them.

"But what I really was hoping was that someone would take a step back and say, 'This kid is hurting.' Instead, they got embroiled in a battle. I felt that if they stopped me that would show some kind of caring about me. But I wanted more than that. I wanted more than being stopped. I wanted them to see why I had been doing that. I wanted them to ask, to take a moment to stop the battle, stop the game on their end and spend more time with me. Maybe too, I was hoping that the school people would discover my crazy home life and do something about it."

7. Developing Roles in the Family

A role is a way of relating, but unlike the survival technique, it is usually assigned by the family and is rigid and unchangeable. Sometimes children develop their own role, but this is uncommon. Roles include good child, rebellious child, scapegoat, mediator, family hero, and others. Roles can also be a wonderful adaptation for survival and offer protection from abuse and trauma as well as some nurturance. For example, the good child, if "good enough," may receive special privileges. A mediator may receive strokes for stopping a fight, even if the reward is only to have the screaming stop for a while. Roles give a niche, a place to belong, and a way of dealing with the crazies in the family. On the other hand, some roles can be devastating and isolating, such as the scapegoat, who gains little, if anything, for being blamed for all the family's problems.

"I had to be there for others or I was worthless, totally worthless with no value to anyone. This is what I learned in my role growing up. My only value was as a helper—to pack for a trip, to clean, to cook, to support Mom, and be a good girl. The real me was underground and well protected. I knew I had to protect my real self, and my role did help keep it away from the family's ridiculing and criticizing. They needed me, so they were not going to hurt me.

"There was no place for me—nowhere, except I had this role that allowed me to fit and be okay, at least on the surface. I also received much-needed praise in this one area of my life, even if it was just for cleaning or helping. It was at least some support, acknowledgment, and attention, which I desperately needed."

"I was not against whatever my father had to do at that time, even when he was having DTs [hallucinations] with his alcoholism, but I think my role was to let him know that I was scared and shaky. I had to deescalate him. My parents would be yelling and I'd start with, 'Stop it, Daddy. Stop it.' My mother would say 'Don't you hear the kids?' Because all three of us would be yelling, 'Stop it!' That would deescalate him because he was really violent."

"I'd been conditioned by adults to deal with matters such as legal documents and adult type discussions. For example, they'd tell me, 'Here, read this. Do this. Talk to this person. Tell them to set it up.' I could mouth all that was needed but really did not have the comprehension, either socially or emotionally, to know what I was doing. I was the prince of the realm, and the rest of the people were as a court in very subordinate roles. I felt powerful and in control and had a supporting world.

"I got all kinds of privileges being the 'brain.' I remember that I was paid by an aunt fifty cents on Saturdays to take my cousin to the movies because my family needed the money. I was not really good working with my hands, doing chores, or being mechanical. I was not even very quick on my feet. But, I was the kingpin. So, I was paid to be this little escort for my cousin for two years. It was terrific. I would take her to shows, and I would see Hop-A-Long Cassidy, Tarzan serials, and Superman serials."

"My mother described my relationship with my siblings to me one time. It became clear to me that I escaped the pain through becoming a surrogate mother in my family. My mother helped me feel as responsible for the baby's care as she was. When company would arrive, she stated that I would insist they come and see the baby's crib in my bedroom.

"My parental role of caretaking and responsibility continued to grow as the family did. The effect it had on me was that I felt robbed of my childhood. I grew up too quickly. I can remember refusing to play with dolls by age eight. Any dependency needs I had were overlooked because I was taught to focus on the needs of the younger children. I can remember being blamed and punished when the other children got into trouble. This reconfirmed my feeling of responsibility for their actions. As a result, I internalized feelings of guilt when things didn't run smoothly in the family. However, I never gave this up because there was a lot of power in the role and self-esteem in knowing I was needed and depended upon. Teaching and leading the way for my siblings helped strengthen my feelings of adequacy as a person."

"I worked to have people like me. It was a way of nurturing me and getting what I needed. If I could nurture others, then I could get some of it for me. Also, it was a way of being needed and being with others. It was a basic way to connect. It gave me a role, a relationship, a connection. Besides, if I were not a caretaker, then what? How would I relate to people? What I did was a form of therapy with people. I would listen to their problems and help them with their feelings. Hence, I would pick out people I could be in that role with in order to get what I needed."

"I was the family hero. I was the one who announced to the world that our family was not only okay, but terrific. It went like this: if I was such an accomplished person, then my parents had to be wonderful because they raised me. I got almost straight As and was involved in all sorts of school activities. Teachers liked me; kids liked me; and I got a lot of praise, support, and a feeling of being special. It also gave me a separate identity from my family, thank goodness!"

8. Seeking Relationships with Significant Others

Significant others are the most important factors in surviving. Most transcenders actively seek relationships that involve them with a more nurturing, protective world. These important relationships offer love, acceptance, support, kindness, and a feeling of being special. Significant others also provide role models, examples of alternate lifestyles, and hope for the future by demonstrating another way to live. The nurturing and protection that come from relationships are remembered vividly for years. Even what seem to be the smallest of gifts from others are priceless gifts to the transcender. These offerings are desperately needed to maintain the self and provide substance for growth. Sometimes, the gift was only offered one time but remembered for decades.

This area is so important that its effects extend into the adult healing and growth process. Individuals find survival as well as healing less difficult and painful when there is even minimal nurturing from at least one human being over the years. Here are a few of the offerings from significant others that transcenders remember.

Significant Others Outside the Family

Many significant others were from outside the family and offered support and encouragement.

"I always had to have one really good friend. My friends have always been very important to me since I was little. They offered nurturing, support, love, acceptance, and being special to someone. They liked me, and I liked the mutual respect. We liked being together, and I liked that feeling because I obviously was not liked at home. I was much more comfortable, accepted, and at peace with my friends, having a good time or even talking about something serious, than being home waiting for things to explode."

"I was a Girl Scout. It was a wonderful experience and helped me a lot. The troop we were in was very friendly and sociable. I started out as a Brownie in second grade and went until the eighth grade. I had the two greatest leaders, who were very kind and loving. One of the leaders was one of my best girlfriends' mother, and I loved going over to her house. The activities were good, but it was the relationship with the leaders that really counted. They were kind and nurturing and they treated me so well. They were really special ladies."

"I used to idealize other kids' parents. I had a pal with an alcoholic father, and I thought his parents were just the greatest thing in the world. Basically, their main attribute was that they were not mine. Also, they were very bright and artistically oriented, and I thought they were really neat, creative people. I adopted them as my family, and I used to spend all my weekends there during most of high school. In essence, I left home emotionally and physically. I basically worked to create my own family and find supportive people since my family was not going to be around for that."

"I had a high school teacher that stopped me in the hall one day, when I was about in the ninth grade, and said to me, 'Do you know you're going to be a great politician someday?' I looked at him, because I was probably some type of officer in every class, and he said, 'You're really a politician; you're going to make it.'

"I was sort of hurt by that and I guess it showed on my face because I thought of a politician as being someone nasty, and he said, 'No, no, I swear, you go for it.' He just said, 'You can do anything.'

"That was just something he stopped me in the hall one day to say. In my senior year I was very popular, and I was this and that and really ran the whole high school if you want to get down to the brass tacks of it. He stopped me again and said, 'See, I told you years ago you can do anything if you want. You're a politician.' He kept using that term, but I knew what he meant. I came to believe I really could do anything."

"I found families in church who really liked me and were so sincerely thankful for all the work I did for the church. I felt gratified that someone appreciated me, because my parents never did. Never! Ever! There were some families in the church who were very important to me because they made me feel so much a part of the church and their lives."

"It was interventions by people, feeling people, that really helped. Sometimes just the little things would help keep me going, not like they were ongoing, fulltime confidants, but somebody who would notice that something was wrong and give that little extra bit to say, 'You're okay. You're special to me. You're important as a human being. You deserve to live and be okay on this earth. You have something special to offer in some kind of way.' That made such a difference to me."

"Our foster mother showed us caring and love through what she did for us. She would take us to town, let us buy our own clothing, make sure we got to church, help us get work we got paid for so we could have some spending money, and make sure we were clean and dressed properly. It doesn't seem like much, but it was more than we had had before, and it felt like caring."

"I blew up during a softball game and got really angry at this teacher. He got angry back at me, and I screamed at him. He took a step back. He was getting all hooked up and getting all involved with this sixth-grader. I think he realized what he was doing, and he stopped and said, 'Hey, come here,' and walked into the school with me. He spent just ten minutes talking to me and said, 'You really seem upset about this game, but it seems like something else is going on besides just being upset on account of this game.' I'll never forget him. He was not even my teacher in school and he cared so much more. He was able to give, just a little bit. You don't have to bend over backwards. I think that was what was missing—the bending over backwards or the ability to do that with my parents."

"I was looking for a different way to live, like shopping new avenues. I had a feeling there had to be a better way. Something about my family just didn't hit me right, so I was always looking and watching how other families lived. I watched how other mothers related to their daughters, and I'd think, 'Oh, aren't they lucky?' Friends in high school were important to me because they opened my eyes to other values and lifestyles outside of my family and neighborhood."

"I would go to the neighbor's and sit in the backyard. I remember being a friendly kid, and sometimes I would start to shoot the breeze. They'd ask me if I wanted a glass of pop [soda] and that was such a big deal for me. I'd want to go back to that house again but I was so afraid to let the good stuff in (to be nurtured). At the same time, I ate it up and needed it desperately. I also had to keep this stuff secret all the time because of what my family might do if they found out."

"I remember how delighted I was when a kid in the seventh grade invited me over to his house. I still remember his name. I felt so damn good. I had a bacon, lettuce, and tomato sandwich, and after twenty-five or thirty years, I still remember this kid inviting me over and even what I had to eat. I can still remember sitting in the kitchen and his mother saying, 'Well, what do you young fellows want to have for lunch?' It was Christmas, and I remember 'Winter Wonderland' playing on the radio. They had a little Hot Point refrigerator, and I thought, 'Gee, they have a nice refrigerator. Gee, why don't we have a refrigerator like that? All we have is an old Kelvinator at our house and here is this brand new Sears Hot Point.' That lunch offered me acceptance and being seen as a person, as a little kid, and not as the illusion I was living at home."

"In junior high and high school, my steady boyfriend kept me from being lonely. He took up a great deal of my time from the age of fifteen to age eighteen. He was always there."

"I had this huge cat that weighed nineteen pounds, and this cat was a dear friend. I can remember many times going to my room, closing the door, and curling up with my cat, just sobbing and saying, 'You are the only one I can talk to.' Then I would blow it all out. This poor cat had to take all this in. As I look back on it, it was one of the ways I could release all this pain inside me."

"I remember a French teacher in high school, and I was getting worse and worse grades. I would get an A one quarter and an F the next, just because I was angry at authority. Anything that symbolized authority, I hated. I was also reading all this heavy existential literature and getting more and more depressed. So my French teacher said, 'Why don't you lighten up?' She gave me a Book-of-the-Month Club novel about a World War II adventure and spent a little time with me just to let me know that she knew I was hurting. She thought I was very special and bright and hoped I didn't blow it all by being Mr. Rebel. Boy, did that make a difference! I felt support and knew someone had really noticed my situation."

Significant Others Inside the Family

Not all significant others are outside of the family. At times, a family member offers some of the needed protection and nurturing even though the relationship may also include pain.

"It was pitch black out. It was nighttime, and my father always left us outside in the dark. I don't remember necessarily feeling afraid because I always had another kid there, my sister. We were company for each other, and we helped each other keep the fears away."

"My father had the personality of Dr. Jekyll and Mr. Hyde. He worked three jobs so we could live in the suburbs and avoid the ghetto. He was also a former professional basketball player and instilled feelings of competition in us. His method of relating to us was mostly through harsh judgments and criticism. He was narrow-minded and set in his opinions. On the other hand, he had a great sense of humor and was artistic. He also played the accordion and entertained us with his talent. He was ethnocentric and had a strong sense of family. My warmest family memories seem to be involved with my father and food. I felt a strong sense of family each Sunday, when all of us joined my father to spend the entire day making homemade noodles, ravioli, gnocchi, and pizzas. After working all day, we would share family dinner by eating enormous amounts of food. I always found eating and food to be comforting."

"My mother would often starve me in order to punish me. Once in a while, my grandma would get me something to eat if Mom had locked me in my room and would not let me eat. It's a kindness I'll always remember."

"The attachment to my mother for so long was symbiotic and beyond the normal stages of symbiosis. What this relationship did for me was to somehow add to a deep level of awareness that I was special. This is one of the reasons why I am a survivor.

"My mother believed I was more of an intellectual than my brother. She noticed my bookworm tendencies, which my brother lacked. I was also more artistic than he, which was a similarity I shared with my mother. We both liked to paint. She and I had a great sense of humor and an art for telling stories. We both loved to dance and dress up swank and go out on the town. I think we both shared the need to be somebody, and my mother knew that need in me would give me ambition and push me to make something of myself."

"My grandmother just loved me dearly, kept me going, and gave me a feeling of being special in my life. I guess she lived vicariously through me, and I took after her. She was quite an aggressive lady in her day, and I think she saw her youth in me. She was my father's mother, and basically he treated her the same way he treated me. He never bent over backward to really go see her and do anything with her. I cared very much for her, and she enjoyed seeing me with all my success and achievement. She thought the sun rose and set on me, which gave me a lot of special feelings. She was very complimentary on anything I did and made sure she was at every activity she could attend to see me. She was a focal point in my life. It was obvious that I was her favorite. Yeah, I'd never been anybody's favorite, but I was her favorite. I felt very special. I still have that feeling of being special inside of me, and it still helps me."

"My father gave me a sense of good morality, and I knew he loved me. When I say morality, I mean a sense of right and wrong; a sense of caring about people and a sensitivity to their needs. He gave me a consistency in the sense that he really tried to provide someone who was caring and nurturing while we were shipped from one place to another. He even tried to give me the little extra things."

"I was visiting my aunt and uncle on their farm, way out in the middle of nowhere. I was very close to them. My former stepfather showed up out of nowhere, and I was devastated. It really upset me to see him again. All I can remember is my aunt coming into the living room after he left. I had tears rolling down my face. She came over to me and kissed me on the cheek and said, 'I love you,' and it was so comforting. It's been years and years ago, but I will always remember it."

"My two oldest sisters and especially my brother offered me someone to whom I could relate; get feedback;

reality test my anger, disappointments, and rage; and to get assistance from. It was a true reciprocal friendship."

"Before my father left our family when I was seven, he clearly favored my brother, and I had very little interaction with him. I handled this situation emotionally by transferring my father figure needs to older males in the family. One older male relative I had gave me piggyback rides, took me fishing and camping, and during some summers, my whole school vacation was spent with him. My stepfather provided some fathering, and I also had a stepbrother ten years older who enjoyed having a little brother tagging along after him. He responded by playing the big-brother role. He was kind to me, and it helped fill the emptiness and pain left by my father."

9. Developing Competencies

In the process of developing competencies, transcenders gain confidence, friends, healthier role models, meaningfulness in life, enjoyment, proficiency, and a foundation for self-confidence and creating a different lifestyle. Competencies are vital to helping the transcender develop positive self-esteem, success, support, and hope for the future. The development of these competencies often involves activities such as academics, sports, work, and anything that helps the individual feel important and accomplished. These activities provide a way for transcenders to get out of the house, stay away, and connect to more nurturing people.

"I didn't belong in my family in one way, but in another way it's okay because I did get something from it growing up. I did get something that formed a foundation from my old neighborhood. What I gained was a gift of words—a gift of language in order to survive. I became very proficient in listening to Polish. I can't speak Polish, but I can recognize the language and pick out some words. Our neighbors next door were Greek. Down the street were Lithuanians; some were Polish and Slovaks. There were blacks in our neighborhood, and Jewish people ran the deli. I learned to listen and developed a gift for listening. Now, being a therapist, this gift is a constant blessing."

"I had music, and that's the thing that really kept me going through school. I was in band, and when I was in high school I started playing in dance bands. Music was something I was really interested in and good at and enjoyed doing. I first started taking lessons when I was in junior high school, and when I went into senior high, it was a whole different thing because I was in a great band. It was just really a fantastic band. That was what gave my life meaning. It offered something to do, something I really enjoyed, and the friendships with the kids that were in it. It offered another life."

"I just found out that I had leadership ability and could keep everybody happy. I just had a way of handling people, and found I could lead without one part of the group getting angry. I kept everybody pacified and had the ability to keep things together. I became popular naturally. It started in fifth grade when I almost won a trip to Washington, D.C., through the national and regional safety patrol. They selected the candidates on their attributes. Things snowballed from there."

"I started working in eleventh grade for a cooperative program (part time work counted for school credit) in school. This is the only encouragement I ever got from my mother about school or help picking classes. She told me, 'Whatever you do, take shorthand and typing.' So, I took shorthand and typing and immediately became a secretary and have been one since. In eleventh grade, I worked for a board of education as a clerk doing odd jobs and typing after school. It gave me a lot—spending money for school, competencies, and a feeling of confidence."

"I had earned the respect at school in the student council, and I was president of the prep club. I earned a lot of respect, and it was a really good feeling. People became real impressed with the fact that I was doing all these things. These feelings gave me the extra impetus to keep doing and achieving."

10. Playing

Through play, transcenders can be something that isn't part of a dysfunctional family—a regular kid. They can giggle, laugh, and just be. Play includes anything that the individual perceives as play: informal sports, organized sports, theater, reading, mental challenges, playing alone, playing in the neighborhood, playing with toys, games, or even work that is perceived as play. From play, transcenders gain escape from the dangers and traumas of the family, release from tensions and stress, and relief from the seriousness of life. The experience of playing offers good feelings about oneself, encouragement, nurturing, and acceptance. In addition, play helps transcenders create hope and important support for the vital and often fragile self. In essence, transcenders experience and nurture their authentic self.

"The reason I liked school so much was I could get away from all the hard work I had to do. I'd go play, especially at recess time. We'd go out at recess time, and all we'd do is run, play tag, baseball, kickball—play, play, play. That's probably one of the reasons I liked school—the play part. We played baseball and I was on the varsity baseball team for four years in high school. We won the county championship the last year. I also used to go skiing and do some tobogganing. All of these things helped me forget some of the things that happened earlier in my life. Playing helped a lot."

"We'd act and we'd laugh and we'd giggle. There was not much fun when we reached a certain age in our house, and I would just crave that fun. I used to like to play with dolls, ride a bike (just loved to ride bikes), talk, giggle, and play lots of typical little girl games. I could be a real normal everyday kid and go play."

"We would have a crop cutting, and everybody in the whole community would come out with their wagons, men, teams of horses, and their tractors. We would load up all the machinery and things and take them up on the farm. We used to sometimes see if we could be as big as a man—a big, grown man—and see how fast we could pitch the bundle of oats, wheat, or barley into this big threshing machine. All the straw would be blowing way up in the air out of the big chute or a big pipe, and we would pitch it fast enough to plug it up and make the machine stop. Then we used to get a big kick out of climbing up onto the engine—it was a steam engine—with the owner and blow the whistle. That was fun."

"I played by myself and did a lot of fantasizing. I played with my dolls, created objects out of clay, and pretended they were real. I pretended I was the hero. I would imagine what my life could be and how I really wanted it. It helped me escape the reality of my family. I could also release and deal with all sorts of feelings. For example, I even played out my death. I imagined what it would be like to die and how my family would miss me, cry endlessly, and feel bad that they had not taken better care of me. It was a way of having a family that did care and love me. This playing kept the inner me alive while I was growing up. This playing also eased my intense loneliness."

"The pain! God, the pain! I was so anxious, and I just knew that to ease it all I had to keep playing on sports teams. I played baseball, basketball, tennis—really, anything that was available. It also brought me friends, eased the loneliness, and released the anxiety."

11. Developing Spirituality

Many transcenders turn to their spiritual base as a source of guidance, strength, support, and help in dealing with their dysfunctional families. Most importantly, spirituality offers a belief in a power greater than themselves and their situation. Transcenders are in touch with their spirituality and find a force powerful enough to help sustain them through the onslaught of their world and through their pain.

Expression of spirituality for transcenders can take a traditional form of religion, like Christianity, Muslim, or Judaism, or it can be unique to the individual. There are transcenders who attend regular religious services and find an entire support system by doing so. Other transcenders find it difficult to attend religious services on a regular basis because of a lack of family cooperation, so they create their own rituals at home. Many view God as their real father and look to Him for all their needs and as a replacement for their family.

"God was involved in my life from the time I was a toddler and is part of my earliest recollections. My firm belief in God has been a large part of my ability to survive. There have been many times when I needed to believe that not only was there a God but also an afterlife—a promise of something more than the misery or the dilemma that I was in."

"When the oppression, stress, fear, and frustration became overwhelming and came to the point of explosion, I'd sometimes explode by yelling, screaming, and airing all that was within me. Other times, and more often, I'd pray—pray so deeply and internally that my being—my root—bared itself in seeking help from God. After the intense praying I'd feel better. Nothing had really changed, but I'd feel better, and my explosive frustration would subside. In its place would be a sadness but also a peace. This sadness would be a deep and alone sadness; yet there was also my commitment, which grew stronger. I said someday I'd be me. Someday I'd pick a different way of being—someday! God supported me and helped sustain that commitment to myself."

"The church helped me a lot as a kid. I don't think I would have survived if I had not had it. I'd go to church every day and I'd pray. God was real to me. He was going to help me. I was able to focus on God through His pictures or religious objects, and it helped me to sort myself out from the crazies."

"Church was wonderful for me. I gained in personal growth, in my own feelings, and the feelings I'd get from attending and being part of a worship service or environment. I also had a lot of really good friends there. The minister was a friend of mine, and I had a lot of other good friends from the church. And musically—I'm very moved spiritually through music. It really nurtured me, and the church was so full of wonderful music."

"I used to get to the point of cracking and have no strength left to battle my family. My connection to God gave me comfort and strength. Once I was comforted, I could again enjoy the good that was in my life. It was a type of surrendering. I knew He was taking care of me."

"God was and is my core. If I went beyond my energy, beyond my ability to cope and beyond feeling sane, I could always go to God and find energy, support, love, and deep caring. I would find relief and rest as well as understanding and acceptance from Him. Thank God! The way my family was structured, with such control, it was the only thing I found that deeply helped. I was strengthened and renewed through my relationship with God, and I just knew He would not let me crack up. It was a strength and comfort. I could talk to God about anything."

Summary

All transcenders develop and use techniques to protect themselves from the traumas and terrors they experience as they grow up in dysfunctional families. They also use techniques to nurture themselves. The more assaultive the world, the more effort is needed.

In the beginning, their skills may not have been adequate, but through determination and perseverance, they develop to a level strong enough to maintain the self, gain hope for the future, and, when possible, promote growth.

Survival techniques are like a haven in the midst of a stormy sea, helping to maintain a belief and sense of the self by creating barriers, escapes, resistances, and defenses that hinder, limit, and, at times, stop the violence toward them. In essence, by the use of these techniques, transcenders gain enough protection and nurturance to survive.

CHAPTER 5

The Self: The Heart of the Survivor

Transcenders are in a struggle for life—a struggle not only to exist but to be authentically themselves. Five philosophical and psychological concepts are at the foundation of survival and are important in understanding the survival process. These are the heart, core, or essence of transcending and surviving. These concepts help explain how transcenders did what they did. It is from these deep cores of the self that transcenders create their ripples. They are the self, the will, the internal frame of reference, Being-in-the-world, and transcendence. I have worked to simplify these concepts. For those readers who would like more information, please see the noted references at the end of the book.

The Self

The *self* is me. It's my essence, my soul. It is who I am. We are like snowflakes with no two of us alike. No two people are alike, ever! I believe each human being is unique and an endangered species. We are born with different talents and abilities and will experience the world differently and learn different things from those experiences.

Every experience we have is processed, or filtered, through our self. It is through the self that we learn, feel, grow, and make decisions. It is where our thoughts, feelings, situations, talents, beliefs, values, morals, view of life, behaviors, and spirituality exist. The entire original package and our world are integrated into the uniqueness of who we are. It is through the self that we learn and grow. It is sometimes called our personality, but it is more than that. We decide what kind of person we are going to be in the self.[1] The self is the core—the essence of life—who and what we are. It's the foundation for all growth. It is through the self that the original package is expressed. Existential philosophers have called it our Being.[2] In spiritual areas, it has been called the soul. The self is the sum total of me. It is from this core that transcendence and the turning-point decision are created and survival occurs.

Transcenders decide and maintain the turning-point decisions through the self by feeling and thinking about all the available information they have experienced that has impacted them. From this processing of feelings and thoughts, survivors decide—powerfully decide—to "make it" and be different from their families.

To make it, transcenders have to protect the self and its authenticity from the onslaught of neglect, abuse, criticism, and all other forms of aggression. In addition, they need to find nurturing that is essential for growth and development. As children, transcenders learn to nurture and protect themselves with very little support from their families. They take in, absorb, and savor tidbits of nurturing that at times seem like crumbs. These offerings are used for growth over many years and, as seen in Chapter 4, may come from almost anyone and anything.

Transcenders, in spite of the onslaught of their world, maintain a spark of their precious unique self on some level. Sometimes it is underground and hidden, but it is through the self that they work to maintain this spark until it is safe to surface. The essence of life knows it has to protect and nurture this spark, or life will not exist in any real form.

Often, while growing up, part of the self is compromised in order for transcenders to survive. However, there is always a part of the self no one can touch. Later, sadly, this very important decision to protect the self during childhood causes intense pain when it's time to develop a growing, close, and trusting adult relationship. A close relationship can only happen if the person feels safe and ready to work through childhood issues. If there is no safety, the self stays hidden.

The Will

The second concept to be explored is the *will*. The will is a basic, vital ability of the self that is controlled by the individual.[3] The will is like the center part of a cell, the nucleus. It has a central position in the self and functions to guide, regulate, balance, direct, and use the forces and resources of the self and the environment.[4] The will has sometimes been defined as the ability to organize or focus so work or play can be accomplished.[5] It is the guiding force to achieving goals, making actions occur, and overcoming obstacles to action.[6]

The will guides behavior, growth, and the development of the ever-growing self. The will has to manage forces such as emotions, impulses, desires, thoughts, information, values, morals, intuition, imagination, and potential. The will works to organize all of this as well as all the available information and resources with the purpose of making decisions, setting goals, and creating behaviors.[7] Without the ability to will, there is no turning-point decision, no survival, and no transcendence.

The will can vary in strength, flexibility, and resourcefulness. It works to get our needs met and is the place where we decide what we will do and how we will behave.[8] Decisions can be as simple as deciding to take a nap or as hard as making the turning-point decision. Our decisions are meaningful to us but not necessarily understood by others because each of us is unique, and no one can fully understand another person.[9]

We make a decision to use our will. This decision is deliberate and for a purpose. We have an experience and then focus on and process our thoughts and feelings about it. We may decide we need more information or we may just use the information and resources available. From this thinking and feeling, we may make a decision to do or not to do something about it.[10] It may go into a constancy (see Internal Frame of Reference, below) or be filed for later use. The action we take or don't take is meaningful and unique to us.

The turning-point decision is an excellent example of the process of willing. Transcenders process what they think and feel about their families and life. They then process and evaluate all the details of their experiences. Next, their will works to organize the information according to what they need, and a decision is made, the turning-point decision. From this comes a goal to be different. From there, personalized survival techniques are created and used for years, decades.

The will uses all available resources of the person such as energy, power, intensity, mastery, control, discipline, concentration, focus, determination, decisiveness, resolution, promptness, persistence, endurance, patience, initiative, courage, organization, integration, and wholeness.[11] All these qualities help create survival techniques and set goals for the future.

Some transcenders with whom I have worked have well-developed, strong ability to will. Their will, in order to survive, gained strength, patience, persistence, and the ability to use and integrate available resources through the years. Their will helps guide and direct them, satisfy their needs (as much as they can), accomplish their goals, and find direction for growth. The will also connects them to higher levels of living, such as the desire to help themselves and others, to accomplish meaningful work, and to develop spiritually. In essence, it acts like a lighthouse to keep them focused on the continuing journey of surviving and transcending.

Healthy willing—willing that does not hurt us or others and directs us in healing and growth—is important in making decisions and dealing with conflicts. Obviously, transcenders face many difficult decisions while growing up. They learn to use their will to make at least enough adequate decisions to keep going and even to develop some of their talents and abilities.

The more the will is used, the more it is trained to develop and function in all states of life, including crises. Over the years, the will becomes finely tuned, strong, adaptable, and efficient.[12] For example, a child may not be able to always avoid difficult family situations that lead to abuse, but after years of practice, avoidance can become easier and sometimes almost routine. Sometimes, through the healing process, transcenders have to learn to use their will differently because it is trained to protect.

This decision is important to survive in childhood; however, it may block adult growth and cause problems in relationships. After leaving the family home, for example, at one point in my life I may have decided never to talk to a person after they said something that hurt me. Now, perhaps years later, I need to learn to talk to that person and not run away like I thought I had to in order to protect myself in childhood.

Importantly, the will enables us to affirm, negate, forget, and become free from the past.[13] This becomes crucial in the healing process. At times the abuse is so awful, overwhelming, difficult, and painful that a child cannot deal with it. Transcenders may block these memories in childhood in order to protect themselves. The memories are put into a memory block, out of awareness, until later when it is safe and there is help to deal with them. In the healing process, when the transcender's life is safer, saner, and freer to remember, these memories can be recalled and healed. A child does not know how to do deal with these traumas at the time they occur and must focus on surviving.

Another quality of the will is what philosophers call the *will to meaning*. This part of the will guides us to our personal search for a life with authenticity, meaning, and purpose.[14] Everyone has a special purpose that is unique and specific to him or her. This purpose is directed by who we are, our abilities, values, and so forth. If it is overlooked or blocked, the person may cease to grow, develop, or survive. When this happens, he or she may become depressed, feel worthless, and lost in the world. In the dysfunctional family, it means, "I'm going to survive these tortures, and I'm not going to let them win. I'm going to make my life better and be different than my family!"

The beginning of the training of the will may occur early in life. It is not unusual for transcenders to go back to childhood memories (we have to go back and heal where the hurt began) and find they made a major decision to survive as early as during the first five years of life. I believe we can remember early experiences and the feelings that go with them. Somehow, some transcenders early in life gain the needed perspective that their family is not going to be there for them, that they are going to have to take care of themselves. This decision is amazing. I wonder if it is at this point that the infant decides whether to be a failure-to-thrive baby or a growing, dynamic self? The following is a poem written by a transcender who reexperienced her infant decision:

Deep, deep,
Into the depths of my being, my soul
Lay the child, the infant.
The small, quiet, strong infant
She knew she'd die.
No breast, no food
No food, no life.

The choice was to live or die
The infant made it.
She decided to live—somehow live.
She set her mind to do it—

To live in spite of them
It was in this choice
Her will developed and became strong.
She had to live—choose to live
          Or   Die.

The Internal Frame of Reference

The *internal frame of reference* is part of the self and is very important to transcenders. The internal frame of reference is how we view our world, seeing it from the inside out. It is how we perceive us and how we perceive ourselves in the world. This view contains our thoughts, feelings, values, beliefs, morals, attitudes, purposes, goals, desires, self-concept, trust of self, trust of others, and view of self and others.[15]

Our internal frame of reference is usually active, growing, and in constant change. This part of us works to integrate our experiences of persons, places, and situations into a larger understanding of us and the world and life. That is, when we have an experience, we give meaning to it as it relates to us. Every person's internal frame of reference, like the self, is unique and personal. None of us have the same view or can totally understand another person's frame of reference because we have not had the same experiences in life.[16]

The decisions of how to behave come from the internal frame of reference. We behave according to our personal belief system, thoughts, and feelings.[17] For instance, if I believe the world is a safe, nurturing place, I will be open to exploring and experiencing the world that is available to me. However, if I view the world as dangerous and difficult, I will relate to it in a fearful, shy, or defensive manner, and I will not be free to explore my world and what is has to offer me.

The internal frame of reference can change to help us with our everyday experiences and to behave differently as the situation demands.[18] For example, in the morning I may view my mother's mood with fear and choose to avoid her. Later that same day, her mood may change, and from my past experience, I know it is okay to be around her. When healing occurs after surviving a traumatic childhood, there is usually a change in the person's internal frame of reference because the old view of life has changed.

For transcenders, the internal frame of reference is vital. If transcenders view their world outside of the family as a place to be nurtured and protected, they can be open to exploring it. If they see an opportunity of getting out of their family, they can create another lifestyle—another world. Basically, decisions about what we do and how we act come from how we see our world and ourselves, which is based on our experiences and decisions we have to make to live.

Constancies are part of our internal frame of reference; we use them to make perceiving easier. Constancies help us group and organize information we have learned about the world. We group or make constancies when confronted with similar situations and information.[19] Having a constancy system is like having many huge filing cabinets full of files. Each file contains information on a certain area of our life—infancy, relationships, school, friends, love, work, Mom, Dad, turning point—just like we have a file for bills. Files are stored in the constancy until we need them at some future date, at which time we take them out and use them. We may pull out all or part of the information from a file, depending on what we need. We may take out the whole file to reevaluate the information, such as the turning-point decision. This reevaluation is an important part of therapy and helps us grow and not become rigid or narrow-minded. Some information doesn't change, like confirmed values, morals, and the turning-point decision.

Constancies are grouped according to beliefs, values, morals, knowledge, feelings, needs, dangers, and previous perceptions and experiences. Constancies contain information and decisions about our world, and they work in order to protect, nurture, and conserve energy.[20] Constancies enable healing and growth and make life easier. These files minimize guessing and keep us from having to develop a new choice each time a similar situation comes along. They help us use information easily and quickly as situations arise. Educators refer to this as a *transfer of learning*. When a similar situation arises, we can quickly sort through our "files" and pick the one(s) we need at the time.

An excellent example of a constancy is the turning-point decision. A transcender's turning-point internal frame of reference may be, "I'm going to be different from my family." This constancy contains all the information that was used to first create the turning-point decision, such as experiences of abuse, neglect, hurt, rejection, and information about other ways to live.

If transcenders had to sort through each piece of the constancy every time they needed to reinforce the turning-point decision, they would lose vital time, energy, and strength. They also might not be able to get out of a dangerous situation fast enough to avoid injury. Transcenders do, on occasion, sort through a lot of the information in the turning-point constancy to reaffirm and strengthen their decision.

What is unusual about the turning-point constancy is that it does remain constant and stable for years—sometimes a lifetime, even after many reevaluations. For many, it becomes stronger as they get older. The transcender's world teaches over and over again that the turning-point decision is not only right but has to be kept strong and be a primary focus for survival and growth. This constancy helps guide transcenders to safety, growth, development, and achievement all through their lives.

Caring is another part of our internal frame of reference. We care about ourselves and our world, and because we care, we relate and are involved with people and activities. We are also curious and want to know about ourselves and our world. Unless stopped or taught to be afraid, we automatically want to explore, discover, and experience our world through our senses, thoughts, and feelings.[21] If we visualize a two-year-old exploring his or her world, we can gain an understanding of this area.

To discover and explore there has to be some sort of world to explore.[22] The family is important concerning what it allows the child to be exposed to. Is the child too free and in danger of being injured? Is he or she so controlled there is nothing to explore?

This varies for each and every transcender. What the transcenders' families do allow is vital to having experiences that might nurture and protect them. These experiences are always unique and specific to each person. Transcenders see a choice in their world. This choice is vital to transcending because it is different from their family and offers substance for growth. These choices can lead them to schools, churches, significant others, organizations, and sometimes bring to their attention even a thought, comment, feeling, or behavior from another person.

For transcenders, caring and discovering often bring complications that interfere with what they need for protection as well as nurturing. They have to close themselves off, at some level, to the family violence and craziness while at the same time being open to experiences that offer nurturance. This is a difficult process for a mature adult, let alone a child who works to maintain his or herself for years in this way. The miracle for many is that their caring for their world somehow continues and often gets stronger.

The danger in the process is closing off the self to all aspects of the world, including other people, thus distorting the person's senses, thoughts, feelings, and reality.[23] This distortion occurs because we need contact with others to test, adjust, and find the truth of reality. It is absolutely necessary to completely close down, at times, when there is severe abuse or when the person feels totally overwhelmed. However, if the individual continues to be closed off, his or her reality may be altered and unhealthy. To survive, transcenders must be open to some positive experiences in their world in order to gain a healthy grounding while at the same time screening out violence to the self.

The internal frame of reference is a dynamic part of the self that is learned and developed. We have the ability to learn, unlearn, and change. Transcenders use this ability to survive. We can change our internal frame of reference as the situation demands. Learning anything depends on our view, or perception, of the learning. Sometimes we have to let go of the past senses, thoughts, and feelings to learn a new area and respond to what is presently needed.[24] Transcenders need to remain flexible and alert to modifications in their perceptions of the world and simultaneously stay true to their turning-point decision. This flexibility is necessary to maintain the turning-point decision and develop survival techniques. The problem in this area is that transcenders can learn to be so flexible and adapt so much that they may lose their grounding. Or, they may also become rigid and inflexible. Many times, as a therapist, I have heard them say, "Tell me how I should think and feel, and I will." Thankfully, this grounding strengthens as healing occurs.

Because we have the ability to learn and change the internal frame of reference, transcendence can be taught to individuals who have not identified their family as dysfunctional when it actually is. The change often occurs by using three steps: (1) gather many details about the family until it is clear to the person that the label *dysfunctional* fits, (2) evaluate previous constancies that can then be reevaluated and changed, and then (3) help create a freedom for a different way of living.[25]

In addition, transcending/survival techniques can be taught to help individuals in painful situations. Here are the steps: (1) learn to detect subtle details that signal danger in the family, (2) learn to put all these details into a turning-point constancy, and (3) learn to use techniques that protect and nurture the self.

In essence, individuals can be taught to survive and transcend their dysfunctional families, and this can be done at any age/stage in life.

Being-in-the-World

As stated before, our self, or being, is the essence of who we are. We express ourselves in our world through our senses, thoughts, feelings, and behaviors. In return, the world offers experiences with senses, thoughts, feelings, and behaviors. Philosophers call this relationship between us and our world *Being-in-the-world*. The world in which we live is basic and essential to us. We are always in a world. Every person has a world, and it is unique to that individual.[26] For example, if I am locked in a closet for most of my life, my world is that closet and all it contains and is. Our world consists of people, places, and situations—we experience the entire environment. It is a unified, integrated whole no matter how fragmented it feels or appears. Our world is not the essence of our self or our Being. However, it is important to know our relationship to our world so we can understand who we are and why we have developed the way we have.

As we experience our world, we develop a unique relationship between it and ourselves. It is in this relationship that the self is maintained and supported while it grows and changes through coping, manipulating, encountering, and producing in our world. We can also work to satisfy needs and develop our potentialities. Our potentiality is the entire original package that includes talents and abilities that can be developed and actualized. Our basic caring and curiosity encourage us to know and understand ourselves and the world by exploring, seeking out, and finding a world beyond the family.[27] Transcenders often find what they need to survive beyond the family in a world more in tune to them—one that nurtures their authentic self.

If our world is rich in experiences and full of meaning, our potentialities can be discovered and developed. If our world is restricted, our potentialities may also be restricted because there is less opportunity to explore and learn about ourselves. There are three important facts to remember about being-in-the-world: (1) our self and our world are two different entities; (2) our self and our world are dependent on each other; and (3) our self and our world are in constant interaction/relationship. This relationship is circular. One supports the other in a continuous cycle.[28]

People and opportunities come together in everyday situations in the world. We experience the world, and from this experience we are given opportunities to develop our potentialities. In turn, we gain support, guidance, confidence, encouragement, and so forth, which help us in the next experience. The more positive experiences we have in the world, the more we gain the strength, self-confidence, and skills needed to continue. This cycle can help transcenders survive and grow. Sadly, not all experiences are positive and helpful; some hurt and hinder, but we can even learn from these negative ones.

We have the power to distance ourselves psychologically and physically from the world and all it contains depending on our needs or situations. We can experience our world closer or farther away by using our abilities to hear, smell, see, touch, think, and taste. We can choose to experience our world at a distance, whether it involves people, places, or situations.[29] Distance or close experiences occur in groups, organizations, television, reading, the Internet, face to face, or through emotions, to name a few. For example, we can be lonely in a crowd or feel close to someone who is miles away. We can feel extremely involved or put the distance of a continent between ourselves and the experience.

We determine the distance of the experience as well as its meanings and relationships in our life. Transcenders, when they can, actively seek out and respond to healthy experiences and choose to gain all they can from the experiences while distancing themselves from traumatic, damaging encounters. For example, transcenders bring needed healthy role models close so they can experience and select more appropriate values, feelings, thoughts, and behaviors. These encounters may come from teachers, coaches, employers, heroes, neighbors, friends, other parents, and so on. Through these experiences in the world, the transcender's internal frame of reference is enriched, expanded, and shifted, as well as supported. Conversely, the transcender may choose to distance an abusive parent emotionally and/or physically for protection and to bring a healthier person close for nurturance.

Transcenders also have an awareness of freedom, even if limited, to see a choice in how they want to live. They see the need to protect and support their authentic self through the turmoil of their family's life. This sense of freedom is at least internal and sometimes, through leaving the house, external. They see a choice and actively choose, when they can, experiences that offer support, guidance, development, achievement, and encouragement, so they can gain the needed energy to continue their struggle to live.

Another important part of Being-in-the-world is *assertion*. This is the individual's ability to be in charge of his or her mood or overall feeling. Mood is a state of mind. It occurs within a person and can change from one moment to the next. We are always in a mood in our world. We can be in charge of our moods as well as change from one mood to another. To do this, we use assertiveness, knowledge, understanding, and *countermoods* (those moods that are different from and, perhaps, in opposition to the present mood).[30] For example, if a transcender is at home when a fight occurs and he or she becomes angry, the transcender can choose to change the mood and distance him- or herself from the fight emotionally and/or physically. He or she can choose to become part of the family fight or shift away from it. The mood then can shift from anger to a choice of more freedom. This does not mean pain is not experienced. It does mean it may have to be felt later by reevaluating the turning-point decision.

A core part of Being-in-the-world is understanding ourselves and the world. This understanding works to expand and support our internal frame of reference, self, and purpose.[31] If I don't understand my world, I can become confused and disoriented. Once something is experienced and understood, we gain knowledge, wisdom, and insights that help us keep going, helping us form a larger basis for living in the world. Webster defines wisdom as learning from experience, knowledge, and understanding and using it to make sound judgments. The continuing challenge of living an authentic life is to take previous knowledge and understanding, add new information, and create new growth and insights. Transcenders use this information to help cope, manage, and learn in transcending. It enables them to deal with their challenged existence and develop potentialities at a deeper level. Without it, they could lose themselves in the confusion and chaos. Transcenders at whatever age appear to develop an understanding of self, family, and their world in order to create abilities to cope, manage, and gain hope.

What happens if we lose ourselves in the confusion and chaos? Philosophers call it *being thrown* from our authentic self. When we are thrown, we become more a part of the world and others than of our authentic self.[32] We lose our authenticity or realness, and we fall away from our original package. Being thrown can happen when we decide to give up a part of us for someone else in an unhealthy way. This does not apply to everyday kindnesses toward each other. It does apply to changing who we really are, how we think and feel in order to meet our needs or someone else's. Even though transcenders work to maintain their authentic self, part of them has to deal with the crazies of the family for survival. Dealing with the family's crazies often throws transcenders away from their authentic self. For example, although the caretaking of others may offer protection and nurturance, it may also focus so much on others that it puts the caretaker in danger of losing a part of him- or herself. In this case, he or she becomes the other person, not authentically him- or herself.

Transcenders do what they need to do to survive in their family and later reclaim the lost parts in adulthood. Healing and reclaiming is the process of finding oneself and getting emotionally straight. Healing is the process of changing old unhealthy patterns to healthy ones. The old patterns that were needed in childhood are not, hopefully, needed in adulthood. These old patterns of behavior often block healing, growth, and healthy relationships, and they need to be changed. For example, the coat that you wore as a five-year-old no longer fits you as an adult. The human being is adaptable, and change is possible at any age.

Transcendence

The final philosophical and psychological concept explored in relationship to the transcender, which is also a survival technique, is transcendence. *Transcendence* is a process of creating and discovering new opportunities, usually in the midst of any kind of pain. It can be described as going beyond, or surpassing, the present situation.

Sometimes it involves going above and beyond ourselves as well as the situation. It may be described as going beyond known limits. At times, it is seen as another higher state of consciousness.[33] Many transcenders would tell you, "It is going to another focus, one that takes me out of the present horror into the future where there are possibilities and hope."

It is an expanded state of consciousness that enables us to go beyond the everyday trauma to create a new world.[34] There, we can separate from the pain in order to develop as unique individuals. When we transcend, we become open to discovering other meanings and purposes that open us up to our world with all its opportunities. It is a more creative, spiritual, and productive state of the self that occurs at a higher level of thinking and feeling.

I believe transcending is a form of detaching from the present to a more nurturing, protective place for the transcender. We can transcend feelings, thoughts, behaviors, situations, experiences, and families. At times, transcendence can be a strong idea that drives us forward, such as morals we want to live up to or strive for. Transcendence also helps us gain a strong idea of values to which we can hold on in life—values that go beyond the everyday, immediate, concrete, and material to deeper levels of the self, such as ideology and spirituality.

Transcendence is like shifting gears to another level that puts distance between us and the everyday and brings us closer to deeper, higher levels of opportunities and potentialities. Through transcendence, the individual gains encouragement, protection, inspiration, and refreshment by embracing higher beliefs, values, and ideals.[35] Being a transcender is all about going above and beyond—being the authentic, ultimate, best self.

We can transcend by perceiving, remembering, learning, achieving, surviving, and organizing our personality. This can be done through self-awareness, death, pain, trauma, abuse, neglect, sickness, one's past, needs, opinions, environment, God, spirituality, values, feelings, or another person, as well as normal behavior. Transcendence may deal with subjects, time, space, human limits, evil, identification, fear, uniqueness, opinions, one's world, culture, the natural world, the cosmos, facts and values, and so forth.[36] Transcendence above all, leads to love.

How does transcendence happen? Some of the conditions that enable transcendence to occur include: (1) the individual concentrates on an object, task, problem, personal need, or other person to which he or she can respond, whether this is perceived as possible or impossible; (2) there is a need that demands attention and focus; and (3) there is a concrete and/or psychological obstacle to overcome.[37]

Transcenders find many obstacles to overcome, needs to satisfy, and problems to face. They use transcendence to shift from the family situation to a level of living that offers hope, inspiration, protection, and support. It is through the transcending process that they become aware of their potentialities and another way of living. Transcendence offers them a way to find their personal meaning and authenticity from life's experiences. It offers a way to gain an understanding of themselves, their life, their situation, and their handling of their families.

Two people describe the process of transcending as follows.

"I sensed a basic striving from within at an early age. I told myself to be happy I must strive to be the best I could. I knew that I wanted, deserved, and expected more from life. There must be more than what I had at home. I did not know why I knew; I just knew and went after it."

"Transcending a destructive family is like living within prison walls while expending constant energy trying to recapture and maintain that sense of self, that natural state of freedom and purity, when one is born. Although there is a feeling of being trapped by the extreme limitation and boundaries established, whether this be extreme poverty; negative family values; harsh criticism and/or punishment; or miserable, gloomy, and unstimulating environments, somehow there is an inner knowing, or sense, that I will be okay, that I can overcome these barriers. I will push ahead and survive."

The transcending process seeks the truth of a situation and the discovery of our specific unique meaning. Our ability to will enables transcendence to occur by using available resources to go beyond the present to a higher, or different, plane of existence.[38]

Here are some examples from transcenders.

"In the tenth grade, I had a history teacher who was young, attractive, and enthusiastic. I used to watch her; examine her closely. I liked her and thought maybe that's what I could be—a history teacher just like her."

"'You can't go to college and waste all that money. You'll just get married anyway. You have to work too hard for your grades,' Mom said. I received a scholarship and I went anyway. Something told me she was wrong."

"I remember saying that when I got older I would have a housekeeper. Others laughed at me. They didn't believe me. I felt angry that others denied what I said I wanted. It challenged me to continue achieving."

Summary

Through willing, transcenders guide energies, use resources, and make decisions that are sustaining and growth-producing. The transcender's internal frame of reference connects to his or her Being-in-the-world because it is in the world that the transcender finds resources, opportunities, and energies to continue. Transcendence is the process of gaining energies, touching potentialities, and invoking hope for the future. Transcenders, incredibly, through their self and will, choose to live and create meaning out of chaos and conflict. They sustain continued growth and, in some form, maintain their authenticity. For transcenders, not to survive is a source of terror—a form of death. To survive and transcend is life itself.

CHAPTER 6

Adulthood: The Process

I believe that human beings are given natural life processes as part of the original package to help them experience the world. We are programmed from conception to develop physically, mentally, emotionally, and spiritually into our fullest potentiality by using these processes. These processes help us to learn from our experiences, to grow, and to heal from traumas. They are *powerful* interconnected life forces that help to lead and guide us ever forward in our growth. At times, these processes flow easily and effortlessly from within us. At other times, we are in an intense struggle where everything is an effort.

When trauma occurs, there is disruption in our life, and our entire being works to heal and reestablish a normal flow. If, for whatever reason, healing can't occur, our natural flow is altered. Dysfunctional behavior then develops to cope with unhealed traumas. In dysfunction, we learn to live with the unhealed trauma as if it were natural and normal. It is neither. What we are actually doing is working around the unhealed trauma by avoiding, masking, transforming, and/or storing it in our body. This is not natural to us, and our authentic flow is stopped and/or altered. I believe that the essence of the healing and growth process is to heal from traumas and reestablish the natural flow of our being.

Healing and growing occur as a well-choreographed unit; movement in one area triggers movement in another.

They combine to make a wonderful process that is an authentic, dynamic, and everyday function. Ideally, the healing and growth process results in the development of our authentic self. According to my research, the essence of the process happens as follows: first, we experience a traumatic situation. This experience could be a past unhealed trauma or a present experience. The experience affects us in many different ways—physically, emotionally, mentally, and spiritually. It triggers discomfort or pain on many levels. We then struggle and feel our pain. Our struggle may be very intense, or it may be an easy flow. After feeling the pain, we go over the information and work to gain all the meaning it has for us and our world. We take responsibility for these opportunities to learn and apply them to our lives. This is growth. Growth, in turn, creates patience; patience creates strength; strength creates wisdom; and all of it creates the character of our authentic self.

This is authentic living. We don't have failure; we just have learning and growth from experiences. No matter what I do, no matter what I experience, I gain. I grow. I learn. I develop. I personally view life as a huge experiential school. I am a life learner. With this view, I never lose. No matter what happens to me I am never the victim, never the failure. I am the learner. No matter what, I am not the diagnosis that was given to me—depression, personality disorder, reactive attachment disorder, etc. I am me. Every time I heal and grow, I take one more step forward to the development and strengthening of my authentic self.

My research consistently shows that in the healing and growth process, transcenders go beyond surviving their family and work to develop their authentic self. They truly transcend. As adults they work hard to create a life they dreamed about as a child in order to surpass the dysfunction of the family. They work to heal and grow as authentic human beings. In this chapter, the basics of the transcender's process of healing and growing are presented.

Definition of Terms

The following are definitions I have learned through my schooling, professional experience, and research that I believe will help you understand the healing and growing process that is presented in the next three chapters.

Directives in life: To love and be loved physically, mentally, emotionally, and spiritually. Love supports, encourages, and helps growth to occur. We must live fully in love to be truly authentic and what our Creator envisioned. This is agape love or spiritual love.

Feeling feelings/emotions fully: To feel our feelings/emotions to their fullest extent in the present moment. Feelings are always felt in the present because we are in the present when we feel them. They are never in the past. The experience that first created the feelings is in the past. However, the feelings are felt in the present. When feelings are fully felt and experienced, they are then complete and settled in the past. This is the magic of feeling emotions. They must be felt in order for us to release the pain they cause and its connection to any trauma. The more we ignore, avoid, and push away our feelings, the stronger and more painful they become. Feelings are stored in our body until we feel them, and until we feel them we don't heal or grow to our potential. As we feel, pain is released (like reverse osmosis), and important, life-changing insights (understanding) into the past and their effect on our present living occur.

Growth: The movement of individuals toward becoming *all* that their Creator originally intended. This includes feelings, thoughts, learning, potentialities, talents, spirituality, and love.

Healing: The process of releasing pain and changing old patterns to develop and enhance our original creation with the addition of growth. Healing allows the darkness of the trauma to give way to the light of being. I do not believe that our Creator ever intended for us to stay in our pain and darkness. I believe that the original package intention is always to work through the pain in order to heal, learn, and grow.

Learning: Learning is what we know and understand and *are* in the process of knowing and understanding about ourselves, our world, and others in our world. Learning supports and enhances growth. We learn by staying in our struggles and gleaning all we can. We then move on to our next experience and all that it contains.

Love/caring: A commitment to carrying out our directive with ourselves, others, and our world. It is a commitment to care in order to help healing and growing to occur emotionally, mentally, physically, and spiritually.

Revisiting: Revisiting is the reexperiencing, remembering, and refeeling of the past in order to gain an adult perspective on and understanding of what has happened to us as children. Revisiting takes place from an adult perspective looking back at oneself as a child. Revisiting is handling all the unresolved feelings as well as problems and conflicts (issues) left from the experiences of childhood. These feelings may include anger, sorrow, pain, resentment, loneliness, shame, hurt, and rejection, as well as guilt. Issues include relating to family members and dealing with unresolved problems from childhood. This is not retraumatization.

Struggle: The internal wrestling with behaviors, emotions, and thoughts that works to create growth in the individual. Old patterns of being are challenged by life experiences to create a new, third way of being that fits. A struggle in the healing process usually occurs when the old is challenged or no longer works and the new has not yet been learned. Sometimes, the struggle needs only a little effort, while other times an incredible effort is needed to move forward. The struggle continues until a new way is created or the individual goes back to the old behaviors.

There is always some sort of discomfort or pain that throws the individual into a struggle that shifts the old and creates the new. Otherwise, there is no reason to change, no reason to grow. Without the challenge, the old way is not seen as obsolete and no longer useful. Struggle may feel like suffering at times, but there is a difference. In struggle, I am moving forward; in suffering, I just stay in pain. The following is an excerpt from Tiffany's journal that focuses on her struggle with being good and bad. In it, you can get a flavor of the struggle and its back-and-forth energy.

Tiffany

"I don't want to be a bad girl. I want to be a good girl. I'll try harder, then Mommy will love me. I'll be the good girl she always wanted me to be. I'll work hard, Mommy. I promise. Just please love me—please, please love me. Please don't be mad at me. I need you. I love you. I know you never liked me—you wanted me to be someone else, not me. You wanted me to be that perfect girl. Help! If I do that, I'll lose me again, and I don't want to do that—not again. It's too hard to come back. Why can't I just be me? Why am I not okay? Why not? I seem lovable. I seem okay to me. Why am I not okay to you?

"Please love me just for me. I can be different. I'll try. I'll change me. I'll be good. Please help me to grow up. Why didn't you? What was so awful about the real me? But I have been judged by you. It's not fair! I'm not bad. I am okay. I am good. God created me good, so I'm good, but you think I'm bad—so I'm bad. BAD! Mommy says I'm bad, so I'll have to cover it all up. Cover up all the bad so no one can see it and so people know that Mommy is okay. I must hide. I'm embarrassed at all of me. But I'm not bad, I'm good and okay. I don't know who's right—me or Mommy."

Trauma: A physical, emotional, mental, or spiritual assault. Traumas usually include intense feelings of fear, terror, anger, and hurt. Often, there is disbelief that the event is actually happening. For example, a child when assaulted by his or her parent is in a state of shock: "This can't be happening! How could my parents, who are supposed to love me, do this?" Then, at times, thoughts such as: "God, they're going to kill me!" All these feelings usually have to go underground and are stored in the body until later in adulthood when it becomes safe to feel.

The terror involved in a trauma can be so powerful that the blood in the body may leave the head, hands, and feet and go to the vital survival organs, such as the stomach, heart, and lungs. The hands and feet may feel cold, and the head may feel light, as if having a head cold. Individuals can faint if the trauma is severe enough. If this state lasts very long, there is energy only for basic survival and nothing for academics or other pursuits.

Traumas, if dealt with in the healing process, can be healed. After healing, there may be a scar, but the majority of the pain is gone. Healing one trauma may trigger healing for other deeper and older traumas. For example, if I feel the fear of one beating, I can release stored fear from other beatings. Healing may also bring into awareness a trauma that has been blocked from my memory.

The Healing and Growing Process

Healing is often called recovery in the mental health field. I believe true healing is more than just recovery; I believe that it is a deep and life-changing process interconnected to the growing and learning process. Together, healing and growing work through the pain and darkness of trauma to create life in freedom and light. They are an integration of releasing the pain, learning, and applying the learning to our lives so we live more authentically in our natural flow. The two processes work together to help us discover our true selves from the inside out.

When we heal and grow, we gain one of the most valuable resources we can possess, wisdom. Wisdom comes from the experiences we have had in life and from which have taken the time to learn. Wisdom, true wisdom and not just information, comes from fully living life. When we have lived life with all its joys and pain and have grown with it, we have earned wisdom.

By growth, I mean learning from all my experiences and taking risks in my unknown areas. It means expanding my limits and not accepting my self-imposed prison bars as permanent but exploring them to see how far I can develop.

An example of pushing these self-imposed limits is a decision I made when I was a teenager. When I was fifteen, I was *painfully* shy and couldn't talk to teachers. I would turn beet red and become speechless if they tried to talk to me. I made a decision when I was seventeen that I would no longer be shy, and no matter how painful it was, I would step out and be assertive. I had no idea how I would develop as a result of making this decision. I just knew I had to be out of that awful pain. I told no one, but continued to make choices that were more assertive. I learned a lot. Decades later, when an assertiveness program was announced in my church, my daughter begged me not to take it because she said I was already "too assertive." If I had not taken those first steps as a teenager, I would never have known how I could develop, and inside I'd still be that shy, speechless teenager. I now speak nationally! The greatest gain in my process to overcome my shyness was that I learned many things about me, the real me. One of the things I learned is that I am not really a shy person. I enjoy people but also love and value my quiet, alone times.

The essence of the healing and growing process is eliminating what is not authentic and enhancing all that is authentic. I compare it to Michelangelo and how he created his awesome sculptures. According to history, he first imaged the creation trapped in the stone and wanting to get out. He then removed all that was not the image while enhancing all that was. We have within us the image of who we are that may be trapped in our stone. It is my professional opinion that we have within us all we need to develop our original package. We, like Michelangelo sculpting, need to remove what is not us—the damage caused by traumas—while embracing and developing our authenticity. In this way we find our strength, growth, original package, and relationship to self, others, and God.

Healing takes on many different forms. It is basically anything that safely promotes positive change from the effects of trauma for an individual with integrity and safety. It may be through formal therapy but not necessarily. The healing process is unique to each person. I've seen healing begin with just a phone call to set up an appointment, a client receiving a special card in the mail, or with a hug or a smile.

It is my opinion that the essence of healing is love/caring and acceptance. Basically, like a dear friend of mine says, individuals need to give authentic love in any form to themselves as well as receive it from others. This is the highest form of love/caring that helps people heal and grow, called agape love.

Our dynamic healing and growing process works to keep us emotionally, mentally, physically, and spiritually healthy. It uses all our available resources to guide us in healing from traumas by learning from experiences, continuing to grow, and then keeping straight in all areas of our lives. By being *straight*, I mean developing and being our authentic selves—having our integrity. It means we are honest in our communications, thoughts, and feelings, and we back them up with authentic behavior. Who we are inside matches who we are outside. When we are straight, there is no game-playing or dysfunction in relationships with ourselves or others. In essence, we are real.

Authentic living involves a constant healing and growing process. This process helps guide us in handling *all* our traumas and experiences throughout life. It works to integrate our perceptions and knowledge of each experience to create growth, development, and learning, all of which becomes wisdom. If we resist our process, as we all do at times, we experience frustration, depression, anger, and lack of learning. While processing an experience, we may have pain, sorrow, and other intense difficult feelings, *but* we can gain learning, growth, peace, joy, love, and wisdom over time.

Healing occurs on many levels at the same time. For example, I may feel sadness when a friend dies and, at the same time, feel the sadness from the loss of never having a healthy family. Or I may be angry about something at work, but when I express the anger its intensity tells me old anger is also being released because I am feeling more anger than the experience triggered. I may not always know what healing is occurring, but I can become aware that it is happening.

After any kind of physical, emotional, mental, or spiritual trauma, there is an incredible surge of focus and energy to release the pain, reestablish the natural flow, and grow. Our internal processes work to establish a normal life again. These processes of healing and growing may become blocked when we are either unwilling (because it's intense and painful) or unable (because it's not safe) to work through an experience or trauma.

Working through a trauma involves feeling and learning from it. When we are not able to do this, the trauma and the damage it causes become trapped, or "frozen," in our bodies. These frozen feelings then interfere with the flow of energy, feelings, and learning. When this happens, we can't function efficiently, and we become stuck.

Research now tells us feelings are stored at the cell level in our bodies.[1] When we try to adapt and handle the trauma by denying, masking, running from, substituting for it with an addiction, not trusting ourselves, or depending totally on other people for our needs, we create dysfunction. Being our authentic selves by staying in our process can be exciting, joyful, sad, intense, difficult, and at times, very painful. But it is the only way to really live. It is only by knowing ourselves that we can heal, grow, learn, and be real. This does not mean we won't have rough, difficult times that challenge us down to our core. It does mean, however, that as we heal and grow, living becomes easier because we have *all* of us available to handle our world and its obstacles—without the old pain.

When we are authentic, we learn to trust our selves, feelings, intuition, and process, and we learn from our experiences. We know that our authentic self and process are not only okay but fantastically wonderful and perfect for us. The tragedy in our society today, let alone in a dysfunctional family, is not knowing this. We, as individuals and as a collective society have forgotten how to support ourselves and others in the healing and growing process. Sadly, society believes that the only way to feel good about oneself is through financial and/or status success. In my many decades as a therapist, I have come to believe that the only way to *really* feel good and be successful is to be our authentic growing, dynamic, in-process self.

With each experience we face in life, we have the choice of growth or nongrowth. In this choice, we face going forward and developing new parts of ourselves or staying stuck on some level. Each of us is personally responsible for our choices. Even in the midst of healing and growing from a dysfunctional family, an individual can make the decision to stop. We may stop for many reasons: too painful, too life-changing, too terrifying, too threatening (like having to leave a relationship), or just too time-consuming. But by not growing, we are saying, "I don't want the rest of me and I am choosing to stay stuck!" Nongrowth sounds like, "That's enough! I have had it. I don't want to grow. I don't want to change. It's too scary. I'll stay where I am, in the pain. I'll keep my identity of being sexually and verbally abused." If we continue to say no, we are at risk of becoming unrecognizable because our real selves are no longer truly alive. We are then in danger of becoming nonproductive *and* definitely narrow-minded and set in our ways.

Nongrowth creates a slow, painful, and tragic death of our authentic self. If I choose not to grow, I have not only denied my internal spiritual vision of all that I can be; I have also denied and squelched my original package's opportunity to grow and develop. This choice takes an enormous amount of energy and a concerted effort. Nongrowth means using energy in ways that do not embrace the natural flow of the authentic self. Instead, energy is used to keep everything in place.

Growth, thank goodness, is so powerful, and its benefits feel so good, that we usually want to continue growing once we have experienced it. I may struggle and suffer in growth, but I gain the authentic life that goes with it. In nongrowth, I have a form of death. In growth, I have life of the self.

Everyone is unique in this area. Some individuals seem to have only a little determination, strength, or courage to face the healing and growing process. Others are so determined that they leap into any experience that supports and encourages growth. Transcenders are usually among the latter and have the ability to use even a little encouragement as support to go forward.

Sometimes we erroneously give the responsibility of our process to another person. By doing so, we give away our personal power and become inappropriately dependent. If this happens, the message is "You take over. You know more than I do. I'm too scared and don't know how to handle my own life." Usually this occurs because we have been taught by rigid and/or abusive families that we can never be responsible for our lives. This is actually an illusion because only we *can* be responsible.

When we choose to support and encourage our process, we develop our unique original package, and our potentiality is virtually limitless. In addition, we gain personal power and freedom, which create healthy interdependent relationships. Interdependency is being appropriately dependent and independent at different times in the same relationship. There is a flow between the two extremes as the individual needs. My needs in the relationship as well as my significant other's needs determine whether I will be more independent or dependent. Sometimes, depending on my mood and situation, I'll need to be very dependent, such as during heavy grieving times or after surgery. Other times, my significant other will need to be dependent on me. At still other times, I will need or want to function in the world very independently of anyone.

Once we learn to live in our natural process, we usually can't and don't want to return to our old unauthentic ways of living. We are on a continuous self-discovery journey. We become excited about what we just learned and look forward to what we will discover next about ourselves and the world. We also learn to trust ourselves at a deeper level. We find within us comfortableness and have a deep knowing that says, "I have what I need to be okay." We also find strength—a deep internal strength of being.

As stated previously, every person's process of healing and growing is unique, special, and prefect for that person. My process is not going to be like yours nor yours like mine. You can't live authentically in my life nor I in yours, but we are perfect in our own processes. However, there are shared components to the healing process.

Steve

The following is a description of Steve's process:

"I was swimming the other day when this last struggle began. I became aware of an old memory, its pain, and how it was interfering with my training. I struggled with it, and I worked hard to make it go away—it didn't. It went unresolved. I then tried to avoid it. Avoiding it didn't work any better than the last time I tried it. The memory demanded that I stay there and deal with it. I was back to the pain and the wrestling.

"The struggle was intense, deep, lonely, isolating, and just plain awful. My brain reached desperately for a solution. There was none. I prayed for one. I wanted one. I wanted to get out of the pain. I felt like Jacob wrestling with the angel. I didn't want to ever surrender to it. It was awful. I screamed, 'I'll never surrender! You'll never win. No! No! No! Never! I'll fight until I have no more energy for the fight.' The worst part was the fear of not knowing what was to come or to what I was surrendering.

"When I did finally surrender and allow myself to go into the feelings, there was a peace. At times it was awful, but there was also a peace—a knowing that I would learn, grow, and find relief from the pain through feeling the feelings. I knew I could handle whatever was coming just as I have handled other struggles. I knew I had to go straight through the process so I could gain all that I could from memory. I did not want to have to repeat this struggle again—there would be enough other ones to deal with in the future.

"As I went through it, I cried, got angry, and released a variety of feelings. Part of me still said, 'Get me out of this.' The other part of me said, 'Stay, learn, grow, and gain strength.' I knew it was the only way. As I stayed, I gained wonderful insights into my life and my behavior. As these insights came, the pain eased and the confusion lifted. I then found myself making changes automatically in my life—healthy, wonderful changes that gave me more freedom and an increasing sense of inner power, strength, and energy.

"I love the energy and power. It's a sense of 'I can handle myself in this world. I can climb mountains, conquer problems, and yes, even go through another growth process.'"

Trauma Layers and the Healing Process

Healing is a process of dealing with the many layers of emotional pain caused by traumas to reveal the real us. According to my research, it appears that layers are caused by the actual traumas as well as by the protective barriers created by transcenders to defend themselves. When an individual is not able (or allowed) to work through a trauma, the experience and all its feelings are stored in the body as a layer. Energy, insights, and learning are lost because the experience can't be processed. This, in turn, makes living in reality and making appropriate decisions much harder if not impossible. Let me give you an example of the process of creating a layer. Every time transcenders were previously abused they may have felt pain, anger, rejection, abandonment, suspicion, mistrust, loneliness, and/or shame. It was not safe to feel these feelings because, if they had, they may have been even more severely abused or they may not have been mature enough to understand the abuse. So, the feelings and thoughts from the trauma are held inside in what is called a layer. When there is another trauma, more pain is held inside on top of the previous layer, creating another layer. Layers function this way: the more trauma, the more stored layers; the more layers, the more terrifying the feelings; the more terror, the greater the need for protection from feelings and what may feel like the original trauma happening all over again. I believe that our bodies remember at some level each trauma, feeling, and thought about the experience, no matter our age when the trauma occurs. If it happens when we are young children, we may not have words to describe it, but we have feeling senses and perceptions.

Tucked inside with the trauma layers are layers of protection. Transcenders have to figure out not only how to protect themselves physically and emotionally from the family but also how to protect and keep themselves away from their own feelings. They have learned that feeling certain feelings, and sometimes, perhaps, any feeling, is dangerous. They believe that if they allow themselves to feel the feelings they will be more severely abused. Also, they believe they will become so overwhelmed that they may not survive. This fear can be so strong that feeling or even acknowledging the feeling can trigger terror and thoughts of suicide. Often, the hardest part of releasing a layer is dealing with the fear. The layer is literally surrounded by a powerful ring of fear, like an electric fence that protects the person from the feelings and, in turn, helps ensure survival.

Protection layers come in many forms: (1) beliefs, such as "My family is perfect, and they loved me very much" (denial); (2) extreme overweight (armoring), fragile, or superbody build (physical barrier); (3) resistant, rebellious, or obnoxious behavior (necessary to keep others away); (4) loving, kind, caretaking behavior (necessary to have others like them so they won't be abused by them); (5) memory blocks (keeping pain out of awareness); and (6) dissociative disorder or multiple personalities created in extreme abuse situations. The "personalities" are really just parts of the same person that hold feelings and pain away from awareness, often in memory blocks labeled with specific names.

I believe that to be emotionally healthy we have to acknowledge, feel, and release from the body each trauma layer. Each layer has to be understood and integrated, or else our body stores them until we do understand and integrate them. The layers don't just go away. Through the healing process, transcenders often become exhausted by the many layers that keep surfacing and need to be revisited. They wish they could stop the process for even a little while because it has become so painfully difficult. The pain does end when all surfacing trauma layers have been released and healed.

In the active healing process, transcenders work with their many stored layers for what seems to them to be an eternity. This healing time is put into perspective when compared with the many years their families have degraded, neglected, and abused them. The more abuse and neglect, the more layers; the more layers, the more healing time required.

Layers may come up in no particular order. As a therapist, it has been my experience that the least threatening will usually come first and the most threatening last. These layers are triggered by the therapy process, as well as by life events. Once the layer is released, the transcender feels freer, stronger, more capable, and more relaxed. Often, I am told the transcender also feels physically lighter! Transcenders also gain new perspectives (internal frame of reference) as well as changed thoughts, feelings, and behaviors. An in-depth knowing that *"that was then, and this is now"* allows a more accurate perspective and a more authentic perception of the trauma as the transcender works through the layers.

Paul is able to identify his order of layers. This is not unusual, but not every transcender is able to do this.

Paul

"I first feel anger. After I feel it and release its power, the feeling of hurt predominates. Fear follows the hurt. I become frightened of what seems to be everything: people, traffic, going out, staying in, the dark, everything. Sometimes, for instance, in the beginning of my healing process, the fear turns into terror. I experience the terror of my little boy who lived through those awful years. What surprises me is that after the terror I experience a lack of trust in everyone around me. Somehow I figured that once I got through the terror I'd be in a nice, more peaceful place. My hoped-for peace is really the feeling of betrayal, deep betrayal. Then comes a layer of wariness that protects me, the real me. Underneath this protection is the deep original hurt and incredible sadness. Once through this original hurt, I do feel better, and I reach a place of peace. I find the only way to get my layers to shift is to feel each thoroughly."

The following is one way a layer is created: (1) an experience occurs that triggers feelings; (2) most of these feelings are shifted out of awareness; (3) feelings cannot be safely expressed so they are denied, buried, and/or transferred; and (4) the feelings create a new painful layer in the body, and little learning occurs.

A healthy way of processing feelings, instead of creating layers, involves the following steps: (1) an experience occurs that triggers feelings; (2) there is an awareness of the feelings; (3) the feelings are felt to their fullest extent; and (4) learning and insight from the experience are gained and stored for later use, and the pain is released.

The Healing and Growing Process

My research indicates the healing process of the transcender has two powerful major components: (1) grieving the past; and (2) reclaiming the self. This two-part process is very hard and intense because grieving and reclaiming are going on at the same time.

1. Grieving the past consists of feeling the losses from childhood. These losses include what the individuals *did not* have in childhood (e.g., love, affection, support, and a normal childhood), as well as what they *did* have in childhood (e.g., abuse and neglect). *Everything* surfacing needs to be felt and grieved. Denial, anger, rejection, and intense sadness are among the feelings experienced in the grieving process.

2. Reclaiming the self includes discovering, developing, and exploring the original package (i.e., authentic self). Reclaiming frequently involves finding one's authentic self for the first time. It is the growth part of the process. It contains a range of feelings from intense pain to joy. In childhood, transcenders have usually been given little chance to discover or explore their abilities, let alone to develop authentically. Transcenders often view therapy as the first chance to develop their real self and potentialities and work hard to transcend their families. They work to become whole functioning people in a life of their choosing. The process is difficult because, as one transcender asked me, "How do you settle down and live a normal, regular, calm life when you have already lived ten lifetimes? How do you settle down and not want to live on the edge (a place of constant tension, anxiety, and defense, as well as excitement) after living almost your whole life on the edge?" The healing process is a *huge* adjustment in the style of inner living. Some transcenders have few problems; others struggle deeply throughout the process.

The healing and growth process is *chosen, active,* and *purposeful.* Transcenders choose to overcome their leftovers from childhood and apply the needed time, effort, courage, determination, and finances to heal. They use psychotherapy, AA-based groups, significant others, spirituality, nature (eco-psychology), therapy weekends, workshops, and anything else that helps them heal from their past. The commitment to healing is the long-term continuation of their growth, the turning-point, the decision of childhood.

I must emphasize that *there are no quick, easy fixes.* The healing process usually takes years—perhaps even a lifetime. As part of the healing process, each individual must face his or her own dark cloud full of thunder, lightning, and gale-strength winds from past traumas. No one else can do this for the person—no one.

Our natural healing process works to heal the body, mind, emotions, and spirit from the damage caused by abuse and neglect. Each individual has his or her personal way of recovering and healing from the trauma of a dysfunctional family. Therapy is often needed to help transcenders uncover and develop this process as well as to give them support throughout the process.

Rarely is one method or one therapist ever enough, although individual therapy with more than one therapist at the same time is not recommended unless one does individual and one does group therapy. Healing requires the use of many different techniques, as well as a variety of people in different capacities at different times. In addition, there is no one thought or feeling that is "it" in the healing process. No one thing straightens out all the past and its hurts. It takes a concerted effort over a number of years with many feelings, thoughts, therapies, and people.

This process of healing is full of contradictory feelings. It may be so intense and painful that transcenders lose hope of ever making it, and at the same time, the process is so freeing and loving that transcenders experience uplifting, energizing freedom and joy.

There are four stages that lead transcenders to their goal of healing and growth as adults: (1) leaving home; (2) transitioning; (3) seeking outside help; and (4) healing and growing in a therapeutic setting.

Stage One—Leaving Home

Freedom at last! The first step in transcenders' healing process is to *leave home* as early as possible. Transcenders move out through college, marriage, work, military, and running and/or moving away. They now use their childhood technique of getting out and staying away to move into well-earned personal freedom. In addition, the turning-point decision to be different from their family once again becomes a powerful focal point in helping them leave. This leaving is absolutely essential to transcending.

The average leaving age is immediately after high school. However, age is *not* important because transcending can occur at *any* age. What is important is that transcenders leave and realize their survival now depends on not going back to the old family entanglements but forward into their own long-dreamed-of world.

The experience of leaving is different for each transcender. Leaving can be easy or difficult, depending on the family's dysfunction. Some families try to stop the leaving by playing emotional games. Games may include the family's becoming so dysfunctional that the transcender feels trapped. The family members may act out violently or become "ill," withhold monies, housing, or anything else. On the other hand, some families welcome the leaving, kick the transcender out, or don't even notice they are leaving. However and whenever it happens, the transcender leaves.

Adulthood and freedom for transcenders hold a mixed blessing of excitement and fear. The excitement is that they are free, unbelievably free, to be themselves and create the life they have been dreaming about for years. The fear includes powerful concerns about themselves and the world. For example, "Who am I?" "What do I do now?" "How do I handle this world?" "Am I going to make it?"

Some transcenders are very conscious of the excitement and freedom and aware of what they are doing. Others have no awareness or only a vague knowing. Tiffany and Marie describe their experiences.

Tiffany

"I left for college immediately after my senior year in high school. I was so relieved, so happy and excited. I finally was free of all those people who wanted to control me. Finally! I waited all those years, and freedom was finally here. I could try out all those things I had been dying to do. Wow! It was great! I did all sorts of things I could never even dream of at home.

"Sometimes I just sat and enjoyed the calm in my life. I began to learn how to get along with other people. I talked with other students discussing the latest topic. I began to learn that I really did have some brains and abilities. That was a big awareness for me because for years I thought I was just conning everyone. I really thought I must be dumb. My nickname in the family was Dopey.

"At the same time, leaving home was terrifying. I didn't have all the skills other college students had. I didn't know how to relate to others without the dysfunction. I didn't even know who I was, not really. There were so many questions, like 'How do I do this? What happens if I don't make it? Will I have to go back home?'

"I had a lot of fear, but I also had a promise to myself to keep going and not be like my family. I learned as I went, but it was a very mixed bag of feelings."

Marie

"Here I was, almost twenty-one years old, living at home, working, paying room and board, and feeling like a prisoner still locked within the crazies of the family. I was not allowed to drive, have my own bank account (Mom took all the money), date, or go anywhere without my mother's approval. And, according to my family, the only way a 'nice girl' could leave home was to get married.

"I had a job I really enjoyed working for a doctor. However, it became more and more embarrassing to me because my mother kept checking on me and would even call his wife. My mother thought I must be doing something 'bad' with the doctor. I couldn't take it any more. I had to get away, yet I knew if I left home, my mother would send the sheriff after me saying I had stolen something from the house. Actually, she had told me she would do this if I ever tried to leave. I never prayed so hard in my life as I did for an opportunity to escape. A couple of guys had asked me to marry them, but I didn't love them. I couldn't see trading one prison for another.

"I decided to join the Air Force and get an education after I saw an advertisement on television. I had completed two years of college and really wanted to finish my education but not half as much as I wanted to get away from home. The doctor I worked for asked me if I had ever thought about joining the service as a way of getting away from home. I confided in him what I was planning. The doctor helped by 'firing' me so the Air Force would look like a great opportunity to my mother. She saw it as a great chance for me to finally become a 'lady' and learn to do what I was told.

"I couldn't believe it! I was really going to leave home. I was finally going to get away. Each night before I left for basic training, I'd lay awake thinking, 'What have I done?' I felt a lot of fear. I knew that no matter how hard it was, it could not be as difficult as my life within this prison.

"At this time, I had no conscious awareness of the sexual or physical abuse, let alone being forced to participate in the horrible satanic rituals. All I knew was that my mother was unable to love me because I was such a bad person. I felt responsible for my parents' unhappiness, their divorce, and even felt guilty for being born. I hoped, in addition to getting away from all my failure feelings, my mother would be happier if I was not around every day to remind her of what a failure I was. And yet, way deep inside, a part of me questioned whether I was the one who had failed. Regardless, I had given up on the little-girl hope of 'today is the day I'll be good enough to be loved.' I could no longer stand the verbal abuse and the put downs. I was getting out.

"I was very aware, largely due to my parents' brainwashing, that even though I was leaving home and getting away from the craziness of my family, I would have to be very careful not to let people get to know the real me. I still believed if they knew what I was really like, they wouldn't want me around. This was parent tape number one. *[Note: tapes are certain ways of feeling, thinking, and behaving that are heard, taught, and learned from others and clicked on under certain circumstances as if they were a tape.]*

"I also knew that people couldn't be trusted. I had already learned that in my world, even though I was not conscious of the reality that had given birth to these feelings. I knew I was bad, dirty, and cheap. Regardless, the free world had to be better. Besides, if I kept up the façade of the smiling, happy, helpful, responsible person, then people wouldn't have a chance to find out what I was really like. Besides, I would be able to lock the bathroom door, have my own bank account, and for the first time in my memory, I could make my own decisions.

"Most of the other Air Force trainees were just out of high school, so I had a little edge on maturity. Many rebelled at the strict discipline. I found great comfort in structure and discipline—far less rigid and certainly more logical than the kind I experienced at home. I can't say that basic training was the easiest thing I'd ever been through, but I fell back on my 'let's see what you can learn from this experience' perspective. It had gotten me through so many things in the past

"After several hours of testing, I was surprised to find that my test scores were high enough to qualify me for the next officer candidate school. Didn't my parents say I was dumb? A few days later, I was told I had the potential for receiving the outstanding-trainee award and was expected to receive this award at graduation. I can remember thinking the officer that told me this didn't know what kind of person I was, but if she thought I was capable I was not going to try to change her opinion. The outstanding trainee is voted on by peers and staff, each vote carrying the same weight. No one was more surprised than I when, on graduation day, my name was called to receive the award. This opened the door to the fact that maybe I was capable.

"I was so excited and couldn't wait to call home with the happy news. My mother's reply was, 'Oh, they don't know what you are really like, or I'm sure they would have chosen someone who deserved the award.'

"I was devastated. I realize now that my true freedom from my family really began several months after my mother was killed in an automobile accident. After realizing she was really dead, I felt like I had just been born. I could have never survived if I had not left my crazy family. Her death opened the rest of the door to life for me!"

Stage Two—Transition

The second stage in the transcenders' healing process is the transition period. The *transition period* is that period of time after leaving home and before formal therapy in which the transcender is adjusting to life without the family. It can last a few months or many years. Transcenders rarely know how to live a normal life in the world, and it is during this time that they learn through good decisions and successes, as well as through many mistakes. Tremendous learning occurs. They learn to handle their freedom, set up dreamed-about lifestyles, and begin to really know themselves. Their mistakes include wrong choices in relationships, marriages, and jobs. Transcenders again use their powerful turning-point decision, as well as personal-growth promises from childhood, to push themselves to learn and grow in their adult world.

Transcenders do not accept their mistakes as something permanent but rather as learning experiences. They work hard, do not give up, and continue to create a life that is more in line with what they pictured in childhood. Some transcenders seek therapeutic help immediately and do anything possible to enhance their lives and accomplish their goals. Others work hard with themselves and in significant relationships to create healthy, nurturing lifestyles. However it is done, transcenders work to overcome issues, problems, and dysfunction stemming from childhood leftovers.

The transition time is a unique adjustment period for each transcender. It is a time of experimenting and learning what they want, as well as what they don't want, in their world. Transcenders also begin to learn how to get along in the world without the family and its dysfunction. During this time they also experience many small transitions—that is, they work to leave old behaviors behind and develop healthier ones. This takes time. They experience fun, relief, confusion, pain, sadness, joy, fear, etc., as well as growing relationships. Some find enormous success during this time, others little.

Stage 3-Seeking Outside Help

At some point, many transcenders find themselves not living the way they intended but, instead, living in emotional turmoil and pain; and then *seek outside help.* Leftovers from childhood may also intensify as transcenders experience the world. Transcenders experience emotional pain from mistakes made in relationships, work, and working to create a healthy lifestyle, as well as from "ghosts" of the past. *Ghosts* are people and memories of the past abuse, pain, and loneliness that seem to haunt people in their present life and in the present moment. These memories and their influence on behavior interfere with transcenders' lives and trigger resentfulness, anger, confusion, guilt, depression, fear, and discouragement.

At times, the emotional pain is so intense that functioning on any level becomes difficult. Transcenders may believe they will never have the life they wanted and dreamed of as a child. They may even fear they have turned out to be like their family. (Sometimes, transcenders have traits like their family members because they carry their genes and are influenced by the people who raise them, *but* these emotional and personality characteristics are not usually permanent and can be changed during the healing and growth process.) It is this combination of emotional pain, mistakes, frustrations, depression, ghosts, fear, the awareness of the leftovers influencing their lives, and their childhood promises to themselves to grow that drive transcenders into therapy. This stage usually occurs around thirty to forty years of age. There is no right or specific age for any part of the healing process. All ages are relative and *not* important. I mention them only to give you an idea of time. Any individual can choose to be a transcender of a dysfunctional childhood at any time.

Chris

Chris, the scapegoat of his family, describes his experience before entering therapy.

"I wanted relationships in my life that were healthy and fun. I needed to be accepted and loved. In relationships, however, I always had problems. They always fell apart and became incredibly painful. I was always left lonely and feeling punished.

"In one relationship, the woman and I loved each other deeply. We shared wonderful times and could talk forever. It was so good, for a while; then it fell apart. We ended up fighting and soon began to hate each other. I needed to be accepted, but every time she'd get close and offer the love I needed, I'd shove her away. It would look like I was a bad guy. In reality, I was terrified to be that close, but at the same time I needed the love she offered.

"This relationship, as well as others, continued to go downhill. I decided I was a total failure. I knew I was not worth much. I had so much pain I couldn't stand it. I also decided that my parents were right—it was all my fault, and I deserved to be punished by people leaving me.

"Finally, the pain was so great, I had to do something. My world was falling apart. All my relationships ended up in pain and anger. I knew something had to be wrong with me. It couldn't always be everyone else all the time.

"By the time I finally got into therapy, I couldn't maintain any organization. Even my finances were going downhill. I was unbelievably lonely and depressed. I believed I had no friends and knew I didn't have a family. I believed no one loved me.

"The subject of therapy came up when a friend and I were talking. He told me how he had been helped. I listened because I knew his childhood had been just as bad as mine. I also saw changes I liked in him, and I wanted the same changes. He was happier and calmer and even beginning to have some good friendships. I went, and I'm glad I did. I now understand my childhood and have changed my pattern of relating to me and others.

"In therapy, I learned that I set up relationships to fail. That is, I set the person up to reject and dump me. Just like my family did! My family did a good job of teaching me how to do it. My family also taught me it was all I deserved—to be rejected, unloved, and lonely. I now know those were the leftovers from my childhood, and I have changed most of them. I'm beginning to have healthier relationships and feel better about myself."

Therapists offer transcenders information about the healing and growth process. They help transcenders know what feelings are normal at different stages in the process, and they give support and help through the process. For

example, there is a stage when transcenders believe they
have become just like their parents and need reassurance
that this is not true. (This belief occurs because as healing
continues, feelings, thoughts, and behaviors come up that
do look like the family's dysfunction. Transcenders, happily,
are able to change them.) There is also a totally confusing,
feeling-"crazy" transition time that occurs when new and
old patterns of operating are functioning at the same time.
Transcenders need reassurance and guidance during
these difficult times. They especially need to know they
are doing well and are going to make it.

Stage Four—Healing and Growing in a Therapeutic Setting

The last stage in the healing and growth process is *psychotherapy.* Psychotherapy is therapy focused on helping
the individual heal and grow mentally, emotionally, physically, and spiritually. The general steps involved in therapy are described below. Each individual has his or her
own unique process within these general steps and may
need different techniques at different times, but the
process is the same. The steps are *not rigid,* and as in any
process, they can mix, overlap, skip, change order, repeat,
or occur at the same time. The grieving and reclaiming
processes are going on at the same time and are detailed
in Chapters 7 and 8.
Here are the steps:

1. *Develop a trusting relationship with the therapist as
   well as themselves.* Most individuals who grow up in
   dysfunctional families have problems trusting other
   human beings. They either can't trust or trust too easily. Thank goodness, appropriate trust can be learned,
   earned, and developed in healthy relationships. In

therapy, it is vital that a healthy, trusting, working relationship be established with a healthy, dependable therapist who knows the healing process in order to promote the learning of trust and the working through of intense feelings and important issues.

Part of a trusting relationship for transcenders is to feel genuinely accepted, cared about, and supported during their process. At this point, transcenders need to ask, "Does what the therapist say and do match? Does he or she really care for me as a person and not just a paying customer? Does he or she see the pain I am in?" It is *very* important that transcenders work with a therapist who is genuine and helps develop trust.

Equally important, transcenders need to gain a trust of themselves and their healing process. It is essential that trust in themselves develops, because trust has either not been developed or has been severely damaged while they were growing up. Trust of themselves becomes increasingly important as transcenders heal deeply trapped layers.

Developing a trusting relationship with oneself and others takes time. Even minimal trust sometimes takes more than a year to develop with the therapist. A deep inner trust of oneself and others may take years. Patience on the part of the transcender as well as the therapist in this area is a must. Remember, it took a long time to grow up. Transcenders are worth the time it takes to heal.

2. *Explore the background.* At the same time the trusting relationship is developing, an exploration of the transcender's background is begun. An infinite number of details about growing up are remembered, described, and examined. Many of these are painful memories that also trigger the very important grieving process. These memories encourage the grieving to start by helping transcenders gain awareness. They are able to

acknowledge they had a horrible growing-up period and experienced a lot of pain, sadness, and loss. This awareness helps transcenders to stop blaming themselves and to see the family's dysfunction and destruction more clearly. All of this, in turn, strengthens and helps the healing and growing process to continue.

3. *Reclaim the self. Reclaiming* is the finding and developing of the original package—the authentic self. Reclaiming of the self begins the day transcenders decide to rid themselves of leftovers, be more themselves, and get into therapy. The process works this way: everything that transcenders discover and feel about their family releases trapped internal layers. Each layer blocks part of the original authentic self. As the layers are released in the body, the authentic self is unblocked in some way and has a greater freedom to be. Also, as each layer is dealt with, more awareness of the traumas occurs from a more adult perspective. The more the authentic self is acknowledged, the more it can be developed.

4. *Grieving the losses.* As transcenders continue to explore and describe the past, old grief is triggered. Grieving at this stage is extremely intense and painful and is very important. *Many* hours of intense, painful crying often occur. Often the crying seems like it will rip the person apart and go on forever. (It doesn't do either, it just feels awful.) There are also feelings of denial, anger, fear, and confusion.

Transcenders express it this way: "I feel as if I could cry for years without stopping." "If I start crying, I'll never stop." "If I give in to it, I won't be able to function or ever be the same again." "I just know I'll die." There is no guarantee *when* the crying will stop. There *is* a guarantee that it *will* stop. When it will stop depends on that particular individual, how much effort they will put into their healing, and how many layers that need expression have been created over the years. After the pain is felt fully, the tears stop. Time off from routine activities as well as a medical leave from work may be important at this time for some individuals. This is not to be seen as a weakness but an acknowledgment of a powerful time in the healing and growing process. When transcenders question this I ask them, "Wouldn't you take time off if you had an intense *physical* illness?" They need to learn to take care of themselves.

5. *Internal clearing and ending of tears.* As the intense grief reaches its end, an internal clearing begins to occur. Transcenders begin to see their families as well as their role(s) in the family with less pain and confusion. What happens is this: as the pain is felt and dealt with, it moves out of the body, leaving the person freer to view the family in a different, clearer perspective. (Remember: That was then, this is now!) Literally, their view of their world (internal frame of reference) is now more honest, less inhibited, less confused with conflicting emotions, and more in tune with what really is and was in their family. (Emotional pain distorts how we view our world, as well as influencing our behavior and decisions.) It is during this step that individuals get a clearer view of the damage their family has done. In addition, understanding of or insights about past and present functioning (i.e., thoughts, feelings, behavior) are developed. One transcender described this step this way: "I never thought the tears would end. I really didn't believe my therapist. But they did! I now see why I felt so bad! My family really hurt me."

6. *Understanding the childhood.* Understanding their childhood is another essential part of the healing

process for transcenders. As adults, transcenders must know what happened to them as children in order to heal. They work hard to develop an understanding of what has happened to them as children and the influence it has had on their adult lives. As adults, they go back to childhood traumas to heal the inner part of them that was so hurt and still feels like a hurt child (inner child). They reexperience their childhood with all its grief and reclaim the parts of themselves that were lost in childhood. Transcenders must refeel, reexamine, reclaim, and grieve that which is part of the traumatic past.

Understanding the past has to include the mental, emotional, physical, and spiritual parts for transcenders. Understanding their past helps them to accept what has happened and love their entire self that was hurt by the past. They learn they were helpless children who were abused by people who were out of control, emotionally ill and/or ignorant. They are able to forgive themselves for not being able to stop the abuse or for being "so stupid." Many transcenders believe they should somehow have been able to stop the abuse and failed. As a result, they are angry at themselves and have rejected their inner authentic self. As adults, they maturely explore this anger, and their relationship with themselves heals.

Gaining an understanding of the past also includes working hard to sort out family games. These games include: "We're Perfect but Crazy," "You Are the Crazy One, We're All Fine," "Let's Pretend the Elephant in the Living Room Isn't There," and "We're All Kids, there Are No Adults." Each game needs to be closely examined and explored. With this understanding comes a choice of continuing or stopping the games.

7. *Behavior Changes.* Understanding continues as transcenders work in therapy and become more aware of

the damage caused by their families. They become better able to make healthy decisions about themselves and their world. At times, changes seem to occur easily and naturally; at other times, old patterns are extremely difficult to change, and a concerted effort is needed. Changes occur in all areas of life: relationships, work, play, goals, family of origin, and present family interactions.

Basically, transcenders work to change patterns they had to develop as children in order to survive. These patterns are either no longer needed or they need changing because they interfere with healthy, productive living. Therapists help sort out the patterns that are healthy and needed from the ones of the past that are no longer usable or productive. The final decisions about which patterns to change are always the transcender's, not the therapist's.

8. *Learning to take care of themselves.* One of the important changes that occur is that transcenders learn to take care of themselves appropriately and lovingly. In dysfunctional families, transcenders are not only taken care of inappropriately but, frequently, have had to take care of others in extreme forms in order to survive. Often, they have been taught they don't count and that their only worth is in caring for others.

Transcenders often need to love themselves in special ways. They do this by doing things just for themselves. This is often difficult and, at times, guilt-producing. The guilt comes from the fear of being abused. The message from the family is usually "Don't take care of you. Only take care of me. If you try to take care of you, I'll hurt you." Or, "You don't deserve anything." For example, if I take care of myself, Mom might call me selfish and become angry. If she becomes angry, I could be hit. The guilt that once kept me safe in childhood I no longer need as an adult. In fact, it works against me and keeps me from having close relationships with others as well as myself.

To deal with the guilt, I have transcenders thank themselves for taking such good care of themselves all those years. I tell them to allow the guilt to be and not fight with it. Then they need to tell themselves they now have a better way to keep themselves safe. They have to go on and take care of themselves even if they feel guilty. The guilt then lifts as they move through it.

In the beginning, I recommend *doing little things such as taking a long, nurturing bath by candlelight, going for a walk, being with a friend, listening to special music, or even just being alone. Bigger things may include taking a special vacation, changing jobs, or even moving to a long-dreamed-of home. Taking care of oneself is *anything* that nurtures and expresses love to the authentic self *and* is not harmful to oneself or others. It is a fun discovery journey because most transcenders have not had a chance to learn about themselves. It's a time to find out what they like as well as what they don't like. If something is liked or enjoyed, it may be continued. If something is not liked, it doesn't have to be repeated. The important part of this stage is to make it a *fun,* growth-producing journey—a journey to discover the self.

9. *Time off.* Another significant part of the healing process is to take time off from formal therapy. This time off can be for a week, a month, a year, or several years. This is *not* an avoidance of issues. This time allows the transcender to think about, explore, experience, and adjust to the many new changes that have occurred in therapy. The break also gives relief and solidifies what has been learned. This is not a break from the healing or growing process, just from formal therapy. For transcenders, healing and growing usually continue throughout their lives.

This break in therapy is needed because the healing and growing process is very intense and may take years. Transcenders need to play, laugh, and take a break from the intensity of formal therapy. Also, some transcenders are so determined to heal and grow that they can create self-abuse with therapy that corresponds to and continues childhood patterns of abuse. By self-abuse, I mean pushing oneself so hard for so long that joy and relaxation do not occur. There *has* to be a time to relax and praise oneself for what has been accomplished and for doing things differently from one's family. There has to be time for fun and a more "normal" way of living. Transcenders usually know when they are ready for a break. Life feels a lot better, and they experience joy, changed behaviors, and a sense of "I feel complete for right now."

10. *Return to therapy.* A deeper level of healing and growing occurs when transcenders return to therapy after a time off. Not everyone takes time off, and not everyone returns to therapy. Some return more than one time. Again, it is an individual process. Usually, those who do return experience a deeper, more intense healing. There may be a lot of fear surrounding this exploration, but transcenders go after the healing. Transcenders at this point in the healing and growing process gain a different look at their survivorship. Some even begin to see some positive aspects from their childhood.

   Returning to therapy can coincide with a person's midlife transition (or crisis, as some call it). At this stage, the transcenders' process sends them as far back as the origin of the hurt and damage. Often this is as far back as early childhood. Grieving and reclaiming the losses of childhood are intensified during this period, with results that offer more freedom and more authenticity.

There is a powerful surge at this stage to heal all the hurt at the deepest possible layer. The mind, spirit, and body seem to demand this deep healing to create an integrated, functioning Being. Essentially, it is a deep cleansing of everything that is blocking the authentic self. At times, it's like a volcanic eruption with enormous intensity to clear out everything that is blocking the flow of the original package. Without this, it is difficult for transcenders to get through the midlife transition and begin the second half of life. As with previous steps, all feelings have to be felt and understood.

11. *Completion.* After the previous steps, transcenders usually do not return to formal extended therapy. They have learned to process their feelings, thoughts, and to change unwanted behavior. They have learned to set realistic goals and create positive changes in their world. They have developed healthier relationships with others as well as with themselves. After completion of formal therapy, transcenders continue their personal self-growth journey. They may participate in seminars, workshops, group intensives, classes, and so on for the rest of their lives. They rarely view their development and growth as complete.

12. *Tune-ups.* Sometimes transcenders go back into therapy for what I call a tune-up. A *tune-up* is one or more sessions that focus on the individual's process of growth. It is a reaffirmation of where they are in their lives and/or a reexamination of old issues if needed. Whatever is explored, it is usually not intense or long-term. Each transcender is different in his or her need for tune-ups.

Summary

After these steps, what is left are healed scars and twinges of pain when experiences trigger memories of the old feelings and thoughts. There may even be a revisiting of old memories once in a while, but it is usually not with the past intensity or duration.

There are no fairytale endings. Life is hard and difficult. But life can be good with the ability to connect with the full range of feelings, learning, and growing. The past does not have to haunt every step, influencing decisions and behaviors. There can be a deep, inner peace and a true sense of freedom.

The healing and growing process is centered on the self. Many transcenders feel selfish because they have been well taught to care for others instead of themselves. Healing is definitely not selfish. It is a personal, unique, important process by which transcenders learn to take care of themselves by focusing their energies, time, and money on healing and growing from past trauma. If you are a transcender, take care of yourself, give to yourself, and explore what you are all about. Take in all that you need to heal. It's worth it!

The feelings of selfishness and guilt can be dealt with in therapy. This healing is essential to moving on in your world. When it does feel selfish, remember that unless you take care of yourself first, you will have nothing to give anyone else.

If, during the healing process, you get pressure from well-meaning friends and family to stop the process because it's too painful, because you are not taking care of them, or because the past is over and you should forget it, tell them very politely that it is not over for you. Tell them you feel the pain every day, and it is influencing your life in a negative way. Educate them. Teach them how you need them to be your friend. Remember, as long as it is alive in you and you feel it, it is not in the past. It is in the present moment.

In closing this chapter I leave you with these thoughts: "The only way out of the pain is to go through it, to absorb, probe, understand exactly what it is and what it means. To close the door on pain is to miss the chance for growth. Nothing that happens to us, even the most terrible shock, is unusable. And everything somehow has to be built into the fabric of the personality, just as food has to be built in."[2]

CHAPTER 7

Grieving the Dysfunctional Family

It seems very appropriate that I am beginning this chapter after the death of a dear cousin. It is the day before Easter, and my cousin died on Wednesday night. He died of cancer—an agonizing death with intense struggles. Tom adjusted his life to battle the disease by changing his behavior, living style, eating patterns, and doing anything that had the hope of bringing more energy and life to his dying body.

I am keenly aware of my feelings about my cousin's death. I feel the death. It is an intense, deep pain and longing—a deep missing that nothing and no one can ever change. I grieve the times I will no longer have with him as well as the times that I wish had been different. I will miss the times that could have been and were not. I grieve for what I had and what I didn't have. The missing will be there forever. It may not be at the intensity it is now, but it will be there at a different level.

I feel my whole pattern of living trying to avoid the pain of the missing, loss, and loneliness for my cousin. My old system—my old way of dealing with pain—desperately wants to take over so I can stop feeling the pain. I want to eat more, stay extremely busy, put myself under more stress, and confuse my thinking—anything to stop the pain and be able to go on with my life as if everything is fine. I want my world to be back to a more innocent age. I am also angry at the world, cancer, doctors, and God for not saving my cousin. I find myself screaming at God and the world with tears and anguish.

I really can't stop the pain. That's an illusion. I must go through it, feel it, and learn from it. Even though it is painful and seems futile, there is no other way. That's my new healthier system with authenticity in my feelings. I must own and feel what I am experiencing. Thankfully, my new system wins. But I will never be the same naive person again. I have grown and changed. I have become more patient, more understanding, and wiser. My healing and growing comes from dealing with my cousin's death.

Grieving a dysfunctional family is *exactly* like my grieving for my cousin. It is intense, painful, and lonely, with deep longings and missing for what was lost. Grieving is the part of the healing process that screams with anguish and tears about what *was* in the family as well as what *was not*. There is a missing of times that never were, a longing for times that should have been, and a deep sorrow and rage for the abuse that was. This missing will always remain at some level; it will never completely go away. Its intensity will change, but the missing will still exist. It's like a wound that completely heals but leaves a scar that reminds us of the injury. The intensity of the grief changes when all the pain is completely felt *and* learning is gleaned from it. It may seem futile at the time, but from the process there is not only healing, but incredible growth.

While growing up in a dysfunctional family, one changes many behaviors in order to stop the pain, as well as to gain energy and life, as my cousin did fighting cancer. Individuals work to adjust and keep going. One of the primary purposes of the old patterns is to keep feelings out of awareness and the authentic self protected. Neither is safe while growing up in a dysfunctional family. The grief is held off, denied, avoided, projected onto others, and handled in any way possible in order not to feel and to keep going. This is survival in its basic form. The grieving process that is part of the healing from a dysfunctional family is the feeling of stored, unfelt feelings. Avoiding the grief supports survival *but* creates dysfunction in adulthood because grief demands tears—deep, gut-wrenching, soul-wrenching tears. Stopping the pain blocks this release and it becomes more painful.

During grieving times, we may need to be held and encouraged to cry. We need to be angry, sad, and disillusioned and to express our anguish as well as our anger (appropriately). It is through our tears that we release the pain and trauma and learn to accept what was and is. Without the tears, there is no cleansing, no release, no healing, and no hope for the future. Without the pain, there is no learning or growing. Without the pain, there is no healing.

Transcenders' Grieving Process

My grieving for my cousin contains many areas of loss for me. I have lost a person with whom I shared over forty years of special memories. I have lost a sense of more innocent times. I have lost a dear friend, someone I knew I could call if I needed help. I knew he was in my life and we cared about each other. I have lost part of my family. It feels like nothing will be okay again—not really.

Transcenders have similar losses from growing up in a dysfunctional family. There is a loss of never having had a happy, normal childhood. The loss of innocence from childhood can never be regained, any more than I can regain the loss of my innocence in the death of my cousin. Transcenders also have lost the chance of ever having the loving parents they so desperately wanted and needed. Even if they heal their relationships with their parents in adulthood, the parents of their childhood remain dysfunctional.

Other losses in childhood include those of closeness with others, of trust in others, of having needs appropriately met, of appropriate dependency, of ever fully being a child, of knowing how to play, of knowing who one is, of dignity as a person, of feeling safe and protected, and of being/feeling accepted and loved for oneself. Also lost are opportunities to excel in certain areas. This does not mean you are unable to participate as an adult in a particular area, but you have lost the opportunity of excelling in it as a child. For example, if as a child I wanted to be a top gymnast and had the ability to do so, but my parents blocked all my opportunities, I have not lost the chance to participate in gymnastics at some level, but I have lost the chance to excel due to my age.

Not all transcenders experience all of the above losses. Each transcender has unique losses to grieve. However, *all* traumatic losses must be fully grieved at a deep, intense level and for as *long* as the grief demands. Grieving includes many different kinds of feelings: denial, anger, making deals with God, sadness, and finally acceptance and/or forgiveness of what was and is. These feelings occur in no specific order, may occur at the same time, and may also reoccur. They may also flow from one to another and then back again. For example, with the death of my cousin, I felt intense sadness that shifted to anger, then to denial, then to anger and sadness again. I still haven't accepted it. It takes time to work through all the feelings and then finally arrive at acceptance.

In essence, grieving a dysfunctional family means feeling all feelings fully, gaining an understanding of what has happened from an adult perspective, learning from the experience, and finally experiencing the end product—the blessing of acceptance and/or forgiveness and the ability to do things differently.

Forgiveness: An Essential Part

Forgiveness is essential to the grieving process. Forgiveness is the letting go of my pain, anger, hurt, and the effects of what has happened to me. It is not the denying or forgetting that something happened. It never will be excusing what someone else did. What they did was not all right. They have a debt to pay, but it's not our job to make sure they pay it. It is my closing of the door to the past traumas. It is not the pardoning of the abuse; it is admitting that it is time to move on, to let go of what someone else did. They have to live with what they did. By forgiving, we free ourselves and, in love, let go of what was done to us. We no longer carry the anger of what was done to us, and therefore it no longer negatively impacts our life.

If forgiveness is possible, it aids in the healing and has a spiritual dimension. However, acceptance can be enough for some because it is a letting go of the pain and moving on with one's life. If forgiveness is not possible because we choose not to let go, then acceptance *is* absolutely necessary. There has to be a closure to the past; otherwise, we cannot move on to a healthier future. Forgiveness and acceptance provide this closure. In some cases, like Marie's, where the damage is so intense and so awful, it seems impossible to be able to forgive, let alone accept; however, Marie did forgive her family. She related it this way:

"I was able to forgive them after many years of therapy and healing. I had to forgive to let go of the past. Was what they did all right? No, absolutely not! I had to go on with my life. I had to forgive them for the impact their abuse had on my life in order to free myself. Now, years later, it seems like those things happened to another person, not me."

Forgiving and acceptance is a process that takes time and does not occur overnight. There are even different layers of forgiveness that occur at different stages of the healing process over a number of years. It is both a part of, as well as an aid in, the healing process. Acceptance can be enough, but is not as powerful as forgiveness. What is important is that the transcender lets go of the pain and moves on with his or her life.

The process of grieving a dysfunctional family has no specific timeline. As described in Chapter 6, a process begins and takes its own time. The process comes to completion when it is fully experienced. The person needs to allow it to run its course until the tears, anger, sadness, and agony of the losses end. Unhappiness, frustration, and dysfunction continue if individuals decide not to do their grieving work. The individual will become stuck, alter behaviors, and will not grow. This is called *neurosis* in the mental health field. As one transcender expressed it, "I refuse to let what happened to me in the past control the person I am today. I choose to let it go with love. I am indeed free."

How Grieving Begins

There are a number of ways the grieving process can begin. Like the turning point, a transcender's pain and loneliness in adulthood are often the triggers. Incidents in life can also be triggers. At times, the person resists the process and the therapist must be a guide into the grieving. This can be done by the transcender's describing in detail experiences of his or her childhood. From this comes an awareness of the dysfunction in which the person grew up; this awareness is followed by previously unfelt feelings. A transcender can no longer contain the feelings and maintain the old way of living in the face of the facts. The grieving process is then under way.

Another way grieving starts is by the discovery that old patterns of living and getting along in the world don't work anymore. Transcenders come to a point of saying, "I can't do this any more. I'm not going to make it. I don't have the energy to keep this up." The *this* is having used all their inner drive and energy to maintain the old inauthentic, protective way of living. They know they can't continue, but may not know what is wrong or what to change. This feeling may be so intense and so overwhelming that it feels like they are going to have a physical or emotional collapse. What is really happening is that the transcenders no longer have the energy to use the old patterns of being to stop the feelings that are surfacing. They are tired, and there is no longer enough energy available to maintain the old layers while still moving forward in their lives.

The Decision to Heal

At this point, transcenders often experience a deep, *inner-core tiredness.* It is a tiredness that sleep does not change or touch. It comes from living and working hard to survive for decades. The only relief is to release feelings and change behaviors. No matter how the grieving starts, the losses of childhood must be revisited and grieved.

At this point, a decision to heal or not heal is usually made. Sometimes the decision is easy, but at other times it is painful and difficult. The fear of the pain and destruction is what prevents transcenders from just surrendering to their grief. Remember, there is a core belief based on survival techniques that says to feel may cause insanity or death. The greater the abuse, the greater the fear of feeling will be. The greater the fear of feeling, the more the grief process is held back to protect the transcender.

The decision to heal is made just like the decision to transcend the family. The individual lives with the pain and frustrations and arrives at a powerful decision to heal and continue to grow. Deciding to heal also entails a recommitment to his or her childhood's personal-growth decision. In any grieving process, there is a choice to heal or to block the feelings and continue suffering, stuck in the pain of the past. Transcenders choose to heal!

Steve

The following dialogue is from a therapy session I had with Steve, who was the scapegoat of a family that physically, emotionally, and sexually abused him, as well as neglected him. It shows the process of making the decision to heal.

Donna: "Steve, it's time to do your feeling work from your past. I know the feelings are awful and are triggering intense fear in you. I also know you are feeling suicidal and want desperately not to feel."

Steve: "I can't make it. It's too painful. It's too much. Just too much. I am so sad. I just want to die. *Have* to die. I just have to die. There is no other way. My kids would be better off. Their mother would then have to take care of them. They'd have my insurance. There is no other way. I have decided to die."

Steve did not want to die, he just wanted out of the pain and saw no other way.

Donna: "Sounds like you see no hope for ever getting through this pain. The pain must be horrible. Tell me about it."

Steve: "It's so bad. I can't stand it. I can't live this way. There is absolutely no hope. Not for me or my kids. Suicide is the only way out. I'm crying all the time. All I do is cry. I can't stand it anymore. I just can't do it. I just can't go on. No one cares about me. No one helps me. Not even you. You're just paid to be here. You really don't care. Not really."

At this point Steve wants me to take responsibility for his pain and have me do his feeling work for him. When I hear this, I say and mean the following.

Donna: "Steve, I wish I could take the pain away. I would give anything to have the power and ability to end your suffering. I can see you are suffering terribly, and if I could, I would do your healing work for you. But, it doesn't work that way. I have to do my own healing and feeling work, and you have to do yours. I wish with all my heart I could take the pain away, but I can't."

This type of dialogue continued off and on for a month. Steve worked harder and harder to make me be responsible for him. He did this by going into crisis and, sometimes, running out of sessions. Finally, after much pain, the following dialogue took place over the phone.

Steve: "Donna, I have finally heard you. I know now you can't do my feeling work for me. I even sort of believe you wish you could. [*Trust builds slowly.*] I have decided to do whatever I have to do to get through this. I want to get through the suicide stuff. I wish there was another way. God, do I wish there was another way. But I know there really is not. I just wanted to call you and tell you what I have decided."

Donna: "Steve, I am so excited for you. You can now begin to fully grieve your childhood and heal. Yes, there will be pain and intense struggles, but there will also be joy, love, and learning."

Steve and I continued to work together, and he was able to work through the pain and begin to receive love in his life. He also created new ways of relating to and living in the world. The suicidal thoughts and feelings stopped.

Paul

Other transcenders know where they have to go, and the choice is easy and determined. This was the case with Paul.

"I'll do anything to heal. I want to be better. I want to feel normal and healthy. "Somewhere I lost it. Tell me what I have to do to heal and I'll do it. I never want to go back to the old way again. Never!"

When I am working with clients who are grieving, I feel deeply for them and wish I could feel the pain for them. I can't. It is theirs, not mine. The grief is deep and ages old. It is scary and very hard to accept, let alone feel. In the grieving process, transcenders become more and more aware of what they had and didn't have in their families. They also become intensely aware of their pain and loneliness. The process consists of the adult's grieving the losses, as well as feeling the pain from all the experiences in childhood. The feelings have to be felt and understood for positive changes in life to occur. Following are some descriptions from transcenders about their grieving processes.

Sylvia

"I just knew I was going to die. I felt like I had the worst case of the flu without really having the flu. My stomach was upset. I had diarrhea and a severe headache. These symptoms seemed to take turns torturing me. I was also dizzy and tired. No amount of sleep shifted my fatigue. I walked around in a daze and couldn't think clearly for weeks. My kids complained about my not remembering things they said, and I didn't. I would not even remember them talking to me. I was so inner-focused that I was barely aware of others around me. If they did intrude, I became short-tempered and nasty. I was working hard just to exist with all the pain. I really thought I was going to die."

Tiffany

Tiffany comes from a strict male-dominated family where the abuses were harder to pinpoint; hence, her grieving process began a little differently.

"I always felt sad and abused. It took me a long time to figure out where the feelings came from because my family looked great. I had productive parents and siblings who were liked in the community and successful in many ways. I kept asking myself just what my problem was. What was wrong with me, because it was not them. Or was it? While working in therapy, I finally began to figure it out. It really wasn't me but was the dysfunction of my family. I was never allowed to be me. I had to be the caretaker, traditional girl, and responsible one. I also believe I was a scapegoat for my family. I don't ever remember being just me, except when I was alone.

"What I learned in therapy was that I was still playing the role I had been well trained for in childhood—this time as the adult. However, by this time, there was only a little of the real me left in my life. Before knowing this, I believed I had to be happy because I had everything a person could want. Even as an adult, I had a house in the suburbs, an executive husband, three kids, a dog, and a cat. I looked the image of success and happiness. Because I had everything, I thought I had to be happy. Finally, after a lot of hard work in therapy, I knew what to grieve. I then gave myself permission to feel my deep sorrow.

"Once the grieving started, it was horrible. I longed for the daddy that was always at work and never there for me as a child. I longed to be held and loved. I desperately wanted someone to see me for me. I wanted my siblings to at least talk to me as a real person, not as just my role or object to ridicule. I wanted a mother who would break away from her traditional role and be a complete, whole, functioning, loving person. They all wanted a little girl who performed like a little, perfect, traditional, caretaking robot—especially Mom. She wanted and needed someone to take care of her sadness and loneliness. They didn't want me. I felt each and every loss and pain.

"I even had to mourn my own death, the death of the child I always wanted to be. I imaged myself putting me in my coffin and then sending me to a place to regenerate. I literally gave birth to myself as I died. The false me had to die in order to give birth to the real me.

"My grieving was at such a deep level I thought my insides were going to explode. At times, I'd cry not knowing what I was crying about. Other times, I knew exactly what the loss was. What was neat was that every time I did cry, get angry, and express my feelings, I felt better and more like me—the real me."

Marie

"At the time I began therapy, I honestly wasn't aware of a past to grieve. I knew my father had raped me soon after my parents divorced, and I never saw him again. I was aware that before having children I needed some professional help because I didn't have very positive feelings about families in general and I didn't want to pass my hang-ups to my children. I always felt unloved and unwanted. I also knew there were a lot of gaps in my usually good memory. Nothing, however, could have prepared me for the memories and feelings of the past that were so deeply hidden. The memories began to surface after I was in therapy for a while and it felt safe to deal with them.

"In my fantasy, I had created a loving, caring, 'perfect' family that I had failed. However, as memories began to surface, I couldn't' believe the terrors and tortures. In the early stages of therapy, I hypnotized myself to allow the memories to come into awareness. Frequently, feelings would surface before the memory. Sometimes, I could feel the anger of my therapist toward my parents for the tortures they performed on me. I, on the other hand, would try to defend their actions. After all, it must have been my fault. I was there. If I hadn't been present, then maybe they wouldn't have tied me up, urinated on me, locked me out, etc.

"Another thing I knew prior to therapy was that my father was an alcoholic and we moved constantly. From the first to the sixth grade, I never began and ended the year in the same school. As I began to match memories to feelings, I came to realize that not only was the 'happy childhood' a farce, so were the two people I desperately wanted to be good enough to be loved by—my father and mother.

"Before any grieving could begin, it was necessary to allow myself to remember what really happened. Deeply implanted in me was a tape from my parents and their co-torturers that said: 'If you ever tell anyone the things that go on, no one would believe you, and you will be put up for adoption for causing trouble. And something will happen to anyone that you become friends with because you cause bad things to happen to people.' To me that meant if I ever told anyone, I would have to be punished and die. I often became suicidal during therapy because of this tape, even though I didn't want to die. Sometimes, the pressure was so strong that I had to fight with myself (and sometimes my therapist) to stay alive.

"As I listen to the tapes of those particular sessions (we taped sessions so I could go over and over them to learn about me), I felt ice water run through my veins when I heard myself talk about my own suicide. I explained how and why it had to be done just as if I was talking about the weather. In fact, it was a long time before my voice held any emotion when I would talk about being sexually abused by my parents, being locked out in the cold, or listening to my parents plan how they were going to kill me and make it look like an accident.

"It wasn't until I was ready to put memories and feelings together that my voice on the tape changed from relaying factual information to the terror and sobs of a terrified child. It was at this point that I truly began to grieve what had never been nor ever could be. At the same time, I began to grieve for what I did have—the evil, satanically warped people who acted out their emotions on an innocent child. No wonder I could never be good enough to be loved by them.

"I remember my therapist saying I would have to grieve my past as part of the process of becoming emotionally and physically healthy. I thought she was talking about sad feelings, but I came to know there were no words to adequately describe the horrible, desperate, lonely feelings. I had to relive the past with feelings and memories matching. Each time I did, more garbage came to the surface. I tried very hard to use the old ways of blocking so I wouldn't hurt so badly. Nothing anyone could have told me would have prepared me for the deep, intense pain—both physical and emotional—that was to be a necessary part of my healing, as layer after layer was slowly peeled away to find the real me.

"When I fought the feelings I discovered two things: (1) I had lost most of my old coping mechanisms and was not able to push the feelings back to stop the hurt, as I had before therapy; and (2) the harder I fought not to feel, the more intense the pain. It was only by feeling the hurt that I began not to hurt quite so much. I would go through several days or even weeks of pure hell, which would usually, thank God, be followed by a real growth spurt. I would think, 'Thank goodness it is over,' to only have the hurt and grief triggered at another layer.

"When this would happen, it felt like I was going backward in my therapy, and I would complain to my therapist that I had done this before. I wanted instant cure. After all, the abuse had occurred over a period of fifteen or sixteen years. Why should it take more than a few months to make everything better?

"Just about the time things would start to feel great (that was my own personal indicator of progress), along would come another period of deep sadness and loneliness. Many times I tried to give my feelings away to my therapist, to get her to do my feeling work for me. Fortunately, she cared enough to give them right back to me, reminding me that they were my feelings and my memories, not hers. She was there for me; she could feel with me, but never for me. That was a very hard lesson to learn. Sometimes I got angry at her because before I started working with her I didn't have the lonely feelings. Instead, I had migraine headaches, inflammatory bowel disease, and asthma. Occasionally I'll still have periods of grief and pain, but it will never be as bad as it was during the intense grieving.

"The periods of pain are shorter now and with less intensity. I now know that these periods won't last forever, whereas earlier it felt as if they would never end. I can't say I welcome them, but I'm learning to recognize the painful times as periods of growth. I'm convinced the only way to get rid of the hurt is to feel it with all the intensity that is locked inside. For me, physical and emotional pain are closely linked. As the emotional pain eases, so does the physical. Freedom from the pain of the past is worth the grief. I am becoming a growing, healthy, fully functioning human being."

Chris

Chris, like other individuals with whom I have worked, says he remembers prebirth experiences such as abortion attempts. Some people remember early things that have happened to them at a deep inner level of feeling. It has been my experience that this is not all that unusual, but it is rarely talked about. In the following description, Chris talks about having two therapists. He had a psychotherapist and a massage therapist who helped him do energy and body work. Here is Chris's experience of his grieving process.

"Grieving for me was having the courage to feel and eventually accept the fact that my family did not want or love me. Being blamed for everything that was wrong in my family was horrible to grieve. For years I worked hard and was successful in avoiding those feelings. I was terrified of feeling the rejection, sadness, and anger because I believed if I felt them I wouldn't make it. I also believed I would become crazy or nonfunctioning like my family. I resisted and resisted until I realized that to be the person I wanted to be and have the life I always wanted I had to do my feeling work.

"It was horrible. I was terrified and felt crazy—the exact feelings I had tried so hard to avoid all those years. I cried so hard and so long I thought I'd be in pain forever. Once I had actually done some of the grieving, I felt relief and, amazingly, began to feel joy. I also started to understand my family and my role in the family, and I realized it was not really me they hated. They would have hated anyone born at that particular time and would have assigned them that particular role in the family.

"I learned this when I regressed emotionally and remembered my mother trying to abort me in the womb. It made me realize that she didn't really know me at all. She was just trying to get rid of any next baby.

"There was a time during my grieving process when my therapist had to help me stop self-abusing. Because of the past and all its rejection and abuse, I had learned never to be nice to me. If I got something good, I had to punish myself. My way of punishing myself consisted of keeping my healing and growing process at such an intense level that I was constantly in turmoil. I never allowed joy into my life.

"My pattern went like this: As I grieved, I began to feel better. The better I felt, the more I gained and the more intense I became in my pursuit of growth. I pursued it with such determination that I was constantly in pain. What I actually did was to stay in pain all the time by making a super effort to rid myself of all past pain in a very short time. This punished me by stopping the good feelings. My process became very difficult and self-abusing in the name of growth. I felt a lot of sorrow in this area. Wasn't my parents' abuse and punishment enough? Did I have to do the abuse also? With the help of my therapist I began to see the pattern and the need to relax and play as I healed. With concerted effort, I stopped the abusive pattern and began to live and enjoy my life a little more."

Tom

Tom is a transcender who grew up in poverty and neglect. Here is his description of his healing process.

"When I finally began therapy I was a basket case. I was confused and frustrated, and my life just didn't seem to be going anywhere. The more I tried, the more frustrated I became. I hated myself, my world, and everyone in it. The worst part was I had no idea what was wrong. I had tried everything I knew and nothing was working any more.

"Once in therapy, I was told I was in the process of grieving my past. I was also told I was frustrated because I was fighting and resisting the grieving. My childhood decision to keep going and never, never go back was now interfering with my healing the past. Because I decided to never go back but go forward, I believed feeling the past was going backward. That is why I was frustrated and confused. I needed to feel the past, yet my commitment to myself wouldn't allow it. I really believed that if I felt it, I would become like my family: nonfunctioning, unable to support myself, and dirt poor.

"Allowing myself to feel was very hard. I had so much fear: fear of being like them, fear of not being able to take care of myself, fear of losing my commitment to never go back—fear, fear, fear. I finally understood that in order to heal, I had to grieve. Once I understood it, I was able to work through all of it, and I'm so grateful I did."

Paul

*Paul was severely criticized and ridiculed, and he felt as if
he never belonged in his family. Here are some of his words
about his grieving process.*

"I had so much to grieve. So much. I had to grieve all
of it. It felt like I had to grieve each and everything that
happened to me, every critical word, every ridicule. I
couldn't believe the memories that kept coming up. I had
to feel every feeling about each memory. I remembered
things as a two- and three-year-old. I even had an image
of being neglected as an infant. I really wasn't sure the
memories or grief would end.

"Donna kept telling me that I would not be overwhelmed or die in the grieving process. I didn't believe
her. I knew I couldn't make it. I fought it like crazy. I did-
n't want to feel it because I believed—no, I knew I would
not survive if I did. This was one of the ways I protected the
real me. I firmly believed if I felt the feelings from my
childhood, I would lose control and go insane like my family. It took me a long time to give myself permission to
grieve. I had been raised to not feel and definitely to not
cry. It was tough. I had to make a definite decision to grieve
and feel. My choice was to grieve and continue to grow or
to stop and die at some inner level. The dying was intolerable to me. That would have violated my childhood decision to grow and develop.

"My resistance was, if I felt all the old pain, my world
would end. And it did. My world will never be the same. I
see my childhood as painful and intensely lonely. There is
no more illusion that I had terrific parents. I had parents
who did more than their parents, but who failed to protect
me and nurture me emotionally.

"I was told I needed too much. In reality, I did need. I
desperately needed nurturance and love at a deep level.
The 'too much' part came because I had never had it and

needed all those lost years worth. I didn't need too much. I just had been given too little.

"While doing the grieving work, I just knew the tears would never end. Again, when Donna said they would end when all my sadness had been felt, I didn't believe her. It just seemed that all I did was cry for a long time. After a lot of grieving, the tears finally did end.

"I still remember the pain of the memories. It was horrible. At times, I felt I was going to be wiped out or die. I did neither, but that's how bad it got some days. Through the grieving I lost my innocence at a deep level. I desperately wanted to believe I was cared about as a child on some level, but I wasn't. I know now my parents were just trying to survive while I was growing up. They did not have the patience, time, money, love, or anything else to offer me. This is sad and tragic, but I have come to accept it."

Suicidal Feelings and the Grieving Process

Suicidal feelings, as you may have noticed in some of the transcenders' descriptions, are sometimes a part of the grieving process and usually come from three areas. The first is family "tapes," such as "I want you dead!" and "You're bad and need to die." Tapes like these are deeply ingrained and are acted out on some level even if not in awareness. In the healing process, as the layers of pain are felt and lifted, the transcender becomes more in touch with the old tapes and may become suicidal. For example, Marie was told repeatedly that if she was worth anything she would die. Her parents told her they didn't understand why she was around and they wanted her dead. For a while, every time Marie processed a deep layer, she would become suicidal. Once the process and feelings were understood, her suicidal feelings lessened and eventually disappeared. It's important to remember that transcenders don't want to die but are acting on old, well-rehearsed tapes.

The second trigger of suicidal feelings is from the experiences themselves. When children are being abused, there is a real fear they are going to be killed by the abuser. The child pushes away and buries these feelings of intense fear in order to continue fighting to survive. In adulthood the fear translates to, "If I feel these feelings I will die." Or the individual may view death as a relief from the brutalities of life. In the healing process, the fear is felt and owned.

The third area that arouses suicidal feelings is the grieving process itself. Grief can be intense, deep, agonizing, painful, and lonely. With this much pain, it is not unusual that dying is seen as a way out. This is the reason that suicidal feelings often occur in the beginning of the grieving process, when grieving is at its greatest intensity and the person has not yet learned that once feelings are felt fully, he or she will feel better.

Fear often acts like an electrical fence, putting a protective barrier around the real self. The closer one gets to the feeling, the more danger is sensed and the more fear is triggered. All the fence knows is to protect the person from the feelings because the feelings mean danger and possibly death. The fear is so great the person believes he or she will die if the feeling is touched. This fear, which protects transcenders from emotional collapse in childhood, is triggered in the healing process by the lifting of layers. The closer one comes to the fence (and real self), the more intense the fear and suicidal feelings. Fortunately, this stage usually does not last long, and it dissipates because it is no longer needed.

During this time, transcenders need a strong, available support system that works to protect them from hurting themselves and to ensure their safety. Also, they need to know from their therapist that they are in a difficult stage, but it will pass and they will survive.

They need to understand the fear and the suicidal feelings. What I tell transcenders I am working with is this: "The fear kept you safe while growing up. It protected you from emotional collapse and enabled you to survive. It also, and very importantly, kept your real self hidden and protected from the onslaught. You will survive these feelings even though it doesn't feel like it. The suicidal feelings will end. I want you safe and alive. You have come too far to give up now. It is vital that you keep the promises you made to yourself as a child. You can always choose to die; you can only choose to live right now. I want you to live, and I know you do, too."

To transcend does not mean one is invincible, invulnerable, or resilient to abuse. It means finding the ability, courage, and strength to survive and overcome a traumatic childhood and build resiliency.

Parts of the Grieving Process

Even though each transcender's grieving process is unique in content, duration, intensity, and order, there are similar parts. As you read, be aware that each stage may occur many times and in any order.

1. *Flashbacks.* The experience of grieving, as stated before, is a revisiting of the past as an adult. Memories from childhood are revisited in such a way they seem to be relived in the present moment. Old tapes such as "You'll never amount to anything," "You're no good," "Why don't you just die," or "We never did want you" are played back with incredible intensity and vividness. Transcenders hear or see incidents as if a video is playing back the scene and they are part of it. These relived experiences trigger intense, deep, old pain. This pain *must* be experienced fully in the present moment for healing to occur. Because it is so difficult, I often wish I had a magic wand to take the pain away. I don't. Each one of us must do our own

revisiting work. What is good is that the more the healing working done, the less flashbacks.

2. *Denial.* Denial is refusing to accept what is and pretending it isn't and never was! Memories, thoughts, and feelings that contradict the reality of what really happened are often kept out of the memory entirely. In denial, transcenders want to avoid and not feel what has happened to them. They work to protect themselves. They may also want to continue the illusion that they had perfect and loving parents. The problem with denial is that it blocks healing. Transcenders must come out of denial in order to heal. This can be done gently and lovingly, but it is often difficult and may require time in therapy before memories surface. The reason it is difficult is that the denied truth often contains painful information and feelings. Additionally, transcenders sometimes fight the surfacing memories because there is intense fear built up around the memory to keep it away from the transcender, as described earlier.

Some transcenders are very successful in denying and blocking memories and feelings. This denial may be so successful that memories are blocked for years and surface for the first time during the healing process. The memory block acts as a protection and a survival mechanism that enables the transcender to keep going.

When working with the resistance of coming out of denial, I approach transcenders this way: "Tom, I know the memories are awful. I know you don't want to remember them, let alone own them, but they are yours. When you have a memory and you are trying to deny it, you need to know that is how you survived when you were younger. Thank yourself for taking such good care of you all those years. Then tell yourself that you can now take care of yourself in a different way. Know you can transform that energy used for denial into healing and growing energy." With this kind of support, encouragement, and gentleness, memories and feelings that have been in denial for years or even decades can surface and be healed.

3. *Feel the sadness.* The essence of grief is sadness. *All* the sadness of past traumatic experiences must be felt at a deep, intense level. The sadness is not only for what was, but also for what was not. Transcenders cry from abuse, neglect, deprivation, lost dreams, and lost relationships. The sadness is often described as "tears that seem to have no end—that go on forever." The sadness is so intense it feels as if "your insides will burst." Often the deep sorrow has many layers through which transcenders must work. Relief comes when all the sadness is felt and experienced and all the surfaced layers released. Thank goodness, many similar layers often surface and are felt together and not individually.

4. *Shame and defectiveness.* Shame arises from deep feelings of guilt, remorse, disgrace, and failure. It says, "I am the shame." During the grieving process, transcenders often uncover a belief or fear of being terrible and defective like their families. The belief is often based on old family tapes, such as "You are dumb and stupid." "You are not good for anything." "You are worthless." "What in the world is the matter with you?" "Don't you know better?" "You're head is screwed on backwards." The shame of the family's abuse and neglect is often taken on by transcenders as their shame. The shame is not theirs. The shame can run deep and is often attached to deep feelings of sorrow. Feeling defective and shameful creates deep sorrow and a deep hidden secret that the transcenders, in addition to not feeling okay, are so awful they should hide their true selves from everyone, including themselves.

Feeling defective and shameful is another loss that must be grieved. Essentially, it creates a loss of confidence, security, and trust in knowing that they are okay just the way they are. In therapy, it is the therapist's job to gently yet firmly help transcenders realize it is not their shame. It is the family's dysfunction that is wrong.

5. *Loneliness.* Loneliness seems to be one of the most difficult feelings to deal with in the grieving area. Transcenders must reexperience the loneliness of childhood with all its agonizing tears, fears, sadness, and emptiness, as well as the loneliness of the present. Transcenders lock away this loneliness in order to survive. Feeling it means being devastated and realizing that no one, no one, was really there for them.

For the child, feeling loneliness may mean facing a form of death. We can understand this by looking at the situation of infants. No one's being there means no caretaking. No caretaking means no food. No food means eventual death. This is known at a deep level but is too terrifying to remember until transcenders are in a safe, nurturing space in adulthood.

Steve

Steve describes feeling the double charge of loneliness from the past as well as the present.

"In my loneliness, I feel as if I'm always on the outside looking in—as if I never belong. I feel like I somehow don't fit in. I transcended my old world with its awfulness and pain. I like my new world I created, but parts of it don't fit for me either. It's a lonely feeling. It's like I don't really have any friends. And yet I do.

"The loneliness is persistent and pulls me into itself. I'm alone, really alone. I feel its awful fear. It feels as if I'll die if I feel it. I try to run from it and get as far away as possible but it's always there. When I feel it, it's awful, yet I gain strength."

6. *Going Back.* It is essential that transcenders *heal as far back as the hurt and trauma.* Going back to only known traumas is not enough. Transcenders need to explore and heal traumas that, in the beginning, may be only felt senses. A felt sense is an awareness of a feeling with no specific identity or memory. Often, something is sensed in the body. These senses are then explored and connected to previously blocked feelings and memories. My research indicates that at times these transcenders' related memories can be from as far back as infancy. (I am not talking about creating false memories, but remembering the authentic memory of the transcender.)

Even though we may not have any conscious awareness of some memories or feelings, our bodies store and remember them at the physical cell level.[1] These stored layers cause intense feelings and dysfunction until they are healed. We literally carry them around. Body-work therapists are often helpful in bringing memories into awareness.

7. *Fear.* Fear is another intense, difficult feeling and, like loneliness, is hard to feel and is avoided in many ways. In the healing process the old fears of the trauma have to be revisited. The fear sounds like this: "I'm not going to make it." "She's going to kill me." "I'm going to be crazy." "I pray my daddy doesn't come home tonight and beat me." "I don't know what to do any more." "I can't protect myself from her—she always gets me." "I'm afraid of the real me because I'm not okay."

Actually, fear, like all our feelings, is healthy because it tells us something is wrong. Fear signals danger. It works to get us out of danger and tells us to protect ourselves. It says: "Run. Get away. I'm terrified." Fear is a part of every abuse, injury, and hurt that we actually experience or perceive that we experience. Think for a moment of the last time you hurt yourself doing a chore around the house and get in touch with your feelings about that injury. You are probably aware of some "Watch out. Be careful." Now, think about a situation where someone else was hurting you on purpose. The fear is intense and terrifying.

In survival, fear is like the protective electric fence that literally surrounds the real self as well as the memories to keep us safe. Every time danger comes near or is perceived as being near, the fence zaps it to keep the danger away or to signal the individual to get away from the danger. This fear, which protects the authentic self as the transcender grows up, interferes with the healing process in adulthood. This occurs because, as transcenders lift and get rid of layers, they are moving toward uncovering and allowing their authentic selves to be free, but the fence is still fully operational. The fear cannot tell the difference between the healing process and real danger. Its only function is to protect the authentic self and to keep it safe and away from others. The more layers that are removed, the closer one gets to the authentic self; the closer one is to the authentic self, the more fear there is, and the more intense it becomes.

Transcenders need to know that their original package is perfect and wonderful and what they will find is just that: perfect and wonderful. They need to know this because the shame and dysfunction of the family that was dumped on them said otherwise. They may believe the reason there is so much fear is because they are a terrible, awful, unlikable person, which isn't true.

At this stage, therapists need to help transcenders feel, understand, and release the fear. It is important to relax into the fear and feel it. It then will dissipate. Also, transcenders need to be knowledgeable about what is happening to them. This information alone often is enough to ease the fear and help allow the authentic self to surface. Sometimes the transcender is afraid his or her authentic self is not okay and is defective. I have seen people run away as they get closer to the real self, but I have never seen *anyone* not like their authentic self once it was uncovered and developed. Transcenders may have to work through many past and present experiences. They may also have to change or transform parts they want to be different, but they always come to a realization that they like and love themselves. Again, our original package is incredible and full of talent, life, and love.

Tiffany

The following is Tiffany's description of her fear as she was dealing with her electric fence.

"Sadness—deep intense, unknowing. What's it all about? Fear God, fear life, fear and more fear. What's the real fear? Don't know. Just know that it's all fear. Fear! Fear! Fear! Fear beyond fear beyond fear. Fear of the next step. Fear of breathing. Fear of smiling. Fear of not smiling. Fear of not knowing and yet fear of knowing. Fear of God—what will He want next? I fear I have given all and there is nothing left for Him, others, or myself. It's so scary. Nothing left. Help. I'm losing it. I'm sinking. I'm in fear if I move. I'm in fear if I don't. Fear is everywhere, all around me, in me, yet I can't find it."

8. *Anger.* Part of the process of grieving is feeling the anger from past traumas. As the sadness is felt and experienced, anger (if not already there) begins to

surface. As children, transcenders often have learned through experience that anger is not an okay feeling. There may have been acting-out, violent anger demonstrated in the family, and so anger becomes a frightening emotion. It is either acted out inappropriately (violently), or if expressed by the transcender, it causes more abuse. Therefore, it is changed, avoided, buried, denied, or built up to a rage point. (Rage is built-up anger.) In the healing process, anger involves parents, siblings, relatives, significant others, and God, as well as the self. Basically, the anger is aimed at anyone who caused the abuse or neglect or whoever did not help to prevent it.

The anger sounds like this: "Why me?" "What did I do?" "I hate what happened." "I hate my parents for what they did to me!" "Why didn't they stop it?" "Where was God?" "I want to kill them—no, I want to torture them like they did me." "I want them to know what it was like." "I want them to suffer." "Where were my teachers? Couldn't they tell?" "Why didn't they stop it?" "Why did my parents do it?"

Anger is a healthy and important emotion. It tells us something is wrong in our world and that we need to change it. Anger helps to separate transcenders from the dysfunction in their families. It also helps them clean up confused, clouded areas and gain a clearer adult perspective on what happened to them in childhood. Anger also gives them energy to keep healing. This is what I refer to as the *anger stage.* It's as if a lot of the pent-up anger is released at one time. They get what happened to them. It looks like the transcender has a 360–degree anger machine gun and is letting it out everywhere. I also give cautions to transcenders to release their anger *appropriately.*

Again, therapists need to reassure transcenders that anger is just a feeling and, like every other feeling, needs to be understood and expressed appropriately.

Anger appropriately expressed by transcenders does not hurt the person expressing it, does not hurt anything alive (people, animals, plants, etc.), and doesn't damage property. Some good places to put anger and its energy to use are breaking dishes (unwanted, old, chipped ones bought at rummage sales), screaming in cars with the windows up (not at someone with the intent to destroy that person), pounding with a racket or piece of hose on pillows, mattresses, etc., slamming doors (please don't slam refrigerator doors; the mess is not worth it!), tearing up old papers or old telephone books, or writing *unmailed* letters to people with any language needed to express the feelings fully and then burning them.

Some transcenders decide to confront a family member about past abuse. Confronting another person about past assaults *has* to be done only *after* the force and energy of the anger have been expressed in another way and an understanding of the past has been developed. Confrontations have to be done with an attitude of healing, not destruction. That way, the confrontation is not an "I'm going to destroy you for what you did to me" session but a productive part of the healing process. Confrontation, however, is not always possible, advisable, or healing.

There are many ways to release anger appropriately. Remember, don't hurt yourself or something alive—like another person or an animal—and don't damage property you don't want to damage.

Betty

Following is a good example of an unmailed letter from Betty to her parents describing the hurt, betrayal, and anger caused by their abuse of her as a child.

"Dear Mom and Dad,

"Dad, I was just a baby, just a baby when you first beat me up. Three months old! How does a person—a six-foot

person—beat up a three-month-old baby who can't do anything?! How do you allow yourself to do such a thing? Mom,
when you stopped him, finally, you took over! You starved
me, hit me, yelled at me, and cursed me. What did I ever
do to you? Why didn't you like me? What was wrong with
me? You cursed me! 'You God-damn kid! You good for nothing! No one likes you. No one wants you. God damn you!'

"You wanted my brothers to like me, so I had to become
their slave. Was there something wrong with me? You made
me pack for them when we went on vacation so they could
yell at me when I didn't pack the right things for them.
Everything that happened was my fault. I was ridiculed,
yelled at, abused, and punished for other people's stuff—
your stuff, Mom and Dad. Your stuff! I was just a little kid
who needed love and had so much love to give.

"I'll never give you love again. I have had it. Had it! I
hate you for everything you did to me and didn't do for
me. How could you starve a little kid and make her watch
her brothers get to eat anything and everything they
wanted? How? I was hungry, starving, and they had food—
lots of it. I still struggle with my weight. The more I have
healed the more I have learned why I have an eating
problem. I never knew when I would have enough food. I
either went without or, if the relatives came over, I got
lots, but then was starved again and punished for eating
too much. I was hungry.

"What did I ever do to you? What did I do to deserve
this? I am not responsible for your loneliness or anger. I
am not responsible for your choices. You made your life
and, as you said to me many times, 'You made your bed,
now lie in it.'

"I have now left the family. I will see you only occasionally when I decide to. Dad, never will I put myself there to
be abused again. Never! Dad, you were rarely there for me.
You gave your time to my brothers and to work. You didn't
even give it to your wife. Then you drank and drank and
drank. For twenty years you drank and hurt us by your

neglect and power. The power that Mom gave you was horrible. Whatever you said went whether it was okay or not. You punished, paddled, and pouted.

"And Mom, how could you have cursed the girl you had supposedly wanted?! I still see your hand coming at me and your huge mouth yelling so loud my ears rang. You tore dresses off me when I wanted to stay pretty and not take them off. You cursed me. You were evil. I was relieved with deep anguishing tears the day you died. It was my freedom day from you. Everyone that knew you thought you were a wonderful person. Wonderful! I wish some-one—anyone—knew you like I did. I felt crazy. I would think maybe it was me all those years. It had to be because everyone else was fine. I thought I was the one that was-n't. Now, after years and years of therapy, the truth has come out, and my puzzle has come together. Mom, you were evil. And Dad, you were abusive. And both of you made me the scapegoat."

9. *Joy.* Once an individual has worked through even *some* of the grieving, feelings of freedom and joy begin to be felt. This joy may come after one layer or several layers, but it always comes. It's as if transcen-ders get a break from the dark thunderous clouds and the sun peeks through for just a little while. From this break, transcenders gain encouragement and hope that a better way of living is coming. They also gain additional energy and courage to deal with the next layer. Surprisingly, transcenders may also come to understand that their parents gave them some good stuff as well, that it wasn't always bad.

Often transcenders experience this time as a chance to "catch their breath" and reorganize. They begin to understand at a deeper level the effects of their childhood and realize they have choices—choices more in line with their original package. Gratefully and with relief, they begin to know they are going to make it through the healing process. That was then, this is now!

10. *Repetition.* The above parts need to be repeated as often as the layers surface. Gratefully, layers often surface together so it doesn't take as long to heal as it did to get through the abuse. This is an individual process that depends upon the amount of abuse and neglect experienced, as well as on the personality of the individual. Usually, the more severe and longer the abuse, the more layers, and the more layers, the more repetitions are needed. Repetitions often blend and overlap. One layer being worked on and healed will touch and trigger one or more repetitions. Thank goodness, many traumas are released with each layer.

Repetitions may occur anytime in a person's life. Any incident or experience may trigger a layer— for example, a fight with a significant other, a death in the family, legal problems, a television show, or a trip home. Writing this book, for example, has triggered deeper layers of healing and growing for me. I have learned to use these times for growth. Yes, there are times when I pray, "That's enough, I have had it! I don't want any more." *But I am always grateful* when I have explored and learned from what has been triggered. I find richness and knowledge about myself and the world. I feel freer, clearer, and happier. In addition, I gain wisdom.

Layers that are triggered after the in-depth heal-ing process in therapy are equally important but, thankfully, are usually not as intense, nor do they last as long. Most transcenders learn to see these events as opportunities to clear out more of the past hurt and gain deeper healing and growing.

Donavon

Here is Donavon's description of one of these events.

"When my father died I had so many mixed feelings. Mostly, I was relieved. I also was very angry, but for a different reason than the childhood abuses. I was angry that he died because I could never resolve my problems with him and never have the relationship I wanted with him. He was never available to me, and now he died! It was the ultimate rejection by him—the ultimate rejection of me and our relationship. How could he do that?! How could he leave permanently? It was the final, ultimate Zap!

"The tears and sadness I had were mostly for the loss of the hope of having a relationship. I grieved for the finality of the loss of what could have been and what I had hoped for and prayed would be.

"What surprised me were all the tears. I didn't think I could cry much more about my father. I also thought I had myself well protected from further hurt from him. What a surprise! I cried as if I really cared, and I learned that I did! That was another loss for me—knowing I still cared and could not stop all the pain. I wish I had known this. I might have gone to him and shared my feelings. I guess I had just shut that part off. The whole thing took me by surprise because I thought I was done with the entire relationship."

11. *Acceptance and forgiveness.* At the end of the grieving journey are acceptance and/or forgiveness for the abuser as well as for oneself. As described previously, either one helps; however, I have come to believe that forgiveness has a spiritual dimension to it and is more freeing. At this stage, transcenders feel peace, calmness, and love. There is no longer the intense

anger or deep hurt. There is no longer deep inner body tension. There is clarity about what has happened and a deep understanding of its effects both on the child and on the adult.

This stage is the result of all the hard work of the grieving process. It is the ultimate goal. Transcenders have come to accept who they are and know they are okay and valuable. Some transcenders have a difficult time accepting and/or forgiving themselves for the many things they haven't liked about themselves or what they did in the past. Transcenders have to make a concentrated effort to accept and forgive themselves. The list of their so-called unacceptable mistakes or regrets can be endless. Here are a few I have heard:

- Hurting themselves
- Hating themselves
- Hating important special significant others
- Being jealous of siblings
- Hating in general
- Not being Superman or Superwoman and stopping the abuse
- Being human with all its limitations
- Caring too much
- Not caring enough
- Lack of assertiveness
- Overassertiveness
- Being angry
- Making themselves wrong
- Making others wrong
- Hating their lives
- Being mad at God
- Being afraid
- Not being afraid
- Not being mature enough
- Missing their childhood

- Needing too much
- Needing too little
- Disappointing themselves
- Not being perfect
- Not taking better care of themselves
- Being manipulated
- Many unspoken transgressions aimed at themselves
- Being too sensitive
- Not being sensitive enough
- Not knowing enough
- Leaving the family

And the list continues.

Chris

Chris describes acceptance/forgiveness like this.

I feel acceptance coming in like a peaceful fawn. It is dawning like a lovely sunrise after a storm that is ever sure and true. It feels like the war is over. There may still be battles, but now there is a peace and a knowing that all is well."

12. *Regrets.* With the acceptance come regrets, or a sense of sadness that will always be, but to a lesser degree. These regrets are about childhood. Transcenders wish their growing up could have been different. They regret lost relationships, lost opportunities, the struggle to learn a different way to live, the work it takes to overcome the past, not having more self-discipline, and the lack of warmth and caring while growing up. While they accept the experiences, most express sadness that life had to be that way. The following passages give you a flavor of this sadness.

Bill

"I was unipolar. You are functionally independent but really dependent. I didn't need anybody else, and I damn well didn't. I needed nobody or nothing. I could make enough money. I would find enough jobs. I could do what I wanted to do. I could pay my own way and with some anger. I'm not feeling anger now, I'm just saying that with some assertiveness and a sense of wistfulness; there are sadness and opportunities lost that I can't replace or make up for. It's like what can I do now to make my life more full, more complete, with more people, with deeper levels of connectedness? I feel and reflect with some sadness that I don't have any friends from grade school."

Sylvia

"My mother didn't want to rock the boat, make waves—just roll with the punches. And you could walk all over her, and that was fine with her. I wish I'd had a strict upbringing rather than the lenient one like I had."

Tom

"In the last few years, my parents and I have given to each other and started a new relationship or friendship. It's still painful to think of those years that could have been so much nicer, so much warmer."

Paul

I close this chapter with a statement that Paul made after his intense grieving. It summarizes the process of grieving.

"I have grieved the losses, the missed opportunities. I wished for times that cannot be. I have desperately sought and longed for my mother's arms to hold, nurture, and love me. I have longed for security, caring, and the joy of a warm, loving relationship. I have grieved for it all. It is with tremendous sadness that I looked at the loss and the emptiness of my childhood. There is still a missing, but now I can let go, let God be in charge, and move forward in my life. I can also let my family go for their better good. I no longer have to hang on and struggle. I am free."

CHAPTER 8

Reclaiming the Self

The reclaiming process is like being on your very own personal yellow brick road that leads you to Oz. In Oz you find your authentic self. Along this road, there are many different parts of you that have been previously rejected, abandoned, or never discovered during childhood. In the reclaiming process, you journey along the road and pick up those precious lost pieces of your original package. Some of these pieces are reclaimed, and some are discovered for the first time. Some of them you have known about, but because of the great need to survive, you could not stop and develop them. In a more normal family, parents work to help their children discover, accept, and develop the original package. In a dysfunctional family, parents rarely help children develop and may even damage this process.

Reclaiming of the authentic self is the second part of the healing and growing process. *Reclaiming* is the process of discovering, rediscovering, owning, reowning, birthing, rebirthing, and renewing, as well as being responsible for, our original package. It's a time when the promise of "Someday I'll be me!" is kept. It is an exciting, energizing growth time.

Growth occurs in many areas during this time: our potentialities, abilities, skills, thoughts, behaviors, emotions, self-love, and self-liking. It is a time of dynamic learning and insights into our past and present life. Healing and growing demand reclaiming because transcenders, in

185

order to survive when they were younger, had to hold back, deny, give up, or never discover and develop certain parts of themselves. At this point, it is time to take it all back.

The reclaiming process is a journey of self-discovery that is deeply intertwined with and occurs at the *same time* as the grieving process. The reason for this intertwining is that the authentic self is uncovered, discovered, and freed as grieving lifts the trauma layers. The grieving process forces an examination of self. This examination leads the way to reclaiming because it forces transcenders to find a way through and out of the grieving. It forces them to find *their* way. The more grief, the more authenticity must be present to handle the situation. For a while, the more they discover about themselves, the more grief because part of the grieving process is the loss of the authentic self in childhood. A memory in the reclaiming area will trigger feeling work in grieving and vice versa. For example, if I am dealing with knowing I have an exceptional ability to ski and I'm fifty years old, I have to grieve that I have lost my chance to perhaps be on the Olympic team and, at the same time, I can claim the skiing ability I still have and enjoy myself in the sport.

As this journey continues, transcenders find more of themselves and, maybe for the first time, their real selves. The end of the journey is similar to arriving in Oz, where they get to go "home" and really feel and love what home is all about. On this journey, home is the authentic self. Along the way are "lions, and tigers, and bears"—fears and concerns about what will be found. However, what is also along the journey is the original package full of potentialities, talents, and abilities. Some of the parts discovered fit and feel wonderful. Other parts fit, but feel awful. Transcenders sort through these precious findings, reclaiming, and transforming them.

As in grieving, transcenders have to go back and revisit memories and be responsible for feelings, thoughts, and behaviors. It's as if part of themselves is locked back in these experiences. As the memory and all its feelings are revisited, transcenders gain thoughts and insight into their emotional patterns as well as their behaviors. They gain a deeper knowing and understanding of themselves. Transcenders glean each experience for every bit of learning about themselves and their world. They also gain wisdom.

Again, as in grieving, the reclaiming process occurs while doing the feeling work. It is only then that the layers lift and the person knows what to reclaim. What is reclaimed is personal power, strength, clear thinking, an authentic way of being, and self-love. Also gained is the learning from past experiences that had been previously lost because of the inability to process situations during childhood.

This reclaiming process sometimes takes transcenders back to their early years. Transcenders *have* to go as far back as the trauma and hurt where the abuse, rejection, and abandonment first began. They have to go back and reestablish a loving relationship with themselves at all ages. They also go back to forgive themselves for being little and vulnerable. Sometimes it is at a young age that a transcender gets a powerful glimpse of his or her original package. These glimpses are then encouraged and developed. Early decisions are also discovered and explored along with thoughts and feelings about people in the transcenders' world. In essence, they go back to the core—the beginning—and reclaim all that is authentic and then work to emotionally remove everything that is not.

This sorting-out process includes questions such as "Who am I, as opposed to who my parents were?" "Which part is me?" "Which parts are them?" "What parts of me do I want to change?" "Which parts do I want to keep just as they are?" "Which parts of me are purely survival skills that I no longer need?" "What are my feelings?" "What are my parents' feelings?" "What are my values and morals now?"

This sorting is vital to transcenders. This is a period of time when transcenders focus totally on themselves to separate themselves from the family at a very deep level. This time is vital to healing and growing because it separates and gets rid of the nonbeing, or non-me, and works to discover and develop the real or authentic me. It is the authentic self that can be happy, productive, growing, and deal with life's difficult situations.

Reclaiming of the past is working to deal with the transcender's inner self, or inner child, as some call it. A poem by a transcender illustrates this process:

"This Child"
This child yearns to be
to struggle is her destiny.
To run
to play
to let unfold
a life
a story
yet untold
of dreams
of songs
of rhythm dancing
of fun
of love
of self-enhancing.
Ways of being
yet to be
and yet to grow
and yet to show
the magic of a destiny
of childlike
love and energy

bursting forth creatively.
This child will always
yearn to be.
This child will always struggle
to be free
from all that chains and blocks and stops
the freedom of the child in me
the spirit of the child who's free
the spirit of my destiny
to be
free
to be
me.

As transcenders heal and grow, they learn what characteristics, lifestyles, and people they really like and don't like. Most important, they learn who they really are and what they are *realistically* capable of doing and not doing. The reclaiming process includes developing their abilities, strengths, and potentialities in the world. Sometimes this is all new learning because, when children are prohibited from exploring, unrealistic expectations and views of self and world develop. For example, if I have survived a severely abusive home, I may feel so beaten down that I believe I can't do anything. Or I may believe I am Superman or Superwoman and can do anything and everything. For example, "I was big enough to stop the abuse at the age of six." Either way, it is unrealistic. Potentialities are unlimited, but there are limits as to how they will develop or be used.

An important area in the reclaiming process is love, agape love. Love is the healing power for transcenders. They use love from others and for others as energy to keep going. Love of self (or acceptance of self, which is not the same self-pride), is part of healing and growing. Love of self may be there in some form that can be relied on and used for development. Or self-love may have to be uncovered, developed, or healed from past abuses. During the reclaiming process, love and acceptance of self is healed, deepened, enriched, and brings joy.

Reclaiming is not an easy process. It may be confusing, frustrating and full of pain from the past. Old memories are remembered and have to be revisited. The process is also fun, joyful, and exciting. As the reclaiming process continues, transcenders feel less crazy because they are more themselves and have sorted out more of their families' dysfunction. In addition, they have more of themselves available. Transcenders end up realistically grounded by liking and accepting themselves. I have never seen a person who ended up not liking and loving him- or herself after working hard in the grieving and reclaiming process. Please remember, the two processes do take time.

Definition of Terms

Before continuing, the following definitions of *self* (authentic), *false self,* and *ring of fear* are given to help you understand at a deeper level the process of reclaiming.

Self: The self is our core, our being. It is our authentic self, our realness, the original package. This core is influenced by family, friends, genetics, church, society, and all that is in our world. I believe our self, or core, is present at conception, and how it develops often depends on the environment around us. In the reclaiming process, it is the self that has to be healed and developed. For example, if I am a happy, outgoing child and my world is abusive, I may withdraw and hide the real me. In the healing process, I will need to feel and separate the outgoing me from the decisions I made to protect myself from the pain of being out-

going. I can then reestablish my outgoing authenticity.
(For further discussion about the self, see Chapter 5.)

False self: Growing up in a dysfunctional family creates
a phenomenon I call the false self. At birth, the authentic,
or real, self is present, and in time, depending on the environment, either the authentic self is developed and supported or a false self begins to be created. A false self is
developed when an individual senses or knows the authentic self is not acceptable, loved, and/or is endangered.
This is learned through experiences with the family and
the world. The false self is a creation of the real self that
works to protect, enhance, and make the person more acceptable and lovable to the world, especially the family. It
is created to help ensure survival. The false self has parts
of the real self in it but is not totally the real self. For example, if I am intelligent in my false self, that is part of my
real self. I cannot pretend to create intelligence that is not
part of me. However, parts of me may be hidden, and I may
develop behaviors that help me in my world, such as being
the "good girl" to get praise.

The false self is what is presented to the world, sometimes called the "face" or "mask" we show to the world.
The real self is usually hidden away and protected deep inside the person. The false self is also an off-centered self.
It is usually pictured outside of one's body, whereas the
real self is centered within the body. The tragedy of developing a false self is that sometimes individuals come to believe their false self is their real self. This belief creates
confusion, anxiety, sadness, and a powerful knowing that
something is wrong but not knowing what.

When a person is operating in the false self, I often hear
things like: "I'm just conning everyone." "I really didn't
make those good grades in school." "I just fooled everyone." "I really don't know what I am capable of or what I
can do." "I'm just sort of here." "Just tell me what to feel and

I'll feel it." "I'll do anything for people to like me." "I have no idea of what I feel." "I'm angry, but don't know why."

Steve

Uncovering the real self means going through the feelings that first developed the false self. This is seen in a journal excerpt from Steve.

"There is a secret inner spot where I keep the condemned me. I put it there and keep it contained and hidden. It's the me that's afraid, the me that's not good enough, the me that's judged wrong. The other me tries to keep going and be what others would have me be to get the love I want and to survive. I changed me into something false and not me. I try to be what I could never be—someone else.

"The condemned me is the real me. It is buried deep, deep, deep—so deep in my depths it's almost not real. But there, in the inner being, is me, the real me, the me I love, the me I am. I hide the real me. I don't want to be ridiculed or judged and found wanting. I keep me hidden because I'm precious and it's not safe for me out there. So I stay hidden and show myself only when I feel absolutely safe, and that's only after a long time. Otherwise, it's only when I am alone that it's safe. It's when I'm alone that I can breathe, move more freely, and feel my feelings more authentically."

Ring of fear/Electric fence: Since the false self is developed because the authentic self is viewed as being in danger and not accepted, survival depends on protecting and staying away from the real self. We do this by putting a powerful *ring of fear* or an *electric fences* around the authentic self. This fear works in two ways: (1) it protects the authentic self from the outside world, and (2) it stops vulnerability—the exposure of authentic thoughts, feelings, and abilities. The fear acts like a protective electrical fence. Every time someone—even the transcender—gets close, it produces a zap. Transcenders either fend off, attack, or withdraw when this happens in order to protect the authentic self.

Here's an example of a transcender's words of fear when someone is getting close to the electrical fence: "Beware. Not okay. Not acceptable. Cover. Cover. Cover. Cover it up. Keep it hidden. Label it dangerous. Keep away. Don't let light into it. Hide it. It's hideous. Don't let it out. Beware. Stay away. If you get close you'll die!"

As stated previously, the problem with the electric fence is that what was needed to survive childhood now continues to work against the transcender long after it is needed as an adult. After transcenders move out of the family and into a safer world, the electric fence around the authentic self still operates. It's still telling them it's not okay to be their real self. Depending on the transcender's childhood, this fear may be *very* powerful. Sometimes, transcenders even believe they will die if they come in close contact with it.

Transcenders need to know that their fence is a protection they have placed there and they can turn it off. This is usually done through awareness of what has happened and feeling the fear. From awareness and feelings, come insights and understanding. What often helps transcenders is thanking themselves for the protection and telling themselves it is now okay to be authentic. They can also tell themselves they may now take care of themselves in a different way. This allows transcenders to develop healthier relationships with themselves as well as others.

Steps in Reclaiming the Self

The process of reclaiming takes time, effort, and persistence. At times, it is hard and requires concerted effort to gain even a small entrance into the authentic self, let alone a change in behavior. At other times, entrance occurs almost effortlessly. This section talks about the steps that may be needed to reclaim the self. These steps include:

(1) discovering authentic thoughts, feelings, and behaviors; (2) going back; (3) learning that feelings are normal and expressing them appropriately; (4) establishing appropriate boundaries and limits; (5) transitioning—feeling crazy; (6) working through layers; (7) peeling away the fear and protection layers; (8) learning and discovering; (9) changing relationships; (10) exploring perfectionism; (11) overcoming tiredness; (12) learning about needs; (13) using the will appropriately; (14) getting rid of shame and secrets; (15) developing appropriate trust; (16) examining work; (17) learning to play; (18) developing spirituality; and (19) surviving dysfunctional days.

Before we explore the steps, let's look at the experiences of the reclaiming process from some transcenders.

Marie

"Who am I? What do I like to do, to eat, etc.? What don't I like about me? These are some of the questions I began to ask myself, especially following an intense period of grieving and sadness. I had spent most of my life taking care of and trying to meet the needs of others. To begin doing things for myself, especially at first, felt very selfish, very self-centered. I was so accustomed to meeting the needs of others I had difficulty choosing food in the grocery store that I wanted. It was as if I wasn't good enough and didn't deserve to have my own wants, needs, desires met. As I began to do small things for myself and make more choices based on what I really wanted to do, I also became aware of what my own needs really were. I began to feel my own feelings instead of running away or blocking them out as I had in the past. I began to breathe the fresh air of freedom for the first time.

"My feelings were not always happy, on-top-of-the-world feelings—my former false self. I learned that I really could cry alone and that the tears really would stop. I was surprised to find that instead of enjoying being by myself, there were times when I felt very lonely and very sad. Although I didn't like being there, I felt an honesty and an orientation to reality that had previously been unknown to me. For a while, during the intense grieving period, I felt I had lost my sense of humor. As I grew emotionally, I learned my laughter was a cover-up. I was surprised to hear myself on tape listening to an earlier session say, 'If I laugh about things, it keeps me from having to feel.'

"My sense of humor is still very much intact and now is certainly used more appropriately. There are times when I still want to block out feelings. When I do, the result is almost always the same: more pain in another way and at another time until the issue is resolved.

"I have learned, for the most part, that I like myself. The old fear of being like my mother is almost totally gone. In many ways the reclaiming process has been getting to know me for the first time. I have learned who I really am. I am learning I can make choices. I'm also beginning to learn that I'll never be perfect—former parent requirement. As more and more insight and understanding reveal themselves, I understand—no, I know—I was not the dirty, bad, and cheap little girl who wasn't good enough to be loved. Instead, I know that I had crazy, evil people for parents. On, the other hand, they did give me some 'good stuff.'

"In learning who I am, I am learning who I am not. I am not the abuse and torture I endured as a child. I am not guilty because I was there. I am not responsible for choices my parents made in their own lives. In reclaiming who I really am, I find a child who was a victim and one who will never be a victim again. I had no control over the things that were forced on me as a child. I very much have control over what happens to my life in the present and future. I can now continue to grow, no longer caged in the past, to take new steps and to invite other people into my life. The self I have come to know has nothing to hide and no secrets to live in fear of someone finding out.

"Is the future frightening to me? Yes, but also very exciting. I work very hard not to continue the abuse begun years ago by my parents. Good times, happy times, although greatly enjoyed, can trigger the old pattern of the you're-not-good-enough and the you-don't-deserve-to-be-happy tapes. Instead, I allow my newfound self to enjoy and know that it's okay to be happy—really happy—not just acting like I'm happy. When these tapes start to surface I tell myself that they were originally recorded on an eight-track recorder and do not fit on my newer cassette tape player; therefore, they can no longer be played.

"I lied to myself for years about my life. The quality of my life now, the excitement of my own personal growth, the lifting of the horrible burden of misplaced guilt, laughing real laughter, crying real tears, feeling real feelings, viewing and evaluating the past with the maturity of an adult, giving up old ways of surviving, and developing new and more appropriate ways of functioning are only some of the things I have gained in therapy. This insight into my past truly began when my daughter's therapist said to me one day, 'You might want to pursue your own family background further and go back into therapy.'

"Going back—that is the direction I had to travel in order to go forward so that I could be free and grow."

Chris

"The reclaiming part of my healing was wonderful. Somehow, as I felt the pain the real me began to surface. I'd find bits and pieces of me everywhere. For example, I found that I really didn't like getting up early in the morning; I preferred a job that started later. My mother never allowed us to sleep past 6:00 a.m. I presently have a job where I have to be at work at 6:00 a.m., but I am taking steps to get trained for other work that starts later. I also discovered I like being with other people but need time alone to be with me. Before this, I was with people who kept me from feeling.

"The reclaiming process was very painful at times. I had to revisit all the old experiences of abuse and take back each piece of me I had either left there or my parents had raped from me. Each time I did, I felt more powerful and complete. Each time, I saw how they raped me of myself. They decided I could never choose anything, never make my own decisions. I was to do just as I was told and never, never question anything. Questioning, even one question, meant certain abuse.

"What I found was the real me, the true me. I have never really known me. I was this person who needed to survive and was trained to do so. Parts of that survival soldier were me, but so much of me was hidden. I couldn't believe that I could be accepted or okay. I found that I was. Most important, I found I was accepted and okay by me. I actually like me! I thought I was bad and not okay because I was blamed for everything. Only a bad person could be at fault for so much. Finding out I was okay was wonderful. I felt free and alive.

"I now work to develop talents and abilities that are truly mine, like writing and running. I am also becoming more financially stable and organized, something I never thought I could do. I now know who I am. I am on a self-discovery journey of finding and developing more of me."

As in the grieving process, the reclaiming steps have no set order, can overlap, and can recur many times. The focus is always on discovering oneself and becoming more authentic in one's own world. The following describes the stages of the reclaiming process.

1. *Discovering Authentic Thoughts, Feelings, and Behaviors.* As transcenders grieve the past, they also need to constantly discover thoughts, feelings, and behaviors that are authentically connected to past experiences

and that also occur in present life. During this time, transcenders gain powerful information and understanding of what has happened to them and how it has shaped them. They become aware that many thoughts, feelings, and behaviors they thought were theirs are really their parents'. These may be old tapes that have been ingrained in them since a young age. *Tapes* are certain ways of feeling, thinking, and behaving that are learned from others, and at times, the transcender hears the actual voice giving the old negative messages. When this happens, transcenders often feel they are like their parents and become frightened, depressed, or angry; however, they are not like their parents. For example, when I discipline my child, I may have one of my parent tapes running. That is, I will say and do exactly what my parents said and did to me. Once the tapes are fully examined and felt, transcenders then have a choice to keep the thoughts, feelings, and behaviors, or change them.

As the grieving and reclaiming process continues, they come to realize, gratefully, that they are not responsible for what happened to them in the family. They know beyond a doubt the dysfunction in the family was not their fault. They did not choose to be abused and neglected. They discover they are *really* not like their parents in the negative abusive ways, which is an old, deep fear. This discovery brings relief and joy. Transcenders then work hard to uncover and develop what they authentically think, feel, and want in their world. They then make decisions based on these new thoughts and feelings.

This knowledge and confirmation that they are not like their parents and are not responsible for the family's dysfunction gives them permission, energy, and the courage to explore further—even if only to explore one more scary, painful memory. It is enough to keep them healing, growing and gaining insights.

This confirmation and learning is powerful and vital to their living. Growth continues to come as long as transcenders continue to work and are committed to their process.

2. *Going Back.* As in the grieving, transcenders need to go back as far as the loss of self. They must go back and reclaim parts that were left behind when they were young children, teenagers, and adults. This includes everything: feelings, thoughts, behaviors, abilities, potentialities—everything that is the original package *plus* all the learning that is gleaned from the experiences. Transcenders go back as far as the pain leads them.

   When transcenders go back, they must heal as well as develop a relationship with those lost parts of themselves. These parts have often been disowned, rejected, judged, and abandoned not only by the family but also by the transcender. Transcenders must bring forward to the present moment all the feelings, thoughts, and insights from that age and own them. Doing this brings incredible learning about themselves and their world. They learn why they feel, think, behave, and respond the way they do to certain situations. They learn about their original package. From this understanding, they can then make changes.

3. *Learning That Feelings Are Normal and Expressing Them Appropriately.* Growing up in a dysfunctional family, a transcender may learn feelings are not okay. Not only are they not okay, they are horrible, crazy, terrifying, and they may bring more traumas. In therapy, a *major* learning is that *all* feelings are normal, okay, and very important. Actually, the awakening of feelings is *the most important* element in healing, growing, and getting to know the authentic self. Transcenders also learn feelings need to be and can be expressed appropriately and in a healthy manner without hurting themselves or other people. In my

sessions with transcenders, one of my *most* repeated questions is, "What are you feeling?" Feelings have absolute priority!

Feeling work has priority in therapy because, unless transcenders know what they are feeling, they cannot begin to find out who they really are and gain an understanding of themselves or their abilities. Feelings give us *a lot* of the information we need about ourselves and our world. As transcenders do their feeling work, they become more aware of themselves, their world, and what they want in their world. They are also able to separate themselves from dysfunction. After the feeling work, decisions can then be made with reason, logic, and insights gained from the feelings, not based on just the feelings themselves. Decisions come after feelings, learning, and insights.

Learning that feelings are normal is sometimes very difficult. Transcenders have seen these emotions acted out violently and inappropriately. They have feelings locked inside from years ago and must go back to heal the traumas. This means overcoming the fear, acknowledging the feelings, and actually feeling the feelings. This is hard because they do not usually know how to appropriately feel, and they fear they may express these feelings in the same way as their dysfunctional family. For example, anger is one of the most feared feelings to express because it was the emotion most likely to be violently acted out. Transcenders often don't feel safe to experience anger. Frequently, there is an image of a parent ready to abuse them if they even think about anger. Anger may also be the only feeling that is allowed in the family. If this is true, other feelings become fused with anger. That is, if I am hurt and sad but anger is the only feeling that is allowed expression, then my hurt and sadness will look like anger. It takes diligent detective work to begin to separate fused feelings.

Tiffany

Here is Tiffany's description of how she came to accept her feelings.

"In my family, anger and happiness were the only feelings allowed. So, every heavy feeling became fused with anger, and the lighter ones with happiness. In therapy I worked real hard at separating my fused feelings and figuring out what I was really feeling. I loved learning about me. Whatever fears I felt I quickly worked through the fears because I knew my feelings were 'the me' I had been looking for all those years.

"Some feelings I never acknowledged because they were so forbidden by my family. Jealousy was one of those. It took me literally years to admit to feeling jealous. It is still hard for me, especially in competitive ways. I was taught to be a good sport and not want to win. I am involved in a very competitive sport, and sometimes I really just want to blow everyone away. Then I feel guilty and get mad at myself. I can't even own the fact that I am jealous at times.

"I can still remember the first time I heard about feelings that really made sense. I was in graduate school, and the professor, a wise, loving woman, described her understanding of feelings. She shared that feelings just were. She went on to explain that feelings are not good or bad, but just part of our humanness. We don't have to judge them, make them wrong, or try to do away with them. We do have to accept, feel, and learn about ourselves from them. She further explained that no one can be responsible for anyone else's feelings, but we are totally responsible for our own.

"I felt instant freedom and love. I felt the real me beginning to surface like it never had before. It was the me that has always wanted to be. As I grew and learned, I faced many fears about accepting my feelings that surprised me: What would my parents think? How would people respond to me having real feelings and opinions that came from those feelings? Would I still be loved if I didn't take care of others' feelings?

"I overcame these fears one by one in ways that were not terrifying. I did it with the help of several people who were mentors and therapists to me. They taught me to work with myself gently and lovingly. The abuse and neglect had been done. I didn't need any more of that. What I needed was to love myself to health and growth through acceptance of my feelings.

"Now, when a feeling comes up that I don't want, I may try to avoid it using the old system and respond with anger, but my new way of being with my feelings takes over. I feel, accept, and learn. I grow with every feeling, and my feelings help me to know what I want in my world."

4. *Establishing Boundaries, or Limits.* Boundaries, or limits, are extremely important to transcenders. In a dysfunctional family, the normal physical, mental, and emotional boundaries have never been established, or they have been violated. (More information is in Chapter 2.) Boundaries normally start to develop as the infant grows and begins to understand that the parent, often the mother, is a separate individual. This concept is usually firmly established in the "terrible twos" when the child demonstrates the separation by being able to say "no." When parents do not encourage this separation or violate the physical, mental, and emotional boundaries through abuse or neglect, the child can't establish this separation. The child then easily takes on the feelings and responsibilities of others and believes they are his or her own.

In the reclaiming process, transcenders work to define and establish their true boundaries. Transcenders must create clear boundary lines between themselves and others, especially with family members. They must get Mom's, Dad's, and their siblings' feelings, opinions, and responsibilities separated from their own. To do this, transcenders go through a confusing time of conflicts and battles that could sound like this: "What if I say no and they hate me?" "Will they abandon me?" "What if I fail?" "What are *my* boundaries?" "What are *my* feelings?"

The process is an evaluation of self, values, and morals that leads transcenders to their real selves with real boundaries that are felt when violated. There can no longer be a violating of boundaries and limits in order to be accepted.

5. *Transitioning—Feeling Crazy.* As transcenders continue to heal and grow, new ways of living in the world begin to be created, and a transition period occurs. A *transition period* is when the old ways of living are no longer needed or wanted and new ways begin to be created. The new ways begin to replace the old, *but* they are not completely known and definitely not solidly in place to be readily used in every situation.

During this time, transcenders may feel they have absolutely no ground underneath them. They believe if they take one step in any direction they will fall into a bottomless pit. When life experiences occur, they don't know whether to use the old way (which they now realize is not healthy because they have grown and changed) or to use a new way that they don't know well enough to have become a part of them yet. The old and new literally clash. Transcenders may find themselves alternating between the old and the new.

Transcenders feel intensely frustrated, fearful, angry, disorientated, confused, and crazy during this period of their therapy. I hear reports of transcenders feeling totally confused and not knowing who in the world they are! If you were to ask a transcender during this time, "Would the real person please stand up?" No one would stand up because there is so much uncertainty of who the real person is. It is a traumatic and scary time. At this point, transcenders often wonder why they even began therapy because it seems to have only made things worse.

In handling the transition period, transcenders need to relax into the fear and continue moving forward. Other professionals, as well as clients, have told me that "relaxing into the fear" is absurd and really crazy. Actually, it's neither. It simply means to relax, allow it to be, and to know the fear will be there. Remember the "snow globes" that you shook as a kid to keep the snow flying around the scene in the globe? Relaxing into the fear is like allowing "the snow" to settle. Don't resist and fight with it and don't let it stop you from your forward growing journey. Have an awareness of the fear, feel it, learn about it, but don't become too excited and upset with it. Just let it be. Accept it as part of the transition period that will eventually go away.

The best way to handle the transition period is to not struggle, but to let the cloudiness and confusion clear on its own like the snow! This will happen as the reclaiming process continues. The old ways of being will give way to the new. Transcenders then report feeling better and less crazy.

Steve

Steve gives us a sample of this confusing time.

"When I was in the transition period I knew something was going on but didn't know what. I was so confused I couldn't figure out if I was going to use the old way of behaving or attempt a new way. If I did the old way, I felt depressed, angry, and just plain awful! If I did a new way I felt terrified and so unsure of myself.

"I had no idea who I was—not wanting the old but not really having the new. I didn't know the old was fading and beginning to replace the new. I was told to relax. Ha! Relax when I felt so scared? How could I? How do you relax in the fear? But the more I struggled—and I really struggled—the more frustrated and scared I became.

"My brain was like a white cloud. A cloud that was so thick there was no vision at all. If I was an airport, all planes would be grounded. In the fog, there were people, things, situations, and feelings floating around. I worked hard trying to figure it out. Each time I tried, it became cloudier and I became more tense. I finally listened to my therapist, who said, 'Relax into the fear and confusion and let it alone.' It was the only thing that worked. As I let it be, it cleared."

6. *Working Through the Layers. Layers* are accumulated traumas that have not been dealt with and are stored in the body. (Layers are described in detail in Chapter 7.) Releasing and healing the trauma layers are essential to the grieving as well as to the reclaiming process. From the layers, transcenders gain valuable information about themselves and their world that is very important to reclaiming the self. When layers are not dealt with and are trapped inside, learning and growing from those layers are lost.

   As transcenders work through the layers, learning is gained. The transcender's authenticity is uncovered, discovered, and freed. The process is difficult. With each layer come pain and struggle, but as each layer is healed, joy and understanding also come. As more and more layers continue to surface, transcenders often feel as if they are going backward and regressing. This is *not* regression! It feels like regression because the layers seem as if they will never stop and it sends them back in time. *Each* layer that is felt and worked through is progress—one less layer inside. What is actually happening is the transcender's struggle to heal. Sometimes, the layers come one at a time; other times, it feels like a dump truck full of bricks has backed up and dumped its entire load. Each layer offers learning about the past and about the individual. Each layer is slightly different from the others. The layers continue until the transcender has healed and released all necessary layers from within.

It has been my experience that layers tend to move out of the body like stacked bundles, one after another with many traumas tied together. Layers do not necessarily come in chronological order or in any logical order, for that matter. Usually they come up whenever they can be handled emotionally. Sometimes they come with the least abusive first and the worst layers last. The individual's body seems to have its own agenda in helping to release layers.

7. *Peeling Away the Fear and Protection Layers.* The process of layers moving through the body may trigger intense fear. This fear can be experienced as anxiety or terror, depending on the layer, its memories, and emotions. This fear is part of the layers of protection the transcender had to have while growing up. Transcenders have set up a system to keep the layers of feelings and memories away so they could survive and keep going. The more severe the trauma in childhood, the stronger the fear has to be to hold the layers out of awareness. This protection is vital while growing up.

I describe to clients the fear while releasing layers in the following way. "The layers are going to continue to surface until they are done. The fear you feel is part of your old protection system that kept you safe while growing up. You no longer need it, and we will deal with the fear and the layers as they surface. We learn from them. This allows the next layer to surface and more learning and growing to occur. Each layer needs to be felt and learned from fully.

Each time you do this, you will gain another part of you and reclaim more of your personal power. Know that sometimes the fear will be stronger than at other times. The fear is an indication to intensify our exploration, not a signal to stop. It means you are close to your authenticity. It is time to search for and deal with more of your truth."

Tom

The fear and protection layers are described this way by a transcender.

"I had to leave me in my childhood. I had to bury myself and pretend I didn't exist on the surface. I had to conform to survive and be acceptable. If I didn't, I wouldn't have made it because they would have gotten me. I still won't be acceptable, and they will get me. The real me wasn't safe. I can't be the real me even now. If I let me out, I still won't be liked, loved, or accepted."

The feeling of not being accepted is powerful and often sets up the following beliefs. "If only I could be better. . . . If only I would have taken care of my dad a little more. If only I talked less. If only—then they would have liked, accepted, and loved me. If they loved me, they would have stop hurting me."

From these thoughts come codependency patterns of taking care of others to the exclusion of themselves. What they are doing is protecting themselves *and* trying to get some sort of nurturing in return. Another part of the protecting fear is of revisiting past experiences—a fear I well understand. Who, through choosing, would ever want to go back to trauma after trauma and feel all the old pain as if it were happening right

now? That is what healing demands. It is painful and
difficult. The last part of this area is a fear of what kind
of person they will find, and it may sound like this:
"Will I hate me?" "Will I be acceptable?" "My parents
didn't want me, so why would I want me?" "I must not
be okay."

Some transcenders may believe that if others really
knew them, they wouldn't like them and wouldn't want
to be around them. This is because they believe they
may not be the loving, caretaking person others see on
the outside. They say, "I'm really an angry person." Of
course there is anger. It's anger at what happened to
them in childhood and from the loss of self.

As the feeling work is done and layers are released,
transcenders develop an understanding of what has
happened to them. From this understanding, they
learn and grow. Transcenders can then let go of the
past, heal, *and* realize not only that they are okay but
that they are someone they like and respect. They
learn they have always been okay, that it is the family
dysfunction that made them believe otherwise.

8. *Learning and Discovering.* A major part of the reclaiming process is the fantastic learning that con-
tributes to growth. Transcenders learn about
themselves and their world with truth and authenticity. The learning is endless. They learn they are not
conning people with their abilities; their abilities are
real. (We cannot have a particular talent or be intelligent when we are really not; those are original-pack-
age qualities.) In addition, transcenders discover they
have skills they didn't know they had. They may find
out they can ski, ride horses, or be creative. They
learn the truth about themselves and their families,
and this information gives them a freedom to be
themselves. They also discover a new, clearer per-

spective about their world. The reclaiming process is a discovery journey about themselves.

For transcenders, a major new experience in relationships is discovering other people really will/do like them as they really are. Because the real self had to be hidden in childhood, some transcenders find it very scary to put themselves on "display." As they take the risk and reveal more of themselves, there is more of a chance of having the authentic self inspected and judged. It is something like showing off a new baby—an important part of you is out there and vulnerable. What if they don't like me? Then what? There is nothing else. Ideally, parents praise and encourage their children to become their authentic selves and the children develop a strength that carries them through inspections. In a dysfunctional family, this is usually not true, and the authentic self is made wrong and is hidden. For help in this area, transcenders need to surround themselves with caring, accepting, loving, nonjudgmental people who encourage the development of the real self.

Sometimes, transcenders find that they have to change certain situations in their world because they no longer fit. If changes are needed, transcenders decide through the process of healing and growing what they will change. The changes may be easy or hard, but transcenders are ready to make the changes. For example, Tiffany was working for an organization that was severely dysfunctional. As she healed and grew, she decided she could no longer work for that organization. She had come to realize the company was very similar to her family and she was in intense emotional pain while working there. She also came to realize that she had changed and no longer needed the company (i.e., family). When she left, she felt she was leaving the dysfunction of the organization as

well as that of her family. She was beginning to create
a world of her own choosing.

9. *Changing Relationships.* In the healing process, *all* important relationships in the transcender's past and
present life are explored and evaluated: Mom, Dad, siblings, significant others, bosses, relatives—everyone.
These relationships are explored in detail so that
transcenders gain an understanding of the emotions
and meanings in their life. This is especially true of
relationships that contain pain because they are apt to
be saturated with the family's dysfunctional system.
Often, transcenders find Dad in a lover, Mom in a
friend, or a combination of Mom and Dad in a spouse.
This happens because there is a match or a duplica-
tion of the family's dysfunction. For example, if I need
to be a caretaker because of my past experience in
my family, I will pick a significant other who is dependent. An extremely dependent person, in return,
will pick a strong caretaker. Or if I may feel loved
only after I have been physically abused, I will get
into a relationship that is physically abusive. This is
*no*t to say I want to be abused. It is to say I have
learned to associate love with abuse because that is
what happened in my family. Also, the concept of love
changes as the person heals and grows. Please note:
this is not always the case, and many transcenders refuse to put up with any type of abuse in a relationship.
    Transcenders have learned how to act in relation-
ships from past experiences in the family. Relationships that simulate the family relationships feel right,
or at least familiar, if not comfortable, because this is
what they know and have been taught. To change
these patterns, transcenders must define the dysfunction in painful relationships and separate it from the
healthy, authentic self. They do this by feeling, exploring, and examining relationships to gain a clearer

view of why they are attracted and attached to un-healthy relationships. They can then make powerful, healthy decisions about their relationships. It is a difficult process, but it often moves transcenders out of painful relationships.

As reclaiming continues, transcenders find themselves feeling less crazy and confused. They feel better and more relaxed; they learn how to play; and they become more authentic. Shifts then occur in relationships sometimes almost automatically. Transcenders find themselves attracted to healthier, more authentic people, and they discover healthier people being attracted to them. New, healthier relationships are formed *and* enjoyed.

Some transcenders are already in healthy, growing relationships that are enhanced by the reclaiming process. Others are in difficult relationships that may be healed rather than terminated. Some are in painful relationships that they find they must leave. There is no set rule about relationships. The important thing is the healing, growing, and striving for an ever healthier, happier life.

Healthy, growing relationships are vital to support the reclaiming of the self. Without these relationships, transcenders stay in loneliness, isolation, and often depression. It is these healthy relationships that give positive feedback to transcenders: "I like you for you." "I like your real self." "You're neat." "I love you." "You're not just a role, you're a valuable person"—and very importantly, "Keep going." These kinds of relationships may already be in place or may be formed during the healing process.

In another important area of relationships, transcenders find other transcenders and share backgrounds. As a result, they gain support and no longer feel they are the only ones to whom their experience has ever happened, and so this sharing is extremely valuable in shifting guilt, shame, and loneliness. Through this exchange, transcenders gain thoughts of "If they can do it, so can I."

By support, I mean having people in your life who value, love, help, and give in many ways that show caring for you as a person. For example, there were many caring people who gave of their talents and time to make this book happen during its first publication, as well as during its revision.

Relationships are just as important in healing and growing as they are in surviving the family. Transcenders change relationships by getting rid of old dysfunctional patterns. They move out of unhealthy, painful relationships with a courage and strength that is impressive. From this entire area, transcenders gain love—self-love and the love of others in healthy, appropriate ways. A healthy definition of love is established, examined, and reflected on in all its forms so that it becomes the essence of relationships.

10. *Exploring Perfectionism.* Another stage of the reclaiming process is exploring perfectionism, which sounds like this: "If I work a little harder, if I make straight A's, I'll do everything right. Then I'll be perfect, and then they'll love me." It can also sound like this: "If I'm perfect, then I'll get through life okay. I can't make any mistakes." Or it may be: "I'll try to be just like him; then they'll love me." "My parents want me to be their perfect little girl/boy for them, so I'll be that, then they'll love me." For some people, perfectionism is a reason not to attempt anything that requires a struggle to accomplish. After all, if they don't try, they can't fail.

The belief is if I try harder and am perfect and do nothing wrong, I'll be accepted and loved. Thus, the authentic self is thrown away and a "perfect" *false* self is created. The negative side of this perfectionism means not being yourself but striving to create a perception of a more acceptable, lovable, and less victimized self. It means trying to meet authorities' expectations because the false self is based on what they perceive as more powerful others want. It means being the image of someone else's illusion and fantasy. *But* this someone else may be dysfunctional. Sound crazy? It is! It is *crazy and confusing.* Sometimes the authority wants something one minute but doesn't want it the next. What brings love one time beings rage the next. At the age of five, one transcender was told to drive a tractor in a straight line. He could barely touch the pedals, let alone figure out what a straight line was. He was severely punished each time he went crooked. This is crazy!

Attempting to be perfect does offer transcenders a type of protection from the world: "If I do everything right, no one will hurt me." So they work very hard to do what is right, or what they perceive as right to keep them safe from abuse. Perfectionism also helps to maintain the self-esteem even though it is part of the false self, so transcenders can function in the world at least on some level. In adulthood, as transcenders heal and grow, they find they can no longer even strive to be perfect. It takes too much energy and too much effort. They may also find they no longer need the illusion of being perfect.

Perfection is an illusion. Perfection does not exist in our world. It is not ever a reality. We create an illusion of perfection that is based on someone else's image. In a family that demands perfection, perfect means *never* failing, always doing the right thing, and never being wrong according to that family's definition of right and wrong. For example, if my family made their living robbing banks, I would be wrong in the family if I didn't believe in stealing. "Perfect" for my family would be stealing. We, as human beings are not perfect—never have and never will be. One of the major ways we learn is by experiencing frustration and making mistakes.

The human brain functions in such a way that we are able to learn and grow from our experiences. What we do have is our humanness and our original package. What transcenders discover about themselves is that although they're not perfect they are acceptable and lovable. They discover and confirm that other dysfunctional people with their own issues were at fault!

Changing the perfection illusion involves feeling the fear and working with the dysfunction that caused the need to be perfect. The fear is, "If I stop being perfect, will I be okay?" "Who am I?" "Will I be safe?" "Will I be liked?" The perfectionism fear shows up in things like being afraid to change one's hair style, eat new foods, change the style of clothes one wears, appear in public without being absolutely "perfect," or attempt new skills. The change away from perfectionism occurs in healing, support from significant others, and transcenders' courage to be. What transcenders learn is to be the *best they can be.*

11. *Overcoming Tiredness.* At some point in the healing and growing process, transcenders experience what I call a *deep, inner-core tiredness.* What happens at this stage in the process is that transcenders, who have been working for decades maintaining themselves using survival techniques, become emotionally, mentally, and physically exhausted because of the effort it has taken to survive and create a different lifestyle in adulthood. The tiredness is deep in the inner being, and regular sleep habits do not relieve the symptoms. What is needed is getting *all* the sleep and rest required until physical, mental, and emotional energy returns. This rest sometimes takes weeks, sometimes months. Patience and understanding are important from others as well as from themselves at this time.

What I hear from clients during this period is, "I can't do this anymore." "I can't go on." "I can't seem to get enough sleep." "I just want to sleep and sleep and sleep." "No matter how much sleep I get, it's never enough." "My tiredness feels so old and so deep." "I don't think it will ever go away." "I just can't go on this way."

Tiffany

Here is Tiffany's journal entry during this time.

"I am so tired. It's a deep, deep tiredness. I don't feel especially sleepy, yet I do. It's not exhaustion, just deep, old tiredness—old, old, as if my struggle has gone on a long, long time. Before all this started, I had the thoughts, 'I can't keep doing this. I am so tired. I can't keep doing it.' I didn't know exactly what the it was, but now I do: the 'it' is keeping me hidden, and keeping all that pain inside and keeping me pretending I am okay, not sad. I have to hide the sadness. The sadness is the shame I felt guilt about, so I have to hide it, or people will judge me as wrong and not acceptable.

"Now this tiredness is there—outside. Wave after wave of sadness brings up the tiredness—old, old tiredness. It's not body tiredness. It's eons old. It's inner core tiredness—tired of battling; tired of trying to be someone else.

"*Deep—Tired—Old*—no words—just deep, deep tiredness. Tired of trying to be competent and covering up my vulnerability. My vulnerability is fear of rejection, hurt, and ridicule. I'm not accepted. There's game-playing. Being nice when I feel angry. Cover! Cover! Cover! It's too much now—too much struggle, too much, too much energy, too old. I have to surrender to me. *I have to be me at all costs. I can't go on this way.*"

The deep tiredness does go away when transcenders get enough rest. After the entire system is rested, growth seems accelerated and transcenders have the energy to implement changes. The learning at this step is the deep realization that they can no longer live the old way; they have to find a new way. The old patterns of living have to change to healthier, easier, more authentic ways of being.

12. *Learning About Their Needs.* Needs are very important parts of the reclaiming process. A *need* is defined as a requirement, something necessary for living, something essential. Needs must be separated from desires or wants. A *desire* or *want* is defined as a wish, fantasy, inclination, liking, or fondness. I may desire a castle, but I don't need one. I need to eat. I need to feel. Desires are important in helping create dreams and goals in life but not in maintaining the basics of life.

For transcenders, learning to distinguish their needs from others' needs and meeting them in appropriate ways is important. They have to stop meeting needs inappropriately through dysfunction. *Appropriately* is the important word here and means in a suitable way without hurting ourselves and/or others. Transcenders often have a fear of meeting their own needs because of what they saw when they were growing up. Their families may have tried to meet needs through abuse, neglect, and making others responsible for their feelings, needs, and desires.

Because needs were met inappropriately, transcenders may have lost any awareness of their own needs when they were given the responsibility of meeting the needs and desires of others. For example, if my mother is needy, lonely, and uses me to feel her feelings, I will have a difficult time separating her needs and feelings from mine. In this kind of relationship, I may feel overwhelmed, confused, and helpless. I may also believe her needs are really mine. In the reclaiming process, I have to sort me out from Mom in many ways so that I know which needs are mine to satisfy and which needs are Mom's. It is not humanly possible no matter how hard I try to satisfy Mom's needs. She has to do it for herself. I can only choose to help her satisfy her needs if she allows it. That is my human limit.

Learning about our needs is vital because they teach us what we like, what we don't like, and what we require to feel loved and okay in our world. Needs help us to know who we want in our world and who we don't want. When we explore our needs, we discover and enrich our common bond of humanness with other people. As a result, we learn greater love and patience with ourselves and each other.

An important thing many transcenders learn is that they are human and their needs are very similar to, if not the same as, everyone else's. They discover their needs are not out of proportion or too great. They discover they were given too little as a child.

Marie's parents, for example, did not want her and acted out their anger by physically abusing her when she was hungry and tried to get food. She learned that if she tried to satisfy her needs she got hurt. She learned to be afraid every time she needed. This fear then acted to block even an awareness of her needs. Every time she got close to a need, the fear said, "Don't! Dangerous! Stop! Stop before you get hurt!" Such fear must be felt and understood before one moves on to satisfy one's needs appropriately. In a case like Marie's, it means feeling the awfulness of starving and then eating when she is hungry. She may first have to learn when she is hungry by putting herself on a schedule, like an infant.

Learning to satisfy needs is a journey of trial and error for transcenders—a journey of trying different ways to satisfy their different needs. They discover different ways work at different times; some ways don't work at all. Transcenders also learn that normal, growing, and ever-developing human beings' needs change and evolve as we grow. Needs change day to day and year to year depending on the transcender's world and activity. For example, what we need as infants is very different than what we need as teenagers. Needs also depend on what kind of day it's been. I love to ride horses. Depending on what kind of stress I have had, I have different needs in the riding area. On some days, I have a great need for a hard, challenging lesson. Other days, I just want to take a trail ride. On still other days, I may want to groom the horse more than ride. Whatever my need is that day, it is okay.

13. *Using the Will Appropriately.* The will is the focal point of the self. It's like a librarian who gathers all the available resources and puts them in a certain area to use for accomplishing goals. The will's strength then takes the resources and works to keep the person focused by screening out and fighting any onslaught or distraction from a goal. For the transcender, the will gathers resources that protect and nurture the authentic self during childhood. (The will is further discussed in Chapter 5.)

Most transcenders, in order to survive, have had to develop a strong will. During the healing process, this strong will often interferes with growth because it has been trained to ensure survival. To be used appropriately and productively in the healing process, the will needs to be channeled into promoting growth and healing rather than fighting it. Transcenders may use their strong will at the wrong times and may actually hurt themselves. For example, it may be used to overpower someone they never meant to hurt, to come on like a Mack truck, which could damage the relationship because they themselves were afraid. It may also be used to handle fear.

To change the use of the will, I use the process of thanking oneself for all the help in earlier years by using the will and then adding, "Now I need to use my will in another way." With this kind of wording, transcenders treat themselves in a more gentle way that encourages growth rather than having another battle to deal with. This way of talking unites their internal strength and shifts the focus of the will. Transcenders are then able to decide when to use their will "full strength" and when to lessen its effect. They learn this as the healing continues and they develop more trust in themselves and others. The process of shifting the use of the will is a learning process of trial and error. Transcenders learn how, when, with whom, and with what strength to use their will in everyday life now that life is safer and more secure.

14. *Getting Rid of Shame and Secrets.* In the reclaiming process, shame and secrets have to be uncovered and disinfected. I view both of these areas as old infected wounds that need to be cleaned to promote healing from the inside out. As with any infected wound, the less airing, the more painful the wound and the more energy needed to contain it. If one is to cleanse and heal from shame and secrets, they have to be expressed, or aired. Once they are expressed, the feeling work can be done. The inner pain and energy that have held the secrets for so long can then be released and new life comes from the healing. We can come to know we are not the shame.

In addition, an understanding of the shame and secrets must be developed. This understanding allows transcenders to gain more insight into what has happened to them and gain an understanding of their parents' behavior. Secrets are often generations old and have been passed down through the years to each new generation. With this understanding, comes a choice of continuing the secrets or stopping the generational dysfunction surrounding it. Airing our secrets does not mean hurting others. Airing needs to be done in a therapeutic, healing appropriate manner. We are always responsible for our actions.

In my family, a generational secret was my grandmother's deep loneliness. She was from the old country and could not speak English when she arrived in the United States. She made few friends and kept to herself most of her sixty-four years. Her children, at some deep, inner level, felt responsible for her loneliness. But the loneliness was a secret and created shame. What would have been healthier would have been to talk about her loneliness so we would see that it was *her* loneliness and not her children's.

Chris
The following is Chris's description of his experience with shame in the family.

"There is an awareness of shame and embarrassment of the past in the present. Feelings of hurt and disappointment never seem to dissipate. I still have a gnawing pain when thoughts of family arise. For example, I never invited my mother to my own wedding because I felt embarrassed by her. What would my new friends and family think? I was also secretly happy when my step-dad died so he couldn't come to my graduation. I also couldn't let anyone know my father committed suicide. They would think something was mentally wrong with me too."

One of the greatest feelings comes from airing secrets and shame appropriately. Freedom! After this airing, transcenders have more energy because they no longer have to hold in the so-called crimes. They also have more energy to be themselves because they no longer feel afraid or shameful, and they no longer have to "walk on egg shells." Once again, they come to realize at a very deep level that they are okay.

15. *Developing Appropriate Trust.* Trust, like respect, is learned and earned in relationships. *Trust* is a knowing that what a person says, he or she will do. If I say I will be at the clinic for an appointment with a client, that client needs to know I will be there. If I say I will call, I call. When words match behavior, trust can be learned. Trust of self is vital to the growing self. Trust is supposed to be taught by caring parents from the time we are infants throughout our life. Infants learn trust when they are hungry and cry and parents come to feed and comfort them. From experience, they learn to trust others as well as themselves and their needs. When appropriate responses don't occur, infants learn not to trust themselves or others. They may come to accept being unhappy as normal living and have a hard time knowing when they are sad or even hungry because they were rarely treated with love and respect.

Think for a moment what abused children do learn from their parents. It is not trust of others or themselves. They literally find themselves fighting for their lives with the very people who are supposed to protect and love them. They learn, in essence, not to trust—to be on guard and to defend themselves.

As adults, transcenders must learn trust, appropriate trust, or life may continue to be very difficult and painful. This learning is possible through caring and loving relationships. It can occur in therapy with a good, nurturing therapist who encourages and acknowledges this area of growth. I have often been told by clients that the greatest assets in therapy are caring and acceptance, which teach clients they are not just the next appointment. This does not mean the therapist is perfect and does not make mistakes. Mistakes, however, are *not* abuse and *not* a lack of trust. They are just mistakes and need to be acknowledged, discussed, felt, and dealt with in a manner that encourages trust. Some clients have an all-or-nothing mind set, and if their therapist makes a mistake, that's it. Therapy is over! Processing through the mistake teaches another way to deal with misunderstandings and to help develop trust. Transcenders learn that they, as well as others, are human and that it is okay to make mistakes. They also learn to deal with the intense fear they have about trusting themselves and discover that this is also possible.

Trust also builds when the transcender continues to reclaim and eliminate the betrayal of self. The *betrayal of self* occurs when the false self is created and the real self is abandoned. Reclaiming in this area involves going back and forgiving oneself for the abandonment and then reowning the self. There is frequently anger and fear in this area, and the client needs help understanding that the betrayal and abandonment that occurred helped to ensure survival. In addition, to come to understand they could not stop the abuse/neglect; they were little.

Here's one final note on trust: because they experienced little from their world, transcenders have adopted what I call a tyrant. The *tyrant* is an internal drive, or will process. The tyrant is in charge of making transcenders do what they are supposed to do. If the task is not accomplished, the tyrant usually dishes out some sort of punishment. Sometimes, this tyrant is imaged as a troll or a fiendish type of character with a whip that lashes out and drives the transcender unmercifully. The tyrant is a combination of the parent transcenders carry inside themselves (internalized parent from childhood) and the drive to survive. Part of the reclaiming is either to eliminate the tyrant or to transform it. This occurs when transcenders begin to build trust in themselves to handle their world without abuse and dysfunction.

16. *Examining Work.* Work is another area that must be thoroughly examined and evaluated in the reclaiming process. Without knowing it, some transcenders find themselves working for organizations and/or bosses that are very similar to their dysfunctional families. The similarities include patterns and styles of relating, neglect of employees, abuse of employees by over-work or use of off-hours, scapegoating, verbal put-downs, rigid rules that are not negotiable under any circumstance, and lack of structure or rules so that no one knows what he or she is supposed to do. At times, employees may get into trouble if they take their own initiative even when doing so would be appropriate.

As transcenders grow, they sometimes become aware of how the dysfunction of their work and family compares. It is often a match. Transcenders know it feels okay to be in the organization because it is similar to their family's system of relating. It's familiar and they know what's expected, how to behave, and what to do. I hear, "I like it because I know what to expect. I'm comfortable there." These are feeling responses and may not actually be true, but match the past dysfunction. As they begin to heal and find the authentic self, they frequently find themselves having to make a decision about staying or leaving their employment. Sometimes, they choose another field entirely; sometimes, they leave on early retirement or move to a new company. There are, however, transcenders who are in healthy, positive places to work.

17. *Learning to Play.* Play releases stress, recreates energy, balances life, develops the inner child, and is fun. Play is very important for everyone—children and adults. Some transcenders, thank goodness, use play as a survival technique and find it a vital escape that helps ensure survival. Others did not play as

children and have a disadvantage of not knowing how to play as adults. Play *can* and *must* be learned by those who did not play as children and/or an adult. Learning to play is an important part of reclaiming the child from the past as well as the adult of the present.

Play can be learned in many ways: watching others, attending play workshops that focus on teaching play to adult children of dysfunctional families, participating in play with others who do play, and playing with children. One learns to play simply by playing. In the beginning, it can be uncomfortable, scary, and unnerving. Transcenders may feel that someone is about to come and punish them or laugh at them. These feelings usually come from never having been a "real kid" and not being sure play is okay. Once expressed, these feelings pass, and play becomes more comfortable and fun. If in the healing process there is punishment after play, a close examination is needed to stop this abuse. It may be that the transcender is punishing him- or herself or that the "playmate" is inappropriate.

Learning to play needs to be an experimental, discovery-filled journey that is fun and creative. We need to give ourselves permission to be carefree and full of life and take time to discover ourselves. To start, think of things you have always wanted to do and then do them. If you do something and find you really don't like it, try something else. If you find you like it, continue doing it and enjoy it. If the activity requires certain skills and you want to develop them, do so. Don't expect to have all the skills initially. The goal is *fun*, not stress or perfection. Remember, perfect doesn't exist.

You may enjoy certain activities, but you may not want to develop those skills. For example, I enjoy walking with our dog. I just walk. Some days I walk fast, some slow. I don't want to develop a technique of walking or get into walking races. I just want to enjoy walking. However, with my horseback riding, I do want to develop my skill at riding a horse. I want to become an adequate rider. Both walking and riding are play to me. So are teasing (not critically) and bubble-blowing. If I find I no longer enjoy these activities, I will explore and find other things I do want to do. Nothing is permanent or right or wrong. It's up to you. The only rule is don't hurt yourself or others, and don't let others hurt you.

Play is anything you enjoy doing. It may be having dinner out, talking with a dear friend, being with a significant other, or listening to music. It may be playing in the sandbox with your children. Children are great at teaching play. Watch them and join in. Play may also, at times, be your work. Whatever it is, play needs to help you shift gears to a more relaxed, carefree, fun state where you can enjoy yourself and have fun.

18. *Developing Spirituality.* Spirituality is the core not only of the healing and growing process, but also of humanness. It's so vital to reclaiming the self that the entire next chapter is devoted to it.

19. *Surviving Dysfunctional Days.* Over the years during my work with transcenders, I have noticed what I have come to call dysfunctional days. *Dysfunctional days* are a throwback to earlier times with the family, but they occur after most of the healing is done. Transcenders seem to revert to old feelings, thinking, and sometimes even behavioral patterns. Experiencing a dysfunctional day is like reliving a day in your old pattern of dysfunction with the family.

The good things about dysfunctional days are that they don't last long and, as transcenders continue to grow, they occur less frequently. The bad thing about these days is that they can be unnerving and unsettling, especially if one doesn't know what is happening.

Transcenders may honestly believe they are regressing and losing all the progress from their hard work. Neither is true. Once the dysfunctional day is dealt with, the healthier patterns return.

Dysfunctional days can be triggered by stress, loss, anniversaries of important traumas, visits home, or other difficult times. They may also occur for what seems to be no reason at all other than waking up. Transcenders need to deal with these days the same way they deal with other feelings—feel the particular emotions and work to gain an understanding of what the day is all about. If they are in therapy, they need to explore it in session. If the dysfunction occurs after the individual is no longer in therapy and lasts longer than a few days, an appointment with the former therapist is needed to explore the feelings. Most importantly, transcenders need to learn from this experience and remember these days don't last.

Summary

The process of reclaiming the self is vital to healing and growing. As traumas of the past are reexperienced and explored, the authentic self is uncovered and developed. There is time in this process for catching up with one's self and no longer having to be mature beyond one's years, "knowing before you know." There is finally time just to be.

Through this difficult process, joy does return and emotional health is gained unlike any that has ever been experienced before. Transcenders gain confidence, wisdom, love, and the ability to give love. There is a clearing, a cleaning, and a releasing of the body and soul into true freedom to be one's own self.

As transcenders grow, they put their families of origin into perspective. They are able to laugh about certain things that happened to them in their families. They may even remember some good things that happened in childhood. Amazingly, they are even able to list the ways they gained and grew because of their survival. In the process, they go from trauma, anger, and despair to healing, growth, hope, and wisdom.

Future days are full of challenge. Just because transcenders are healing and growing, that doesn't mean the rest of their life is totally wonderful. It does mean that transcenders have all of themselves to deal with whatever life brings.

CHAPTER 9

Spirituality, Healing, and Growth

I have just finished a twelve-hour day at work. It is one of many twelve- to sixteen-hour days I put in between work, writing, and family responsibilities. Today I had a meeting with staff, picked up the kids after school for an appointment, functioned as a clinical director, worked with clients in therapy, and met with two attorneys to discuss a very difficult, emotional case. Yesterday, I coached my daughter's high school equestrian team. With this responsibility I got up at 4:30 in the morning and ran around with horses and riders until at least 6:00 p.m. Sound like fun? Actually, it is. I love the kids, clients, work, and especially the variety in my life. The only problem with my schedule is that there is little time to rest and I sometimes become exhausted.

When I finally arrived home tonight, all I wanted to do was crash. I didn't want to move or talk to anyone about anything; I just wanted to vegetate. However, our dog got loose and decided to have one of his "biannual" excursions into the neighborhood. On these excursions, he believes he must, like my two teens, stay out most of the night visiting everything and everyone around. I was content to let him roam and planned to greet him in the morning. However, my daughter, who works for a veterinarian, has seen too many dogs that have been hit by cars, and she refused to go to bed until he's safe at home. She wasn't feeling well and was also exhausted. So, I promised to stay up until he safely arrived home. At midnight my husband took over dog-watching duty for me.

I was so tired I was not sure who I was any more. I climbed into bed anxiously looking for my head and pillow to meet. Just as I climbed into bed, I felt God "nudging" me to pick up the pen and write. After many years of having a relationship with God, I know to follow such feelings because it is the best for all concerned. So, I picked up the pen and started to write. As I wrote, the words came in spite of my tiredness—as if God and I were working together.

My relationship with my spirituality, that part of me that relates and is connected to God, enables me to use these resources whenever and wherever they are needed. This is true in giving to others as well as to myself. Being in tune with my spirituality gives me the ability to write this chapter in spite of being tired. Actually, the more I write this, the less tired, more energized, and stronger I feel.

My personal relationship with God enables me to balance the many facets of my life. God loves me, nurtures me, strengthens me, and gives me wisdom and abilities that at times are beyond my human limitations. It is my spirituality that helps me to help others find and develop their original package. In my work, I have seen many miracles—things that have happened beyond human understanding. It is God who creates miracles, sometimes even by using human beings who have the necessary training and talents.

I define *spirituality* as that part of us, our life essence that is connected to and relates to God, the higher power, or higher consciousness. For simplicity, in this book I refer to this as God. Whatever we call our spirituality, it is the relationship between our essence—our spirit or soul—with the living, loving, power that created us. It is through our spirituality that we connect to God, whoever you know Him to be. It is through our spirituality that we can love. I believe that we as human beings are spiritual beings first, then mental, emotional, and physical. I believe it is this core that is the prime influence in life, whether we know or acknowledge it. I believe that as our core of being our spirituality must be nurtured and developed. It is a deep strength that helps us navigate through life, as well as through the healing and growing process. It is vital to everything we do.

By spirituality, I do not mean organized religion. I do mean the relationship one has with God. Organized religion may be part of the expression of our spirituality, but it is not solely within itself spirituality. Our spirituality may be expressed by communing in the woods; meditating; worshipping in our home, in a church, in a temple, in a mosque; or sharing our thoughts with others who believe the same as we do. I can attend a temple, church, or mosque three times a week and have very little spirituality. However we relate to God, we gain healing, growth, understanding, acceptance of self, love of others, and direction for our lives.

Do we need our spirituality? Do we need God? I personally believe that we absolutely do. I know that I do! I remember a time in my life when I didn't have a relationship with God. I would describe myself during that time as an angry, depressed young woman in a deep, dark slime pit. I was a young mother with two children. My daughter was two and my son had just been born. I was recovering from his birth, a C-section. I was tired, exhausted, lonely, and unbelievably depressed. I truly did not know who I was. I was not prepared for motherhood and I really struggled. At that time, no matter how hard I tried to rest to gain energy, be less depressed, less angry, or a more loving mother, I couldn't. The tiredness I felt then is similar to the tiredness I feel now with one major difference—my spirituality, which will give me strength and energy for tomorrow.

As I work with clients, there are times (as in everyone's work) that I don't know how to help or what to offer next. At these times, I usually say, "God help!" It is not unusual to then find a direction in which to go to offer what that person needs. Sometimes what is needed is a thought or intuitive feeling. Other times, I may confront a dysfunctional behavior. Whatever form the help comes in, it encourages healing.

How does this healing occur? The transcender connects with his or her spirituality to heal and further develop the original package. One flows with and through the other, each nurturing the other, each contributing to the healing and growth.

I believe God created the original package and we need to be in a relationship with Him. My experience has been that without this there is an empty spot or void inside of us that only our spirituality can fill and nurture. No one and nothing else fits, fills, or satisfies this emptiness for very long. Sometimes individuals use addictions to attempt this but are not successful. This void in us is connected by what I call a *spiritual umbilical cord.* This umbilical cord connects soul to Creator. It is there when God creates us, and I believe we need to have this connection throughout our lifetime. It is through this connection that we receive support, strength, and love.

Feeling abandoned is really feeling our separation from our spirituality. This separation is often felt as a deep, gnawing, lonely feeling. Philosophers sometimes call this feeling *existential loneliness,* which is essentially that we come into this world alone, live our life alone, and die alone. However, it is more than a feeling of loneliness. From my work with people, I see it as a spiritual vacuum. I believe we have been given this need to help us at deeper level to get through life. I certainly find this the help I need! We all feel a form of abandonment and are spiritually deficient and crippled until we find and develop our relationship with our spirituality. Once this union occurs, the void is filled and deep soul healing can occur.

The Transcender and Spirituality

Spirituality is important to most transcenders. They need to believe in and rely on a power greater than themselves while working to survive the abuse/neglect they endured. Their spirituality helps guide, energize, nurture, and develop their authenticity through childhood and adulthood.

Many transcenders describe their relationship with God as the core of their survivorship, which enabled them to transcend their family. It is this power that keeps them focused on a positive path. In addition, formal worship at churches, mosques, and temples supplies transcenders with a sanctuary as well as relationships with more nurturing people. Marie and Tiffany were two of the transcenders who found their spirituality to be the essence of their survivorship and healing. Here are their words.

Marie

"When I was a small child I decided God was really my father. He would take care of me and keep me safe by teaching me how to take care of myself. Looking back over the years, I see this early adoption of God had a strong influence over my growth and the development of my own value system. The façade of the upstanding Christian life my parents showed the outside world 'took,' in my young life. As a child, even though I was forced to be involved more in the dark, evil world of Satan than of God's warm, caring love, I knew the difference. God's love fed, nurtured, and protected me, my spirit or soul, from the cold, satanic life of my parents.

"I was so alone it was very easy for me to look to God for direction. Fortunately for me, the bad was so bad that the only direction was away from the lifestyle of my parents. The only other direction I knew was that of God. I could certainly not claim credit for trying to be a good person because the alternative was too horrible in my life.

"One of my coping mechanisms that began in my early teens—one I still use today—involves thinking through whatever situation I am in. I search for the answer to the question 'What does God want me to learn from this?' I never felt that God wanted me to be hungry, lonely, terrified, or hurt, but because I was in the situation, it was my responsibility to learn something positive from it and then use the knowledge to help myself or someone else.

"I feel sorry for people who say they don't know how to pray. If God ever took a vacation, I would be in trouble because I talk to Him all the time. Many times in my life, especially in my adult life, I have found myself in situations where I have had to say, 'Okay, God, you are going to have to get me through this,' and He always does.

"I have been through periods of doubt, even anger at God, but it is through this doubt that my faith in God is strengthened, and I know He is quite capable of handling my doubt and anger. As much as I love God, His watch and His calendar are rarely the same as mine. It is when I try to do things in my own time frame, without regard to His, that He lovingly brings me to my knees to wait for Him, much as a lion swats at his cubs when they get a little carried away with their own importance.

"Without God's love, His very real presence, I do not believe I could have survived my childhood as I can now see it. I feel a very strong debt to God and the positive influences He sent into my life. This is a debt I can only begin to pay back by sharing whatever I have with others. Sometimes, when I forget that this is to be done for His glory, not mine, He gets my attention.

"I cannot imagine being strong enough to survive in this world without a sense of God. I know that I could not. Without God's guidance and direction, I would be lost and only marking time in life, only surviving, not living!

"In many ways, God was all I knew as true, safe love. As my healing continued I learned the joy of receiving safe love from other people, and this safe love is God-based. Because healing has necessitated the returning to my childhood, I don't think I would have had the courage to do this without God right beside me. I have no doubt in my mind that He chose my therapist(s) because of their commitment to Him, just as I also know He continues to direct my growth process. My healing work in therapy has been the most demanding task I have ever undertaken. For me, my surviving and healing from the past would not have been possible without a strong faith in God."

Tiffany

"I don't know how I knew to be connected to God. I just knew it was important, very important. I attended church. Sometimes I attended with my family, but most of the time I attended without them. My family would give me rides, but they were too busy to go themselves. I am grateful that they valued church enough to take me every week.

"I didn't go to Sunday school because I felt what they were studying was dumb. I can remember going once and deciding I got more out of sitting in church than being in Sunday school. Being in church was a powerful experience for me. When I went into church, I usually felt beaten, demoralized, stupid, and like I was a bad person. As I sat there and took in the service with its prayers, singing, and nurturing atmosphere, I would begin to feel close and nurtured by God. I prayed intensely and deeply about my life, my loneliness, my problems, and anything else I needed to talk to God about. I also prayed about my badness. As the service continued, my mood would shift, and I would feel lighter, like a good person, and happier. I felt I could go on again.

"After attending church, the week then went better for me because I had this intense, uplifting, nurturing experience. I felt God loved me, and that was all that mattered. Also, I attended church with a good friend. Her family never went, so we became buddies in the process of surviving by attending church together. We both knew that we needed it, didn't really understand why or how it helped, but knew we had to be there. We were both still very lonely, but not alone in our loneliness.

"As an adult, in the healing and growth process, my relationship with God was my stabilizing, nurturing, sustaining core. It enabled me to get through the pain, turmoil, struggles, confusion, and deep grieving. My relationship with God also guided me to all the steps of my process. Without it, I would have been lost and unsure of the direction I was going and too terrified to do the feeling work I had to do.

"During the worst part of the healing, the intense grieving, I could feel God supporting and loving me. With this knowing, I never felt alone; I knew I would not only feel better but I would also become more of the real me. Without God I would have had a much more difficult time. One of the best things I have learned over the years is that I can express all my feelings and thoughts to God. I have been intensely angry at Him and have screamed and yelled at Him. After these times, I feel Him holding me, loving me, and sort of saying, 'Now, doesn't that feel better?' I have learned that what He wants from me is my love and my sharing with Him. It's the not talking to Him and not listening to him that really messes up the relationship.

"Again, I don't think I would have made it through childhood or the healing process without Him. I was still messed up emotionally and needed to do a lot of healing as an adult, but I found the ability to do it because of God's love for me."

Healing and Spirituality

For me, my spirituality has been the core of my healing and growing from past wounds. I have come from the slime pit with all its dysfunction, anger, and pain to amazing healing, growth, and joy. For example, previously my body would become ill when I wanted to retreat from my world. I now have a body that rarely gets sick. Healing, under God's guidance, is nothing short of amazing. I still battle in some areas, but I see those areas as opportunities for growth.

I believe the purpose in healing is to restore the original package, the authentic self. Our authentic self is like the kernel of a seed. Growing up in a dysfunctional family forces the kernel to create a hard outer covering to protect it from the world. These protective coverings in humans are the behaviors and patterns we develop to fend off painful experiences. Sadly, because of this, the behavior frequently becomes dysfunctional in adulthood.

Like maple seeds with their propellers, we are sent forward to have many life experiences. These experiences offer a chance for healing, learning, and growing. As we are propelled forward and experience life, we have a choice of shedding the hard exterior of the seed by healing or staying in old dysfunctional patterns. If we choose to heal, the wonderful kernel, the authentic self, is then exposed and free to be and develop into its uniqueness. Through healing, the authentic self becomes ready to meet the world openly without the tough outer protective covering. We then learn to be free and grow like the seed that produces new life—vulnerable, yet strong; open and alive, illuminating the truth.

This illumination is spiritual light. I believe that spiritual light always overcomes darkness. It gives joy where there is sorrow and happiness where there is pain. I believe that through the healing and growing journey, we are personally called on to develop our authentic self and reach out to others on their journeys. The process of healing means growth and learning not only for ourselves but also to help bring peace and love to our troubled world.

We get to this light by developing our spirituality. The process is one of healing deeper and deeper into the essence of our being, to our truth and integrity. This healing can occur in two ways: (1) we begin to heal from our emotional hurts and then develop our relationship with our spirituality, or (2) we unite with our spirituality and then heal. Either way, it leads us to healing, growth, and a spirituality that sustains us through life.

I believe that our spirituality guides us to live our lives in integrity—the truth of our essence, our original package.

Integrity is being, speaking, and living our truth. We are
challenged to develop ourselves to the fullest extent possible. As we venture forth and grow, we can then reach out
to others. Our responsibility is to work to heal, grow, and
accept ourselves and others in the fullest way possible. We
can send God's light and love by helping, sharing, supporting, setting an example, but not by being totally responsible for others' feelings and lives. Healing, growing, living
in the light helps us continue this unique journey throughout our lives.

Each one of us is loved deeply from the core of our spirituality. Always have been and always will be. No one ever
walks this life alone. God is always there helping, touching, connecting, and healing. Often obstacles in our lives
can be used to help us grow if we choose. These obstacles
can toughen, teach, develop, and encourage us to be
everything we authentically are. Often, I have heard transcenders say, "Who would I be if I hadn't gone through my
childhood? It helped create me. It's part of me."

My healing has given me a wisdom and compassion, an
ability to say, "I know what it's like; I have been there." I
have been where the pain is—the deep sorrow. I can tell
you of its darkness and torment. I can tell you of growth
and of the joy that follows. I can say in truth that healing is
life enriching and is the difference between surviving and
living. Let nothing stand in your way of healing. Nothing!

Anger at God

Being angry at God is part of the healing process. This
anger needs to be acknowledged and worked through.
God can handle our anger. Our anger at God is often expressed by blaming Him for what happened to us. I've
heard it from many clients many times over the years. It
sounds like this: "Why did He allow it? Why didn't He stop

it? How could He do that to me?" Eventually, the anger is released, and a new peace is found. The transcender usually comes to a place of knowing that other people made poor and violent choices. Staying stuck in this anger is not a way toward growth. Working through the angry feelings, learning from the pain and growing from our experiences, however, does lead to growth.

Personal Purpose

I believe that each of us has a purpose to which we must commit in our world. Finding this purpose is an important part of the healing and growing process. It is of ultimate importance because it coordinates with others working together to heal our communities and our world. If we reject this purpose or fail to accomplish it, we have one less healthy, helping person in the world. This means our ripples will be lost. Also, when we fail to work toward all we are capable of being, we lose an important part of ourselves that can lead to unhappiness, discontent, and discouragement. I do not believe that we can be fully content, happy, or productive until we are working to accomplish our personal purpose in life.

I believe that the core of everyone's mission is to support and love each other through our shared humanness. We all need support in our struggle to be authentic as well as in our struggle to love and be loved. Because we are human, we share and know this experience with all its turmoil, pain, and joy. We can also identify with each other's spiritual struggles. We need to encourage each other and work together to accomplish our work. This is true regardless of our career or lifestyle choice. I believe that we need to commit ourselves to continue to keep loving, healing, caring, growing, and accomplishing. This is vital in order to stop the darkness of abuse, neglect, and dysfunction in our world.

Development of Spirituality

Spirituality can be explored and developed by praying, reading, meditating, talking with others, and participating, as well as learning. The only objective is the development of a relationship between us and God with integrity and honesty. Development of this relationship, like growth, takes a lifetime. As our spirituality develops, we gain deeper strength, freedom, and understanding.

The earlier spirituality is developed, the greater its strength during the healing and growing process. Some individuals have developed their spirituality from early childhood. Others need to start their explorations from scratch as adults. Either way, it's a vital power for living.

In your explorations, if you find yourself in a spiritual group feeling stifled, controlled, abused, and/or frustrated, you are probably in the wrong place. God is love. Keep looking, and trust your spirituality to help guide you to the right place.

Some transcenders have problems dealing with organized religion because they have had rough, abusive, and/or painful experiences with their religious upbringing. Individuals raised in these types of religions often experience intense fear and guilt just at the thought of exploring their spirituality. They do not understand that God is much more about unconditional love than He is about punishment and judgment. Spirituality is the relationship with God, not an organization.

Spiritual exploration does not necessarily mean throwing childhood religion out the window; it does mean exploring, evaluating, and figuring out what *you* believe as opposed to the beliefs of others. Some people embrace their childhood religion; others leave it and discover a different way for themselves.

In exploring spirituality, there is one *major* word of caution. Be alert for *satanic-based cults.* These cults that worship Satan are very real in our world. As Marie has testified, they are dangerous and severcly abusive. They may even kill. There are also many cults that are not abusive in this manner but would have us believe their way is the only way and that we will be "damned" if we don't believe exactly their way. I personally don't believe this. I do believe that God deeply loves us and is committed to helping us to heal and develop our original package.

Summary

In closing this chapter, I leave you with these thoughts: spirituality is love—acceptance of self and others in the world. Spirituality is our human essence, our realness, our truth. Because of our spirituality, we are never alone. God's love is for everyone in the world, and He offers it in many ways so that the world, as well as its individuals, are healed and fulfilled. God wants us to heal, grow, and become all that we are created to be!

CHAPTER 10

Where Are They Now?

Transcenders work long and hard to create the world of their dreams. Do they succeed? What are their lives like in adulthood after healing? Are there benefits to transcending? In general, their lives are wonderful in many respects, but they don't have fairy tale endings. Life is life and often hard and painful. These transcenders related having gained special insight and wisdom from their lives, even though some of them would trade these painful experiences for healthy, loving parents. Often their present lives, compared to their pasts, look like Utopia. In this chapter, five previously mentioned transcenders share about their present lives and what they have gained from becoming transcenders.

Marie

"Looking back at all those painful, horrible times, I can't believe I have such peace and joy today. I always believed in the existence of the light at the end of the tunnel but had no way of knowing how bright that light could be! I see my recovery as a daily process and one that I continue to work though.

"Do I feel successful? Yes! I am continuing to heal, feel, and grow with the help of newly learned ways of working with myself. I am proud of what I have been able to accomplish. I am not proud of the things that happened in my past, but for the most part, these things are over. I see now that I had no control over them and am not responsible for them. I am neither the abuse nor the abuser. I was the victim and have now chosen to be a transcender. I have worked hard to survive.

"Until recently, the past ten years of my life have been very physically painful. Numerous surgeries, including a bowel resection and colostomy, did not alleviate the pain of inflammatory bowel disease. It was as if each painful memory was stored inside, still producing pain, with the cause unknown to me. For years I was given injections of Demerol and morphine to help control the pain. Looking back, it's no wonder that the medication was of little help. The pain was the result of an infection known as abuse. To date, no medication has been found to be successful in dealing with that type of pain.

"Before, any feeling I refused to acknowledge was immediately turned inward and converted to physical pain. Now, after more healing, I have learned to own and feel my feelings and express my emotions rather than swallow them. The frequency and intensity of physical pain is much less than in the past. I am still capable of inflicting pain on myself but choose not to! Besides, I don't feel now as if I need to be punished, as I once did. I know I'm not to blame for everything negative.

"One of the sad things about growing up in a family where you learn to insulate yourself in order to survive is that, in trying to protect yourself from the bad things, you also keep out the good. I realize now that there were people outside of my family, especially from my teen years and beyond, who loved and cared about me. However, because of my background and a well-learned distrust of people, I was unable to take in what these people offered me. The door of fear that protected me was locked on both sides, but I held the key to this door within me. Now, I have unlocked the door and know there are people who really do care about me and love me. This is an important discovery, and one I am thoroughly enjoying.

"I have always enjoyed working with people. I love to teach, and my years as an educator have been very meaningful to me. I am particularly skilled in helping others deal with their fears. My own personal background of having to deal with my own terror has provided excellent training not taught in any graduate school.

"One of my joys in life is being able to provide for others the emotional support that I did not have myself. Whether teaching preschool or community college, guiding my students in labeling and appropriately expressing emotions is a high priority with me. Yet, I was over fifty years old when I internalized, for the first time, the idea that anger was a normal healthy emotion.

"Another joy in my life is giving and doing things for others. I am sensitive to the needs of other people—an outgrowth of the need to read others around me in order to survive. It has taken me longer to learn how to get my own needs met, but I am learning how to receive from others. Recently, a group of newfound friends surprised me with my very first birthday party, complete with balloons and cake. I loved it. It feels so good to be cared about.

"Because I have walked in the black darkness of evil, the light of freedom shines even brighter for me. I am free to be myself. I am no longer terrified of beds as I was for so many years, and am now, at times, able to sleep six hours a night. Before completing the healing process, I rarely slept more than two or three hours. I no longer live in fear, waiting for that bad man to find me. Instead, I laugh with friends I have grown to trust and love—friends who know me and accept me for who I am. I see freedom from my growing up as a special gift!

"I see transcenders as very determined souls. My determination has sustained me in the past and continues to provide me with the perseverance necessary to reach toward future goals. I know I can do it, whatever the 'it' is. From very early childhood, I was exposed to circumstances that engraved on my soul the challenge that I would not be like my mother. I have kept that promise to myself. I know I am nothing like the evil, negative person she was, but I do have some of her mannerisms and talents, something I can now acknowledge without feeling as if I'm a 'bad person' because of the genetic similarities.

"My love for nature has also come from my childhood trials. I am very close to nature because nature provided many lessons. A walk through the woods, a sunrise, even the lightning during a storm were my teachers. This ability to look for guidance in the symbolism of my world still continues to nurture and sustain me.

"Another gift surviving has given me is God, or maybe it's the other way around! God has had a very important influence throughout my life. He was/is the only true security I really knew. Very early, I decided that God must think that I was able to handle whatever I had to deal with and that He expected me to turn stumbling blocks into stepping-stones. Many times I would pray, "God, please help me deal with this; show me what I should do,' and without fail, God would make His presence known.

"I have been asked if I was ever angry with God for allowing the abuse to take place. I don't believe He allowed the abuse as much as He expected me to learn from it. Because of this expectation, I understand the whys behind adults who are abused as children and become abusers themselves, and this area is the key to the direction that God is guiding my life in the present and future. There has to be some reason, some purpose for the torture I endured. I have a responsibility to use the knowledge and the experiences from my own life in a way that will help others who may have experienced similar trauma.

"I am now taking the required coursework for admission to graduate school. Within the next two years I will begin my work as a psychotherapist. I will be very surprised if God does not lead me to a position in which I will be working with transcenders—a responsibility for which He has been preparing me for many years. I am grateful that I have gained so much in my life. I want to share what I have gained with others, not as a victim of my abuse, but as a conqueror of it."

Note: Marie did obtain her MA degree and became a psychologist. She has worked many years helping people not only to survive but also to heal from the agony of dysfunctional families.

Chris

"My life is just like I pictured it as a child. I have a family who loves me and I love them. We don't scapegoat each other and never blame each other for anything. We work it out. We work at communication and changing the old dysfunctional patterns which sometimes surface to healthier ways of relating. The love I have is so wonderful. There are times when I can't believe it's really mine. When I do get upset and have an old-type day or what I call a dysfunctional day, I handle it. I try to work through it and learn from it. In this way I gain.

"I feel so free, so free to be just me. I'm not carrying my family's guilt, shame, and blame anymore. It's not mine. They still try to get me to take it, but I refuse. I don't even let it go inside me, because it's not mine and never was. I never thought I could say that and mean it. Wow! I'm really the real me. I am lovable, creative, intelligent, energized, and happy. I like my job, my family, my life. If I ever come to a place of not liking part of my life, I know I have the ability to change it. If there were problems with my children or with my wife, I know we'd just work on them and work them out.

"Yes, I feel successful and happy. Yes, I have bad days, down days, but they don't last. I see them as part of life, not as my life, as I once did in childhood and early adulthood. Life still holds many obstacles for me. My father is critically ill, and I'm having to face all those feelings. I hate the idea that he is still blaming me for everything, even his illness. But I know it's not my stuff. You'd think he'd give up or change now that he is facing death. He'll never stop. There is part of me that still wishes and hopes he'll change so I can have at least one serious, loving conversation. I'd love to be able to talk about the past and try to heal the relationship. It would feel so good to settle all of that before he dies. I know it's a dream. I do feel sorry for him, yet not really. I do feel bad that he is in so much pain; yet he's caused so much pain. He has created his own world. One minute I cry, the next I get angry at him, and the next I pity him. I accept the way he is doing his life, but I don't like it. It's his life and his choices, but I wish they were different.

"I have gained from my childhood even though I wish it had been different. I wish I had had caring parents but have come to accept the fact that I didn't and still don't. I also realize I have gained from my growing up in ways I would not have if I had a normal childhood.

"I think the biggest gain for me is the wisdom and understanding I now have as an adult. I better understand not only me but also other people and the world. My past has helped me see that our world is made up of hurting people who need to be understood and loved. Many times I can offer something to someone who looks like he or she feels the same way I used to feel because I've been there. I think I'm more patient, gentler, and kinder because of where I have been.

"It's a good feeling to know I can handle all sorts of things and continue to learn and grow. I don't feel helpless anymore. I am confident and love my life."

Steve

"My life is now more stable, less painful, and more fulfilling than my childhood. I never go hungry. I can't say it's always wonderful. It's not. I still have my struggles. I have two children and have a hard time balancing my work, family, and growth commitment to myself.

"I had an accident recently that disabled me and triggered old emotional stuff dealing with the fear of having to go back to the old way of living. Just the thought of it terrifies me. I put myself back in therapy to work on some of the fear to help me adjust to the disability. I'm dealing with its effects in my life and the losses it has caused. I'm slower and emotionally stressed. The disability has affected my whole life. I just can't do everything I've set out to do, at least not yet. I'm still working and still hoping.

"I'm trying to work with the disability and adjust to it by rearranging my work and family schedules. I need more rest now, and it's hard to get it. Sometimes my wife becomes upset with me and I feel like I'm going backward; that I'll have to go back to that awful poverty again. I dread that so much. I just can't ever do that again, ever! Therapy is helping, but I still have the disability to deal with and the issues it's triggering from childhood.

"Do I feel successful? Up until the accident, I could have said I felt very successful. Everything was going fine. My wife and I had no major struggles, and I really enjoyed being with my children. We worked out the issues that came up and communicated well. We just handled it all. Now, since the accident, there are stresses and struggles. We are still working to communicate and deal with them; it's just harder. I'm not sure anymore if I feel successful. Some days I know I am doing well and recovering. Other days I feel set back and very disappointed. I keep trying, though. I won't give up. Giving up means going back to the old stuff, and I'll never do that.

"Did I gain from my survivorship? Yes and no. I hated the pain, the hunger, the cold, the neglect, the dysfunction, and the struggle to be me. I wouldn't wish my growing-up and healing process on anyone. But, yes, I did gain. I learned things I would never have learned any other way.

I'm not saying I would want to grow up the way I did. I'm just saying it did teach me some valuable lessons. It's not all a waste.

"I have gained strength, a knowing that I can handle many difficult situations. I don't think I would have known what I could handle and live through if I had had nice, wonderful parents. I also gained a deep understanding and knowing of me. Having to heal from my childhood forced me to learn about me. That in itself is a wonderful gift. From learning about me, I gained an understanding and knowing of others and of humanity in general. I wouldn't wish my parents on anyone. Yet I wouldn't want to give up my growth either."

Paul

"The fighting, criticism, chaos, and all the pain is all that I remember from childhood. Now, I refuse to allow any of that in my house. I don't allow unfair fighting or name-calling in my home. I make sure I praise and encourage friends, acquaintances, and relatives. I will never live that way again or allow anyone I care about to live that way.

"Maybe that's why I seem to be a doer, an accomplisher. Some people call me an overachiever. I call me a motivated, caring person. I'm involved in local and state organizations that work to help children in abusive families. I'm especially interested in helping the parents change. I'm just driven to do something more than just living an average life.

"I get anxious if I'm not being productive. By productive I mean accomplishing something that makes a difference. I'm saying I need to give and help. Thank goodness I have learned to take care of myself and not to overextend my energies, but the giving is a very important part of my transcendership.

"My friends understand this drive in me. They see that it makes a difference. They see that things change. That is one of the things I learned from childhood and the healing process—that I can change things. I learned I don't ever have to live that way again, and if I can change, so can others. For example, a recent career change caught me off guard and sent me back to some old stuff. I know from past experience that I have to feel it and learn from it. I did, and I know my direction again.

"Some people call me a crazy optimist. I call me a hard worker who believes in the ability of people to heal and change if given the chance. The hardest part for me is working with people who do not want to change. That's the discouraging part. The neat part is that a lot of people do want to change, and it's a tremendous high for me to be part of the change.

"Do I feel successful? You bet! If I stopped feeling successful, I'd figure out what is going on and then change something. I will never be stuck again. I have learned too much about me to ever let that happen again. I have dear friends who love me and who I love. I'm healthy, happy, and alive. I will never again accept dysfunction as part of my life."

Tiffany

"I would describe my life as just the way I want it. I have my family, friends, a new semihealed relationship with my parents, and love everywhere. The best part of my life is knowing that if I don't like a part of it or have a clash with someone, I have the power to change it. I can create what I need. This doesn't mean leaving my family or destroying someone else. It means being in charge of my life and having the power to work with important people in my life to make changes that feel good to everyone.

"I am no longer the victim. I'm no longer the trapped, helpless little girl who could do nothing to change her world. I really like me, my world, my career, and my family. The problems I have are like every other working mother's problems. I have a difficult time balancing the different aspects of my life with the available time in the day. I get torn between my needs, the family's needs, and career demands. But I wouldn't trade it. I'm challenged, loved, and happy.

"I have regrets. I wish I had gotten into therapy sooner. That way, I would have felt better sooner. But, I'm so glad I didn't wait any longer. I pray my children are not too affected by my struggles, especially my anger. I used to really want to hurt with my anger. I'm so grateful I'm healed.

"I still have rough days, when I feel I have regressed. I work with my feelings and learn from them. Usually, the rough days are caused by not having the time to feel the feeling or wanting to avoid them. Once I work with it, I feel better, learn from it, and get on with my life. Actually, the rough days are part of my living cycle: feeling, learning, and using the growth I have gained.

"I have learned many things from growing up in my family. I would trade the pain I went through any day for loving, normal parents and brothers. I didn't have them, but it wasn't all a waste either.

"The biggest part is knowing I can live through anything. It's a strength I don't think I would have if I hadn't been subject to all those trials—severe ridicule, criticism, emotional neglect, and not having anyone there to guide and help me figure life out. I lived through long never-ending loneliness, when I worked just to get through the minutes, let alone the hours, days, months and years. My isolation, in turn, has given me a special relationship with myself and a knowing that I can survive.

"There are very few situations in my life that I wouldn't be able to handle somehow. Now, my main decision is to find out what I do want to handle. I have the strength. I'm in charge, and with God's help I decide what goes and what doesn't. There is a new working together with others. I have surrounded myself with individuals who care and listen, many who also have had dysfunctional family

backgrounds. These are people who have chosen to heal and with whom I share a deep understanding.

"This strength I have is wonderful and constantly reassures me. It's ever there, ever constant, telling me that no matter what happens, I will make it.

"Most important is my relationship with God. I know He is there for me in every situation. I have often wondered if I would have turned to Him as much as I did if I hadn't grown up in my family. My spirituality is a prized possession and is part of my knowing that I can handle everything with God's help. God gives me love, guidance, and joy beyond description. He loves me.

"My growing up and my healing process have taught me what I would venture to call wisdom. It is an understanding of myself, others, God, and the world. It's a sense of how we all fit. I have a truth about the world and about myself. This doesn't mean I have all the answers. I'm far from that. I do have the answers for me as I need them. If I don't know, I know how to find them."

Summary

In summary, transcenders overcome, heal and gain from their process. Life is not a fairy tale, and struggles continue. The difference is that after healing and growing they have themselves, their realness, and their authentic self to work to create a healthy life.

CHAPTER 11

Using Transcenders' Information

Our world is close-knit. How often have things happened that made you say, "What a small world it is?" When one person moves, the next person feels it. When one nation makes a decision, another nation across the ocean may feel the consequences. Individuals, as well as nations, must make healthy decisions to help change our hurting world into a peaceful, agape loving one. The material in this book can be used in many ways to help individuals and, in turn, our world. To close this book, I offer some of those ways.

As individuals, we must heal and continue to grow in order to heal our world and maximize its potentiality. It is no longer an option or luxury. Individual healing and growing are necessary to create a healthy world. It is only in this way that we will gain a lasting, loving peace. Just think for a minute of the problems we could solve if we all developed our abilities and spirituality and worked with each other through acceptance rather than judgment.

Collectively, we have the potential to care, love, nurture, shelter, and feed all people that inhabit the earth in a way so *everyone* wins. This cannot be done by governments, laws, or regulations. It must be done by individuals. Each individual must heal, grow, and give love back in many forms. At the moment, we have too many individuals and nations who believe in taking what they want by way of robberies, murders, unfair trade, major debts, game-playing, and terrorism.

I believe that as human beings, we need to care and take our share of the responsibility for helping create the love and peace we so often talk about in our world. This means helping all mankind—people we like as well as people we don't. Let's care enough to start a chain of healing and growing that eventually could encompass our community, nation, and universe. It starts with each one of us.

I believe the healing and growing process as documented in this book can help. The essence of transcending, whether from a dysfunctional family or as a prisoner of war, may be universal. It may be the way to overcome all obstacles in our lives. The process can be and has been taught to adults and children. Individuals with whom I have had the privilege of working have given me a chance to see the process at work in almost every circumstance: family, relationships, and workplace.

Our society has become more willing to give back to the world. The generation that grew up in the sixties has been termed the "me" generation. The "me" time has been an important growth time in our history. We took the time to learn about the Being called a human. This exploration helped us find authentic individuals with abilities, feelings, and potentialities. It has been called selfish and, yes, it is to some extent. However, as in individual healing and growing, our society needed to discover and develop itself. Without the "me" time, we can't fully know the true "we" time. Without the me time, there is nothing to give to others. I believe the me generation has served a purpose in helping us focus on ourselves and develop a sense of me and the abilities we can contribute to the world. Now, however, it is time for us to unite as human beings on this earth and contribute our part without losing our individual authenticity. It's time for each of us to say, "I can and will make a difference in the world."

This helping is not a codependency type of help in which I give all and don't take care of myself. We must still take care of ourselves while giving to others. Caring can be big or little and shouldn't occur only when we feel like it. An example of this caring happened this morning when I was swimming at a nearby health club. My swim time is my "selfish time." I usually go into a state of isolation as I do my laps. If I could, I would put a sign on me that says, "Do *not* disturb or enter my lane." With an exception of a few smiles, I rarely talk to anyone. To share even a "Good morning" seems like an intrusion and too much.

This morning, as I was swimming in "my" lane, I realized I was sending out more than my usual leave-me-alone signals. I was also sending out an anger attitude. I decided I was just in one of those moods and needed to do my laps and go to work so I hurried up my pace. Something, though, drew my attention to the woman swimming next to me. She seemed down and lonely. I smiled and said, "Good morning." As we swam and took some rest breaks, we chatted a little. By the end of our swim, both of us felt better. In addition, I felt an uplifting energy from our contact. It didn't take from my time; it added to my life.

It's this kind of contact I am talking about. If we can give of ourselves and others in healthy, loving ways, we all gain. We can do this in many ways: by running an errand for someone, taking time to listen, taking a child for a day so an exhausted parent can get some rest, etc.

Specific Ways to Use the Transcending Process

The following are specific ways the healing and growing process can be used in our world. I'm sure there are other ways, and I would love to hear about them from you. Here are my thoughts.

1. *Help children who are in dysfunctional families.*
   Throughout our world, we have *many* children growing up in dysfunctional families. Each of us can and

needs to take some responsibility for helping them grow up with love. At present, we have many social organizations: foster care, protective services, mental health programs, school counselors, mental health clinics, ministers, rehabilitation programs, juvenile homes, and special education. What we need is more individual personal involvement. We need each individual to be loving and caring enough to personally do something, even if it is only saying "hi" with a smile. This is how we will stop dysfunction and create healthier individuals and societies.

Individuals such as neighbors, relatives, friends, ministers, teachers, and others can offer a great service. I believe each of us needs to notice a child that is hurting and do something—anything. It doesn't take much. It can be a small or large giving, depending on your relationship with them. Here are some ways:

- Teach them the survival techniques described by transcenders.
- Above all else, take time and listen.
- Give a special compliment, send a card.
- Create a special time doing anything that is fun, such as going to the movies or a playground.
- Report suspected abuse and neglect to the authorities in your county, help stop it.
- Meet and support the parents, because they too may have had a difficult past; they are sometimes the previous generation's abused children. Let them know you want to help them, not judge them.
- Be there for the children in any way that offers acceptance.
- If you have a dysfunctional past, share it and how you transcended; get into therapy if you haven't; this sends out healing ripples to a hurting world. This is supportive and encouraging for everyone.
- Keep telling the children they can make it.

- Help others make it by giving of your time, energy, and/or money.
- Help without judgment, criticism, or ridicule; each of us has our own specific way of healing that is right for us, but may not be right for others.
- Offer a sanctuary or shelter during rough times or just to come "hang out."
- Be patient and loving.
- Be friendly and speak to the child using his/her name.

If you are a therapist and working with a child from a dysfunctional family, I offer these suggestions:

- Work with acceptance. Above all, the child needs love and may even experience it appropriately and safely from you for the first time. Helping children feel love is done by genuinely accepting them in session no matter how "unlovable" they appear.
- Help the child understand that he or she has choices in life and that these choices have consequences.
- Help the child know that he or she can create another kind of life in the future.
- Offer tons of support and encouragement.
- Listen.
- Teach survival transcending techniques.

2. *Teach healing, growing, and transcending.* I believe strongly that these can be taught to individuals of all ages. Teachers, ministers, counselors, and others can all offer help. Individuals can be helped to make a turning-point decision. For example, one teenager I was working with became very upset because her birth parents would not release her to be adopted by her foster parents, whom she loved and who wanted to adopt her. Her family situation was abusive, and she had been taken out of the family years before.

When her birth parents refused their permission for her adoption, she became extremely upset and began acting out. I gently, but firmly, informed her that she had only three more years to put up with the family (she was 15) and then she could do anything she wanted to, including being adopted by anyone of her choice. When she understood this, her face brightened and with support was able to transcend the situation through the remaining years.

3. *Heal from your dysfunctional past.* Just one person who is healing touches many other lives. There are ripple effects similar to when a stone is thrown into the water and creates many ripples. The ripples are incredible to watch because we never, ever, really know where they will go or who they will touch. It's a wonderful feeling just knowing you had something to do with helping another person heal, especially by your example.

4. *Grow as an individual and give your specialness to the world.* It may be a smile, helping hand, listening ear, talent, or an object you create. My dear friend is a good example of a person who gives of her specialness. She has a way of letting you know that you can learn, grow, and are okay. I don't think she ever has given up on anyone. When I have a problem, she works hard with me to figure it out. This kind of support has kept me going when I have become discouraged. Another wonderful lady in my life is a dear friend who, at a moment's notice, will drive my teenagers to their destinations when I am unable to do so. Our ripples are enormous because they are combined with many others' ripples, all working together. Their ripples affect me, which affects others. Often we do not know who our ripples may touch. What is your specialness? Give it to our world!

5. *Choose to love.* Love is a commitment to care and to grow. I believe it is a commitment to looking for and

focusing on the good in ourselves, others, and our world. Love is a *choice,* an action, not a feeling, but a caring. I can love others in many ways. I can love our world.

6. *Work to gain appropriate acceptance and forgiveness in your life.* This frees you as well as others. Again, forgiveness has an *incredible* ripple effect.

7. *Help others to make the decision to become transcenders.* It is never too early or too late to make the decision. Eighty-year-olds have done it, and so have children. Many individuals need to see that there is a choice, a hope, and a way of creating a different world. Not only can we teach survival techniques, we can also help individuals create and make turning-point decisions.

8. *Help transcenders realize what they have accomplished and what a wonderful contribution they are to our world.* Because of their healing, there is one less dysfunctional person in our world. In turn, their children will grow up healthier and not abused or neglected. This adds one more healthy family to contribute to the world. Through the generations, who knows how many ripples there could be!

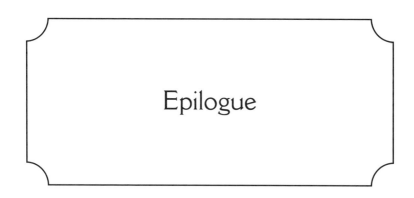

Epilogue

I have experienced much joy watching and being a part of others' healing and growing. What I see is a gaining of incredible strength and wisdom that could be gained in no other way. There is a depth to those who have taken the time to heal and continue to grow. They gain an understanding of themselves and the world. There is also a deep sensitivity within this understanding, a deep compassion not only for themselves but also for others. Such people enable us to battle the disease of dysfunction that ravages the body and soul. It is destroying our world and each of us *must* work to stop it.

Transcenders provide the world with hope for the future, hope that no matter what the circumstance, life—full authentic life—can prevail. After childhood, they live a life with all its elements: feeling, growing, working, healing, thinking, behaving, and loving.

Their journey involves pain, loneliness, and disappointment, as well as happiness, joy, and love. The journey demands from the transcender a decision for life or death. Transcenders decide for life—life with all its challenges, heartbreak, and joy. A life full of the courage to be!

To the transcender:

May you always be—
Strong of will
Strong with courage
Strong in heart.

—Donna LaMar

RESOURCE SECTION 1

Therapy and Finding a Therapist

I am writing this resource section as if you, my reader, are a close friend for whom I wish the very best. Much of this information is basic and well known to therapists and clients who have already been through therapy, but not necessarily to the general public. My purpose is to clear up some of the confusion and misunderstandings about the mental health field.

Psychotherapy, therapy that focuses on the mental health of individuals, sometimes called counseling, is one of the major tools used in the process of healing and growing. For simplicity I will call it therapy. Therapy facilitates knowing and understanding yourself at a deep level. I strongly believe therapy is essential for most people in creating a healthy life if you have grown up in a dysfunctional family. Its strength is that a trained mental health professional gives you an objective outside view of yourself, your family, and your role in the family. This point of view offers a new perspective as well as knowledge and insight into dysfunctional families, specifically yours. It also offers an understanding of how you function and about human existence, that is, the science of humanity.

More important, my purpose is also to help you find an effective therapist. *Effective* means the kind of therapist and therapy you need at your particular stage of healing and growing. As you heal and grow, the type of therapy and techniques, as well as the therapists you may need, will probably change because you change. I have found that rarely is one therapist (throughout the process) or one type of therapy enough; I personally encourage my clients to become involved in different types of therapy techniques such as group, body process work, etc., while working with me.

One therapist, therapy, or technique is not enough because healing requires different things at different times; however, it is *not* advised that you work in individual therapy with two therapists at the same time. You may find one therapist who is able to facilitate your healing all the way through, but don't be disappointed if this doesn't happen. Therapists can be "outgrown." Over time I personally have had three official therapists and countless other therapists through friends, groups, seminars, and workshops. I have grown and learned with each of them and am indebted to all of them.

Outgrowing a therapist, therapy, or technique is *not* regression—it's just that growth occurs! An important note about therapy: when you feel you are outgrowing a therapist, it is important to bring closure, that is, talk about the work you have done with the therapist and make sure you are not avoiding any issues. If you are, stay and work with that therapist. There is such a problem as "therapist hopping," which occurs when someone blames the therapist instead of dealing with his or her own issues. If you are not avoiding any issues and it is time to move on, try to leave on good terms. Some therapists are open to helping you find your next step in your process. Others are not.

I personally am greatly indebted to the therapists and mentors who were committed to helping me on my healing and growing journey. They have helped me establish a life that I long dreamed of—one without past hurts, painful emotions, and dysfunctional behavior. Most important, they assisted me in finding the authentic me. When I now have a difficult or dysfunctional day—and we all do at times—I know how to deal with it because others have helped me know, really know, myself. I realize now that those days are there to teach and offer me opportunities to heal, grow, and learn. Thus, I have learned how to deal with obstacles as part of the flow and continue the growth in my life.

The following sections answer basic questions about locating an effective therapist and handling the logistics of the process.

What Is Therapy?

The more I work in the mental health field, the less I know what therapy is. What I do know is that it is support that facilitates healing and growing. I know it is a process that helps you to face, get to know, and develop your authentic self. The therapeutic process helps you seek your truth, vision, integrity, and authenticity by helping to distinguish you from your family and significant others. Therapy is a way of being in a professional relationship with a specially trained person who will use techniques to enable the individual to heal and grow. It can be emotionally painful and also wonderfully joyous. It needs to be gentle and accepting. By gentle, I do not mean pain-free, but I do mean it should not be abusive to you in anyway. The abuse has already been done; you don't need more!

Therapy is a reparenting, an evolution of you. You face and heal from traumas you have experienced previously in life in order to find and learn all about you. It is a process that offers an opportunity to finally become what you have always wanted to be—the authentic you. The work is hard and requires a major commitment to yourself to develop the original package and learn new ways of being, but it is a joyful reuniting of you with you.

Therapy provides a safe, nurturing, nonjudgmental (without ridiculing or criticism), nonabusive environment where you can feel secure in exploring all aspects of you— even the parts you are afraid of or don't like. If a therapist is abusive or judgmental, it's a signal that you need to leave and find a healthier therapist immediately!

Today, therapy is no longer just for those who are considered mentally ill and have to be institutionalized or on strong medication for life. Today, most therapy occurs with "regular" people who want to heal and grow. Therapeutic techniques have also changed in recent decades from harsh interventions such as electroshock and insulin shock to techniques that are full of support and caring.

Finally, therapy needs to go at your pace, not the therapist's or the insurance company's. Please note: many insurance companies believe that short-term (ten to twenty sessions), goal-directed, behavioral therapy is the only effective therapy. This type of short-term therapy usually offers only symptom relief. For deep healing from a dysfunctional family, I believe long-term (two to three years) is needed. Remember, you were abused for many years. It takes time to heal. If you need a year or more to gain trust in your therapist, take it. If your process moves fast, go for it. If you alternate between slow and fast, that's fine. Whatever your pace, it is perfect for you, and you need to be supported at your rate, not the therapist's or the insurance company's.

What Are the Benefits of Therapy?

The following is a list of benefits experienced by individuals who have been in therapy:

- Decreasing emotional pain
- Increasing emotional well-being
- Increasing self-esteem
- Healing from traumas of the past
- Changing painful dysfunctional behaviors to healthy functioning ones
- Becoming your authentic self
- Developing your skills and potentialities
- Finding more happiness in life

- Creating healthier, more satisfying relationships
- Having more real friends and significant others
- Developing a true and healthy support system
- Finding more personal freedom, power, and success
- Feeling loved and being able to love
- Learning your process of healing and growing that lasts a lifetime
- Decreasing physical pain

Why Do You Need Therapy— Why Can't You Do It Yourself?

Therapy occurs in a relationship with a trained professional who is totally focused on you and your life. As stated before, this relationship is vital to you because it gives you an outside, professional perspective on what has happened in your life. Therapists are trained to help people heal from dysfunctional backgrounds. This individualized time is *your* time. It is not shared with a sibling, mother, father, or anyone else who has taken from you in your life unless you choose to have them attend. Most important, it's your time to be with you and learn about you.

In therapy, the therapist helps facilitate exploring all areas of your life. There will be lots of areas. Therapy is not like sharing and complaining with a friend who is willing to listen. It is a professional helping you explore, with meaning and purpose, what has happened to you in order to promote your healing and growth.

In this relationship, you get feedback based on who you are, not based on your parents' or siblings' opinions. When I am in sessions with clients, my focus is to understand how they feel, what has happened to them, and what they are all about. What is important is the client's world and perspective. It is only in the client's understanding of this perspective that healing and growing can occur. I need to know how the client's mom felt or what she needed *only* as these things affect my client.

The professional feedback in therapy helps you separate from your family and heal emotionally in a healthy, appropriate way. Once feelings are felt and understood, behavioral changes can occur more easily. For instance, one client was convinced that he was stuck forever with his extremely demanding family of origin. As he healed and grew, he came to *know* that he had choices. Once he saw he had choices, he was able to make changes.

Another reason for therapy is that we have often blocked or fused our feelings to such an extent we have to be taught how to feel. In other words, we may never have been taught to identify or feel our emotions. The people in this category often say, "Tell me what to feel and I'll feel it!" Teaching about feelings is something therapy does well. In the beginning, learning about your feelings can be frightening. A safe, supportive place to identify, explore, and feel your feelings is essential for healing.

Another thing therapy does is to aid you in knowing beyond a doubt that you are not only okay, but are the unique, special original package. You usually do not learn this growing up in a dysfunctional family. It is very important that you receive this feedback from another objective human being to affirm, support, and help you heal.

The therapeutic process also helps you uncover and know your needs and wants as an individual and, more important, you learn how to meet these needs appropriately. Finally, therapy helps you learn your natural process of healing and growing and knowing what your responsibilities really are. This knowledge lasts a lifetime.

When Do You Need Therapy?

When should you seek outside help? My general response is: "Does it hurt to be you? Does your world feel awful or painful? Are you feeling stuck, discouraged, anxious (fearful), or depressed? Do you have problems with relationships? Do you change jobs frequently?" If your answer is yes, seek help. The following is a detailed list of symptoms to help identify when therapy is needed by a child or an adult.

Do you feel:

- Confused about yourself and/or your world?
- Anxious and so afraid that it is painful or uncomfortable to be you?
- Guilty to the point where it interferes with your life on any level?
- Ashamed about yourself and/or your past?
- Angry so that the anger sabotages your life and hurts others?
- Numb or have few or no feelings?
- Sad about not living the way you have always dreamed of living and see little hope for change?
- Dislike or hatred for yourself?
- Constantly sad and depressed?
- Helpless in your life and world?
- Like a victim, as if everyone is out to get or hurt you?
- Lonely and isolated from everyone and everything?
- Detached from yourself and/or others?
- You have problems in relationships?
- Multiple marriages?
- You change jobs often? Move often?
- You feel you don't belong anywhere?
- Upset about going to school?
- You have few if any friends?

Do you:

- Have frequent, especially unexplained, physical complaints—headaches, backaches, ulcers, etc.
- Abuse yourself physically, emotionally, verbally, sexually, and/or neglect yourself in any way?

- Abuse others (children, and/or adults) physically, emotionally, verbally, sexually, and/or neglect others in any way?
- Abuse animals?
- Devalue yourself as your family did or does, putting yourself down, and thinking less of yourself than of others?
- Come from a childhood of abuse and/or neglect?
- Have few, if any, childhood memories?
- Have little trust in yourself and/or others?
- Block your creativity or don't believe you have any?
- Have any kind of addiction—work, alcohol, drugs, food, anger, sex, shopping, gambling, and so on?
- Have explosive or uncontrollable anger?
- Have difficulty with authority figures?
- Have continuous health problems?
- Have trouble sleeping or sleep too much?
- Avoid living in the present moment?
- Hate the past?
- Live constantly in the past?
- Have sexual dysfunction?
- Have a poor self-concept or low self-esteem?
- Have an eating disorder?
- Have memory gaps or time losses?
- Constantly wash your hands or behave compulsively in other ways?
- Have painful and difficult flashbacks from the past?
- Have suicidal thoughts or feelings?
- Care-take your friends and family to the exclusion of yourself?
- Have a fear of being crazy or insane?
- Have to create constant turmoil and chaos in your life?
- Constantly worry?
- Have multiple marriages or relationships?
- Make poor grades?

If you have any of these symptoms, or multiple symptoms (usually we have more than one or two) seek help. If you come from a dysfunctional family, seek help.

IF YOU ARE EXPERIENCING ANY OF THE FOLLOWING SYMPTOMS, SEEK HELP IMMEDIATELY:

- Suicidal thoughts, feelings, and/or plans
- Living in an abusive relationship
- Abusing others
- Abusing animals or something that's alive
- Abusing of yourself *in any way*
- Feeling out of control and "crazy"
- Times of raging anger
- Losing time

What Are the Different Types of Therapy?

There are many different types (modalities) of therapy: individual, couples, family, play, groups, and educational. Each modality can have special focuses, such as twelve-step, body-processing, structured, unstructured, relationship, spiritual, and peer. Each type may occur on either an outpatient or inpatient (residential) basis. When you are deciding on a modality and special focus, it is important to choose what you need for your stage of healing and growing. What may work for a friend may not be what you need. Sometimes the only way to find out is to educate yourself and try it. You may have to try different ones to make your decision. The following are brief descriptions of therapy modalities or focus.

Inpatient and Outpatient

Outpatient therapy. This refers to therapy that is done when the client lives somewhere outside of the site of the mental health facility. The client arrives for the appointment and then returns home. Outpatient therapy is done at community mental health clinics, private offices, clinics, and hospitals.

Inpatient or residential therapy. This occurs when the client stays at the mental health facility. Residential treatment provides individual, group, family, couple, educational, and milieu therapy. *Milieu therapy* is therapy that occurs at a residential facility during the entire stay which includes the surroundings and its activities from every moment of the day to help the client learn. Length of stay in the residential setting can be a few days or several months. In previous years, there were only inpatient programs for alcoholism, depression, and severe mental illness. Now, there are programs for codependency, eating disorders, reactive attachment, adult children of alcoholics, and many other areas. One of the benefits of residential treatment is that it provides a sanctuary from life and a time to focus on healing without the interference of outside stresses. This reprieve from the outside world often rekindles hope, relieves intense stress, and dramatically aids healing. It is always important after residential care to continue therapy in an outpatient setting with your own individual therapist.

Different Types of Therapy or Modalities

Individual therapy. This occurs when the individual meets face-to-face with a therapist and focuses on personal issues. The goal in individual therapy is to explore the past and present of the individual in order to gain healing and growth. This kind of therapy explores relationships from the client's perspective, not from that of the family or significant others, and without outside interference. Individual therapy for young children should occur in a playroom setting with a therapist specially trained in play therapy (see Play therapy on next page).

Couple therapy. This occurs when a couple meets face-to-face with a therapist. This type of work focuses on the relationship between the two individuals. Its intent is to heal the relationship and help the couple grow. Each person's perspective is important because of how it affects and pertains to the relationship. The past and present of each individual is explored, as needed, to help the couple heal and grow. Note: some therapists will not see a client in couple/marriage therapy if they are already seeing the couple in individual sessions. Some therapists will; it depends on the therapist and the couple.

Family therapy. This occurs when an entire family meets face-to-face with the therapist to explore interactions between family members. It is preferable to work with all members of the family. However, if all members can't attend, important work with those who do attend can still be accomplished. The goal of this therapy is to help the family unit heal and grow. Again, the past and present are explored along with each person's perspective, as needed, to create healthy relationships within the family.

Group therapy. This occurs when usually unrelated individuals meet face-to-face with a therapist. The goal of group therapy is to help individuals learn how to relate to others in healthy ways. Individuals in the group share life experiences, and this sharing encourages healing. Group therapy offers a chance to share at a supportive, safe, deep level while working on relationships. Clients get feedback from the therapist as well as from other group members. The goals of group and individual therapy work well together. Many individuals benefit by participating in both modalities at the same time.

Play therapy. This occurs when a child meets face-to-face with a specially trained child-play therapist in a playroom setting. The playroom is equipped with toys that have been especially selected for their therapeutic value. A child's work is his or her play. As the child plays, he or she works out emotional issues. Sharing with the therapist occurs at the same time. This type of therapy is extremely effective with children. Adults may also go into the playroom to work on issues and to learn to play.

Educational therapy. This occurs whenever individuals learn anything about themselves. This may be done through experiences such as reading, workshops, seminars, television, and radio.

Different Types of Groups

Many types of groups are available in today's therapy market. Again, as with therapists, you pick the one that best fits you and your needs at the time. The group you begin with may not be appropriate two years later. Groups, like therapists, can be outgrown as you get to know yourself and heal at a deeper level. This is not a failure to fit into the group but a positive statement about your growth as long as you are not avoiding any issues. Also, just as you check out any therapy, check how the group is run, as well as the therapist who runs it. If you are working to heal and grow, a professional should be used in any of the following groups.

Therapy groups. Therapy groups are run by mental health professionals and focus on healing and growing by having members of the group share experiences and interact with others. These groups also help individuals learn to develop healthier relationships. Therapy groups may have many special focuses. Fees for these groups are usually based on standard professional rates in the area.

Structured groups. These groups have a therapeutic process that follows set, predesignated steps. The steps have been developed to address a specific problem area. These groups usually have professional leadership.

Unstructured groups. These groups have a therapeutic process with few or no set steps, which allows the group to create its own direction under a professional.

Body-processing and bio-energetic groups. These groups use techniques that focus on releasing stored memories and feelings through the body. Since feelings are stored in the body, not the brain, this technique often works well. Two examples of techniques include releasing energy by beating a pillow with a racket and/or specific breathing techniques. Professionals run these groups.

Eco-psychology groups. Members of this type of group work with plants (horticulture), animals, and nature to assist in the client's healing and growing. These groups have a wider variety of techniques and activities. This may include nature walks, working with animals, or gardening, for example. The leader should be a trained professional, if therapy is the goal.

Spiritual groups. The focus of these groups is on members' relationship to their spirituality (God) and on their growth as spiritual beings. Among the types of groups offered are prayer, spiritual growth, and specific religious study groups. Both professionals and nonprofessionals run these groups.

The following are peer groups:

Peer/support groups. These groups are usually run by nonprofessionals. The members of the group share problems and help each other by offering support and encouragement. The leader(s) of the group offer only structure and not advice or therapy. These groups are usually free or require only a donation.

Twelve-step groups. These groups include a variety of focuses, but contain a common base in the original twelve recovery steps of Alcoholics Anonymous. They are designed to help individuals with addictions or families living with individuals who are addicted. Types of twelve-step programs include Alcoholics Anonymous, Al-Anon, Alateen, Alatot, Adult Children of Alcoholics (ACOA), Overeaters Anonymous, Codependents Anonymous (CoDA), Emotions Anonymous, Gamblers Anonymous, Love Anonymous (sexual addiction), and others that are being created on a regular basis. These groups are peer group organizations. Fees for these groups are donation only.

What Are the Steps to Starting Therapy?

Some individuals are anxious when they think about starting therapy for the first time. To help reduce your fear, please know that therapy, your therapy, is all about you. Also keep in mind that therapy is a process that helps you discover yourself. It does this by helping you to reduce pain, to heal, and to discover all your uniqueness. In addition, many therapists have been in therapy and know how difficult it is to make the first call. The receptionist at the therapist's office will also know it's a difficult call to make and will help you through it. It takes courage to make the first call to the first therapist, let alone walk in the door for the first appointment. If you are treated abusively or rudely when you call, find someone else.

Starting therapy is generally the same no matter where you go. First call the clinic to set up an appointment. A receptionist or an answering machine will usually answer and ask for background and insurance information. If you have the name of a specific therapist, ask for that therapist. If not, the receptionist will assign you a therapist usually based on the background information you shared with him or her. You may also ask for a therapist specifically trained in the area that you need, such as depression, substance abuse, healing and growing, or dysfunctional families. It is important to work with a therapist who has the training in the area you need. If you do not know what area you need to work in, don't worry. Just be honest with the reception-ist and therapist. The receptionist does not need a lot of de-tails about your life—just general information so he or she can help you get to the appropriate therapist.

During this initial telephone contact, it is appropriate to ask about office hours, fees, insurance eligibility, serv-ices provided, fees for missed appointments, and other questions you need to have answered.

After the initial call, the therapist may call you to set up an appointment, usually within twenty-four hours of your call, or the receptionist may make the appointment. If the receptionist sets up the appointment, ask to have the ther-apist call you beforehand if you want. This telephone con-tact with the therapist is your chance to ask other questions, such as how does the therapist work? Does he or she believe in the client's ability to find his or her own direction? Does the therapist see him or herself as the fa-cilitator or a director who makes all the decisions? Does he or she know the dysfunctional family area? If you are un-sure about the therapist after this call, ask for a fifteen minute interview. Most therapists will do this for free; some will charge a small fee. Please understand that most therapists cannot afford to give you an entire hour for an interview without charging. Therapists make their living by selling their time. More than fifteen free minutes is more than they can usually donate.

Once you are satisfied, or fairly satisfied, make or con-firm the appointment. You may still have anxieties about therapy. This is normal. Once the appointment is made, and it is usually set within a week of calling, think about other questions or things you want to share about yourself in that hour. Most therapy sessions last forty-five to fifty minutes. The last part of the hour is for the therapist to write notes required by insurance companies and states, make another appointment with you, and get a chance to get ready for the next client. Like everyone, therapists need breaks.

Okay, so now your first appointment has come. Plan to arrive twenty to thirty minutes early so that you can fill out all the required forms. These forms usually include a general personal history questionnaire of one to four pages; consent to treatment; consent to release of information *if* you need the therapist to share information about you with anyone else; insurance, financial arrangement sheet; confidentiality (yours); and any other policy and procedure forms needed by the clinic or the therapist. These forms vary, but usually cover the same basic information. You will usually fill these forms out in the waiting room.

After the forms are filled out, the therapist will come to the waiting room and take you to his or her office. Once "in session," ask any additional questions you have left about therapy, the forms, insurance, the therapist, procedures, techniques, and the therapy process. If the therapist resists answering your questions, be aware that he or she may not be very open in other areas either. You should be allowed to ask any questions you want about procedures and therapy. Questions about the therapist's personal life are generally not the subject for *your* therapy and most will not share this kind of information. However, there are therapists that do relate certain aspects about their lives *if they believe* it will help you in your therapy. For example, they might share what their healing and growing was like in order to help you understand the process better. Other therapists never talk about themselves. The choice depends on the therapist's orientation and personal preference. If the therapist spends all of your therapy time talking about his or her life and not yours, confront the therapist. You may have to find another one if this continues.

Confidentiality is extremely important and must be maintained at all times for you to build trust in the relationship. *Confidentiality* means that the therapist cannot, by law, share anything you share in session with anyone else unless your have a signed consent to release the information. This law ensures you a safe place to do your healing work. However, if you are suicidal or homicidal, the law requires the therapist to break confidentiality and take action immediately to keep everyone safe.

After all the initial questions are answered, the therapist will generally ask you, "What has brought you here?" or "What has been going on in your life that makes you seek therapy?" At this point, formal therapy begins.

In therapy, the primary technique is talking about you and your world. You will focus on your background, traumas, thoughts, feelings, relationships, behaviors, and anything else that is important to you. It is your chance to get to know all about the authentic you. If you choose not to share something important with your therapist, you are really choosing to keep a secret from yourself. This will delay your healing process. *Your* pace in therapy is just right for you. There is no right or wrong way to do therapy, just your way, as long as it is not abusive. What you are seeking in therapy is your special way of being with yourself, not someone else's. This special way helps our world have unique individuals in it and not clones.

Things that Should *NOT* Happen in Therapy

There are things that definitely should *not* happen in therapy:

- Abuse of any kind—physical, verbal, criticism, ridicule, sexual, and so on
- Sexual harassment of any nature—verbal, physical, criticism, ridicule, and so on

- Manipulations by therapists to use you for their needs—you are hiring them to help you.
- The therapist's being inattentive to you in sessions—sleeping, taking long telephone calls, and so on. A therapist occasionally may have to take an emergency call.
- Not feeling comfortable with or not trusting the therapist

The following are two warning signs about therapeutic techniques:

- Techniques that are abusive and/or painful need to be carefully examined. Techniques should help you feel your feelings, release pain, not cause more pain.
- Body work usually creates a type of altered consciousness—body consciousness. My warning is this: be careful how many times a month you do it. Going into body consciousness work can be extremely helpful during the healing process because it helps you physically release stored body memories and feelings while bypassing the intellect. Use it too many times, however, and you become a space cadet! If any of the following symptoms start, stop the body work immediately and work on integrating the information that has already been uncovered. Use only "talk therapy" until you understand more and the confusion and other symptoms stop. This may require a number of weeks. When there has been too much body work, clients experience the following symptoms:
  - Short-term memory loss
  - Spaciness
  - Floating feelings
  - Confusion
  - Feeling ungrounded in the present moment

- Impaired focusing ability with tasks or other people
- A feeling of not wanting to be in life and preferring to avoid all feelings and problems by being in an altered state

How Do I Pay for Therapy?

Most therapy may be paid for through insurance or private pay (cash). Before your first call to the clinic or therapist, I advise checking your insurance coverage so you know what it will pay for and what you will have to pay. In addition, some clinics may check it for you. If this is the case, be ready to give the numbers on your insurance card to the office staff. Sometimes this is done during your first call. Most insurance policies cover some part of the per session rate. The rate at which insurance reimburses varies, and each insurance policy must be checked individually. Please remember, the therapist is *not* one of your benefits from your work. Clinics bill as a courtesy to you. You are always responsible for any bill you have for your therapy.

When you call about your insurance coverage, here is what you'll need to know:

- Who is the policy listed under?
- Who is covered under the policy? You? Your children? Your spouse?
- How much will the insurance cover per year? Per visit?
- How many visits per year will be covered?
- What is your deductible, and has it been met?
- How much will you have to pay (your co-pay)?
- Is the therapist/clinic in network with your insurance provider?

- Do you need preauthorization?
- Who will the insurance pay? Master of social work (MSW)? Master's level psychologist (MA)? Doctoral level psychologist (PhD)? Psychiatrist (MD)? Licensed Professional Counselors?
- Where will it cover treatment? Outpatient clinic? Inpatient? Hospital? Anywhere?

Most clinics and therapists require that you pay the same day as the service, as in any medical office. If you don't have any insurance coverage and do not have the money to cover the fee per session, some clinics and therapists, on rare occasions, may see you for a lower fee or sliding scale. On other rare occasions, some therapists will arrange a payment schedule to pay part of the therapy costs after therapy is finished. At times, a clinic may have a master-level intern who sees low-fee clients. There are also community supported agencies, such as mental health agencies (look in the phone book under county agencies) that charge lower fees, which is based on income and ability to pay.

At a private clinic, therapists are paid only as you pay, and they need to earn a living and pay bills just as you do. At community mental health agencies, therapists are paid a salary, part of which comes from special state, federal, and county funds. Other special funds may be available in certain areas. Do some research to find what is available in your area.

If the rate for the therapy hour in a private clinic shocks you, please know that therapists have to share the fee. Therapists have to pay a large portion of the fee to the clinic for rent and services, other expenses required by their profession, and then pay taxes on it. Believing therapists make "big bucks" is an illusion. So, if you have chosen a therapist and can't afford the fee, don't become discouraged or believe he or she is terrible and an unfeeling person. In reality, the therapist is working to make a living and may already be seeing someone for a reduced fee. Ask for the name of another therapist who may be willing to see you at a lower fee or who has other community resources to help pay the fee.

How Do You Choose a Therapist?

There are many different kinds of therapists who come from many different orientations. The most effective therapists have been in therapy themselves, have done their healing work, and are continuing to grow themselves. The orientation I use is what I call *spiritual humanistic psychology* using a variety of techniques. Basically, it is a belief that you, the client, have everything you need to go forward in your life. You are an integrated, whole being that consists of body, emotions, mental ability, and spirituality. I, as the therapist, am a facilitator. I help guide my clients, give them feedback, and teach techniques that encourage the healing process. I can't do the healing or play God in anyone's life. Also, I believe our spirituality is the human life core and it must be developed. The humanistic orientation is also called *client-centered* or *holistic psychotherapy.* It has also been called *Rogerian* psychotherapy after Carl Rogers, one of its cofounders.

There are other orientations, such as *therapist-directed therapy.* In this orientation, the client is guided more by the therapist and is seen as a patient more than a client able to do for him- or herself. Included in therapist-directed therapy is psychoanalysis.

The healing process needs a variety of techniques. Most effective therapists are eclectic. *Eclectic* means the use of many techniques from many different orientations. These are used at different times as needed by clients in the healing and growing process. *Techniques* are specific ways of helping you heal, and not all therapists use all techniques. The techniques may include talking, creative visualization, role playing, psychodrama, behavioral, cognitive, psychoanalysis, music therapy, art therapy, journaling, body-release work, massage, guided imagery, interventions, focusing, eco-psychology—the list goes on. Techniques work together in the healing process. No one technique seems to be enough for the entire healing process for any one person. One is rarely enough to release all the layers that have been trapped for so long from surviving a dysfunctional family.

You, as a client, have the right and the ability to read about and learn which techniques will work for you. You also need to read books that have been written about dysfunctional families and healing. Educate yourself. Your therapists won't know everything you will need on your journey. Some books and techniques you will find effective and may use a lot; others you may try and may choose not to use again. The choice is very individual, only you will know which ones you like and are effective for you. However, techniques must be honest, nonabusive, and work to help you heal.

Most importantly, find a therapist you like and with whom you can work to develop a healthy, trusting relationship, someone you feel comfortable with. If you can't relate to and/or don't like the therapist, you'll probably become stuck. Personality clashes can happen between therapists and clients. This is not failure. The therapist you choose needs to be someone you trust enough to help lead you to the next step and eventually to your truth, your authenticity. The therapist needs to challenge you to go forward yet not be in conflict with you and your healing and growing process; and needs to be supportive of you and your process, yet not create dependency on him or her.

Here are some of my suggestions for finding an effective therapist:

1. Ask for recommendations from people you know and trust and who have been in therapy. Question them

about what they liked and disliked about these therapists. Ask about their orientation and expertise areas.
If you can, get two or three recommendations.

2. Call the therapist(s) to get some preliminary questions answered. Set up a fifteen-minute interview
with each one, if necessary.

3. Ask the therapist about his or her approach to therapy, education, training, view of the client, and what
he or she sees as the therapist's role in therapy.

4. Get answers to these questions: Does the therapist
hear and understand you? Does he or she know the
healing and growing process? Does he or she know
about dysfunctional families? Has he or she done his
or her healing work?

5. Make sure you like and get along with the therapist
because you're going to be spending a lot of time, effort, and money. There should not be personality
clashes.

6. If you start with a therapist and after two or three sessions find a definite personality clash, talk to the therapist about it. The clash may be resolvable. If it's not,
it's okay to seek out another therapist. You can also
ask for recommendations.

7. However, and this is a *very important however*, if you
find that you are *therapist-hopping* (trying many therapists with no one being okay), the issue may not be
in finding the right therapist as much as what you are
trying to avoid in therapy.

8. Check out the therapist's credentials through state
and school organizations, i.e., license boards.

9. If during therapy you begin to feel devalued and/or
misunderstood often, discuss it with the therapist. If
this doesn't work, find another therapist.

10. If you are abused in *any way* and/or sexually ap-
proached and/or harrassed, get another therapist *immediately* and report the therapist to the licensing

board in your state. This behavior is not professional and *not okay.* No therapist with integrity does this. You had enough abuse as a child; you don't need more.
11. Remember the choice of therapist is yours. You have the power to hire and fire.

What Are the Different Types of Therapists?

There are four basic types of psychotherapists:

1. *Psychologists.* These professionals primarily study people from the perspective of the individual and how emotional and intellectual healing and growing occur. They also study how society affects the individual. There are two levels of psychologists: master's (MA) and doctoral (PhD).
2. *Social workers.* These therapists primarily study the individual from society's point of view. They may also study how healing and growing occurs as well as how to deal with the community. There are two levels of social workers: bachelor's (BA) and master's (MSW).
3. *Licensed professional counselor.* These therapists come from a counseling background and work to help people with their issues. There are two levels of licensed professional counselors: master's (MA) and doctoral (PhD).
4. *Psychiatrists.* These professionals are medical doctors (MD) who usually study psychoanalysis in their residency program. They can dispense and monitor medications.

What Is the Therapist's Role?

I strongly believe the therapist's role is as a facilitator; that is, one who helps you find your answers and not an authority on your life. I believe *each* of us has what we need to succeed in life. Therapists do not have our energy, abilities, experiences, feelings, thoughts, or anything else of ours. They can't make our decisions, feel our feelings, or grow our growth. They can't heal for us. Therapists are neither gods nor superhuman. They are human and have obstacles to deal with in their lives just as you do. They have no magical cures. Disappointing, isn't it? What they do have, however, is the training to help people recover, heal, and grow. They offer vital, caring, objective, trained, and professional perspectives on what has happened to you in your life. They help you find your way to a healthier, happier, productive life.

A therapist's role includes:

1. Supporting you through your healing and growing process
2. Helping you identify, clarify, and learn about and from your feelings
3. Helping you learn techniques that encourage and aid your process
4. Helping you develop healthier relationships
5. Sharing information about dysfunctional families and their effect on your life
6. Offering in-session support with difficult feelings and issues
7. Being available in crisis situations by phone or for extra crisis sessions (or having another therapist cover for them in their absence)
8. Being a supporter, guide, and encourager

Therapy is only a *part* of your healing and growing. You must work and develop all aspects of who you are: physical, mental, emotional, and spiritual. Therapy by itself will never be enough. A lot of therapy occurs between the end of one session and the beginning of the next, not just in the

therapist's office. Without this between-session work, healing and growing is slow. Sessions support and facilitate
your healing. The therapist also helps you learn techniques
and gain an understanding and wisdom that will last you a
lifetime.

At times during therapy, there is emotional confusion
about the identity and role of the therapist. Freud calls it
transference. *Transference* occurs when the therapist takes
on many faces from the client's past as the client works to
heal. The client may respond and treat the therapist as if he
or she was his or her mom, dad, sister, brother, and so on.
I have even seen sibling rivalry among clients who had the
same therapist. This is normal but needs to be resolved in
therapy. The object is to heal and not just shift parent and
other issues to the therapist. So when transference does
occur, sharing with the therapist and confronting it are important. Remember, the therapist cannot replace family
members or someone else you feel is lacking in your life.
The therapist also cannot be the target for your venting of
anger. The therapist can help you heal those areas.

The therapist's role is to be with you and provide guidance through the healing process. It is not, however, his or
her role to be there every time you have a feeling that up-
sets you. It is not the therapist's role to be on call twenty-
four hours a day, seven days a week for you in case you
have questions about something going on in your life. Save
it for your next session. True emergencies include being
homicidal or suicidal. True emergencies are not appointment changes or being lonely. In case of a true emergency,
your therapist, or another therapist who is on call in your
therapist's absence, does need to be available to you. This
is usually done through the clinic's clerical staff and/or answering service. In a true emergency, call the clinic, state
it is an emergency, and ask to speak with your therapist as
soon as possible. The clinic or answering service will then
contact your therapist, who will then call you. If your therapist is not available, the answering service will contact

the person on call or ask someone to call you. Some clinics refer all emergencies during off-hours to public crisis numbers or hospitals. If you are in an emergency, a hospital may be the only safe place for you. Find out how your therapist handles emergencies.

Please remember, therapists need time off and have families of their own. Most therapists cannot handle being a therapist all the time, even though they like people. It is their work. Most therapists, after talking and being with clients most of the day, go home to be with their families and relax just as you do after work. Therapy is very demanding, and time off is essential for therapists' health and well-being. It is essential to their performance as a therapist. So if you call after hours, make sure it is an emergency. You can call to make or change *appointments* during normal office hours, and is not considered an emergency. Suicidal or homicidal feelings and thoughts are *always* an emergency.

In general, I tell my clients the following. "You are in charge of your life, healing process, and growth. I am here as a facilitator and road sign consultant to help you in *your* process. If I offer something that does not match your knowing of you, tell me. In that way, we can keep exploring to find out what does fit. You are the one that ultimately knows. I am not God, nor do I play God in your life. Your decisions are yours, not mine. We need to work in areas you choose that are important to you. Your natural healing process is perfect for you and you know it best. I'm here to help you recognize it."

What Does a Therapist Not Do?

When therapists see pain, we want to change it. That is probably the major reason we come into the mental health field to start with, along with needing to heal and find ourselves. If we could do your feeling work for you and you would heal, we'd probably do it. It is not humanly possible for anyone else to do your work for you. What we can do is to help you release pain, heal, and gain understanding and wisdom from your journey. That is where our power stops. We cannot heal for you. Therapists cannot feel for you, think for you, or change your behavior for you. They neither have crystal balls nor can read your mind. You have to do it for yourself, just as I and many others have done.

Summary

In summary, when selecting a therapist seek a healthy relationship. This relationship needs to help you build trust as well as to help you find your original package and authentic self. The techniques used should aid in releasing layers and in promoting healing and growing. They should never be abusive. Healing needs to be done with support and gentleness. Your growth is based on the work you do, not the work the therapist does. It may be painful, difficult, and hard work, but know it is definitely worth it. You will never regret doing it; you may regret not doing it earlier.

RESOURCE SECTION 2

References Noted in Chapters

Chapter 2

1. Beaver, W. R. (1977). *Psychotherapy and Growth: A Family Systems Perspective*. New York: Brunner/Mazel Publishers, 1–388.

Chapter 5

1. Rogers, C., and W. R. Coulson. (1968). *Man and the Science of Man*. Columbus, Ohio: Charles E. Merrill, 1–207.
2. Moustakas, C. (1956, and personal supervision, 1979–1986). *The Self: Explorations in Personal Growth*. New York: Harper, 1–284.
3. Assagioli, R. (1973). *The Act of Will*. New York: Penguin Books, 1–278.
4. James, W. (1962). *Talks to Teachers on Psychology and to Students on Some of Life's Ideals (1899)*. New York: Henry Holt and Co., 1–160.
5. May, R. (1969). *Psychology of the Human Dilemma*. New York: Laurel-Dell, 50–215.
6. Assagioli, R. (1973). *The Act of Will,* Penguin Books: New York, 1–278.
7. Ibid.
8. Ibid.
9. Rank, O. (1950). *Will Therapy and Truth and Reality*. New York: Alfred A. Knopf, 1–98.

10. Maslow, A. (1971). *Farther Reaches of Human Nature.* New York: The Viking Press, 1–336.
11. Rank, O. (1950). *Will Therapy and Truth and Reality.* Alfred A. Knopf, 1–98.
12. Maslow, A. (1971). *Farther Reaches of Human Nature.* The Viking Press, 1–336.
13. Ibid.
14. Ibid.
15. Rank, O. (1950). *Will Therapy and Truth and Reality,* Alfred A. Knopf, 1–98.
16. James, W. (1962). *Talks to Teachers on Psychology and to Students on Some of Life's Ideals (1899),* Henry Holt and Co., 1–160.
17. Rank, O. (1950). *Will Therapy and Truth and Reality,* Alfred A. Knopf, 1–98.
18. Frankl, V. E. (1963). *Man's Search for Meaning.* New York: Beacon Press, 1–224.
19. Combs, A. W., D. L. Avilia, and W. W. Parkey. (1971). *Helping Relationship: Basic Concepts for the Helping Profession.* Boston: Allyn and Bacon, Inc., 1–133.
20. Ibid.
21. Husserl, E. (1962) *Ideas.* New York: Collin Macmillion Publishers, 1–96.
22. Kelly, E. C. (1980). *Urban Educator.* Detroit: College of Education, Wayne State University, 50–75.
23. Kuenzli, A. E. (ed). (1957). *The Phenomenological Problem.* New York: Harper and Brothers, 1–321.
24. Ibid.
25. Heiddegger, E. (trans. Macquarrie and Robinson) (1952). *Being and Time.* New York: Harper and Row, 1–397.
26. Combs, A. W., D. L. Avilia, and W. W. Parkey. (1971). *Helping Relationship: Basic Concepts for the Helping Profession.* Boston: Allyn and Bacon, Inc., 1–133.
27. Combs, A. (ed.) (1962). *Perceiving, Behaving, and Becoming: Lessons Learned.* Washington, D.C.: National Education Association for Curriculum Development Yearbook, 1–162.

28. Rogers, C., and W. R. Coulson. (1968). *Man and the Science of Man.* Charles E. Merrill.
29. Privette, G. (1968). *Transcendent Functioning: The Full Use of Potentialities, Ways of Growth.* H. Otto and J. Mann (eds). New York: Grossman Publishing, 1–227.
30. Heiddegger, E. (1952). *Being and Time,* Harper and Row, 1–96.
31. Ibid.
32. Ibid.
33. Ibid.
34. Ibid.
35. Ibid.
36. Ibid.
37. Hora, T. (1961). "Transcendence and Healing." *Journal of Existential Psychiatry* 1, 500–511.
38. Ibid.

Chapter 6

1. LeDoux, J. (2000). "Emotion Circuits in the Brain." *Annual Review of Neuroscience* 23, 155–184.
2. Sarton, M. (1980). *Recovering.* New York: Norton, 50–86, page 21.

Chapter 7

1. LeDoux, J. (2000). "Emotion Circuits in the Brain." *Annual Review of Neuroscience* 23, 155–184.

RESOURCE SECTION 3

Foundational Bibliography

This bibliography includes many books covering different areas of dysfunction and healing. The list includes references used to develop the research as well as some references offered to help you with your reading selection in the healing and growing process. Many of these books may be purchased as paperbacks or found in libraries. This listing is by no means exhaustive. There are many good books, with many more being published every day. Explore older books. We are too quick to throw out oldies and too quick to accept new books sometimes. Evaluate them. Explore and learn about you. The list is sufficient to help you on your journey.

When selecting a book to read, use your inner sense, your intuition, and your spirituality to guide and help you choose. When I am choosing a book, I allow myself to be "attracted to" one, whether it's on a bookstore shelf, mentioned by a friend, or listed on a reading list. For me this method rarely fails to uncover just the *right* book I need to read next. Occasionally, I buy a book and don't read it until much later—sometimes years later. When I do get around to reading it, it seems to be at exactly the correct time.

If I do buy a book that doesn't fit, I soon know it when I try to read it. I'll start to read it only to find that I am bored and not understanding what I am reading. I then set it aside until later. I know there will usually be a time when the book will be important to me or someone else in my life. When I read books in my time, I gain and learn from them. When reading books, give yourself permission to read *parts* of books. Just because our teachers taught us to read *all* the book from front to back is no reason to keep doing it. If only certain chapters appeal to you, read only those. If you start a book and find it awful, stop and find another. It may either be an awful book or not your time to read it. Trust yourself. Be good to yourself. And most of all, gain and learn from your reading.

One last word on reading books written by professionals in the mental health field: don't believe everything you read! Each book, like this one, is written to relate information. This information is what this one particular author has learned and written about from his or her perspective and beliefs. What the author learns and believes may not fit you or your situation. Your experience may be totally different, and you may not agree with the author at all. Don't leave your intelligence and education out when you read. Process the information and try the suggestions if they are healthy. *Then* evaluate the information and its effects on you. You are the last word in your life, not the author who decided to write in book form what he or she knows.

Many of the following books are also available in cassette form and have workbooks that go with them. Workbooks and work tapes can be a great help in the healing and growing process. If you have questions, ask your therapist. He or she may know the answer. Use them and enjoy growing!

Al-Anon Family Group. *One Day at a Time in Al-Anon.*
New York: Al-Anon Family Group Headquarters, 1974.
Al-Anon Family Group. *Al-Anon: Faces Alcoholism.* New York: Al-Anon Family Group Headquarters, 1977.
Al-Anon's Twelve Steps and Twelve Traditions. New York: Al-Anon Family Group Headquarters, 1981.
Al-Anon Family Group. *Al-Anon: Is It For You?* New York: Al-Anon Family Group Headquarters, 1983.
Alcoholics Anonymous. *The Big Book* (3rd ed.). New York: Alcoholics Anonymous World Services, 1976.

Anderson, Louise. *Dear Dad: Letters from an Adult Child.* New York: Penguin Books, 1989.

Anthony, E. J. *The Child in His Family* (Vol. 3). New York: John Wiley, 1974.

Assagioli, R. *The Act of Will.* New York: Penguin Books, 1973.

Axline, Virginia M. *Dibs: In Search of Self.* New York: Ballantine Books, 1964.

Bach, E. *Heal Thy Self: An Explanation of the Real Cause and Cure of Disease.* Bend, OR: Sun, 1985.

Bach, George, and Herbert Goldberg. *Creative Aggression.* New York: Avon, 1974.

Bach, Richard. *Illusions.* New York: Delacorte Press, 1977.

Bach, Richard. *The Bridge across Forever.* New York: Morrow, 1984.

Bancroft, Lundy. *When Dad Hurts Mom: Helping Your Children Heal the Wounds of Witnessing Abuse.* New York: G. P. Putnam's Son, 2004.

Bandler, Leslie. *They Lived Happily Ever After.* Meta, 1978.

Batson, C., N. Ahmad, D. Lishner, and J. Tsang. *A Handbook of Positive Psychology.* New York: Oxford Press, 2002.

Beattie, Melody. *Denial.* Center City, MN: Hazelden, 1986.

Beattie, Melody. *Codependent No More.* San Francisco: Harper, 1987.

Beattie, Melody. *Games People Play.* New York: Ballantine, 1987.

Beattie, Melody. *Beyond Co-Dependency and Getting Better All the Time.* New York: Harper, 1989.

Beauvais, F., and E. Iettubg. *Resilience and Development: Positive Life Adaptations.* New York: Kluwer, 1999.

Beaver, W. R. *Psychology and Growth: A Family Systems Perspective.* New York: Brunner/Mazel, 1977.

Benard, Bonnie. *Resiliency: What We Have Learned.* San Francisco: WestEd, 2004.

Benson, H. *The Relaxation Response.* New York: Avon, 1976.

Bernie, Eric. *What Do You Say after You Say Hello?* New York: Bantam, 1971.

Bettelheim, Bruno. *Love Is Not Enough.* London: Collier Books, 1950.

Bettelheim, Bruno. *Paul and Mary: Two Case Histories from Truants from Life.* New York: Doubleday, 1955.

Bettelheim, Bruno. *The Empty Fortress: Infantile Autism and the Birth of the Self.* New York: The Free Press, 1967.

Bettelheim, Bruno. *The Children of the Dream.* New York: Macmillan, 1969.

The Living Bible. Wheaton: Tyndale, 1971.

Black, Claudia. *It Will Never Happen to Me.* Denver: MAC, 1981.

Black, Claudia. *Repeat After Me.* Denver: MAC, 1985.

Black, Claudia. *Repeat After Me: Workbook for Adult Children.* Denver: MAC, 1985.

Bleuler, M. "The Offspring of Schizophrenia." *Schizophrenia Bulletin,* 8 (1974):93–107.

Bloomfield, Harold H., and Leonard Felder. *Making Peace with Your Parents.* New York: Ballantine, 1983.

Boon, Corrie Ten. *The Hiding Place.* New Jersey: Fleming H. Revell, 1971.

Bradshaw, John. *Healing the Shame that Binds You.* Deerfield Beach, FL: Health Communications, 1988.

Bradshaw, John. *The Family.* Deerfield Beach, FL: Health Communications, 1988.

Bradsky, Anne. *With All Our Strength.* New York: Routledge, 2003.

Brandon, Nathaniel. *The Disowned Self.* Los Angeles: Bantam, 1971.

Brandon, Nathaniel. *How to Raise Your Self-Esteem.* New York: Bantam, 1987.

Briggs, Dorothy Corkille. *Your Child's Self-Esteem.* New York: Doubleday, 1967.

Briggs, Dorothy Corkille. *Your Child's Self-Esteem: Step by Step to Raising Responsible Productive, Happy Children.* Garden City, NY: Dolphin, 1970.

Briggs, Dorothy Corkille. *Your Child's Self-Esteem: The Key to Life.* New York: Doubleday, 1975.

Briggs, Dorothy Corkille. *Celebrate Your Self: Enhancing Your Own Self-Esteem.* New York: Doubleday, 1977.

Briggs, Dorothy Corkille. *Embracing Life: Growing through Love.* Garden City, NY: Doubleday, 1985.

Brooks, Cathleen. *The Secret Everyone Knows.* San Diego: Kroc Foundation, 1981.

Bowdan, J. D. and Gravitz, H. L. *Genesis: Spirituality in Recovery from Childhood Traumas.* Deerfield Beach: Health Communications, 1988.

Buber, Martin. *I and Thou.* New York: Scribner, 1958.

Bugental, J. F. T. *The Search for Existential Identity.* San Francisco: Jossey-Bass, 1976.

Burke, S. O. "The Invulnerable Child." *Nursing Papers: Perspective on Nursing,* 12(1–2) (1986):48–55.

Burke, T. *I've Heard Your Feelings.* Suttons Bay, MI: Delafield, 1976.

Burke, T. *Loving Who You Are Where You Are.* Suttons Bay, MI: Delafield, 1982.

Buscaglia, Leo. *Love.* New York: Fawcett Crest, 1972.

Buscaglia, Leo. *Living, Loving, and Learning.* New York: Fawcett Crest, 1982.

Buscaglia, Leo. *Loving Each Other: The Challenge of Human Relationships.* New York: Holt Rhinehart and Winston, 1984.

Canfield, J. *Self-Esteem.* Pacific Palisades, CA: Jack Canfield and Self-Esteem Seminars, 1985.

Canfield, Jack, and Harold C. Wells. *One Hundred Ways to Enhance Self-Concept in the Classroom: A Handbook for Teachers and Parents.* Englewood Cliffs, New Jersey: Prentice-Hall, 1976.

Calhoun, M. *Are You Really Too Sensitive?* New York: Dolphin, 1987.

Cantril, A. "Perception and Interpersonal Relations." In A. E. Kuezli (ed.). *The Phenomenological Problem.* New York: Harper, 1959.

302 If Marie Did It, So Can I!

Capucchione, Lucia. *The Creative Journal.* Athens, Ohio University: Swallow, 1979.

Carnes, Patrick. *Sexual Addiction.* New York: CompCare, 1983.

Carnes, Patrick. *Out of the Shadows: Understanding Sexual Addiction.* Minneapolis, MN: CompCare, 1985.

Carnes, Patrick. *Contrary to Love: Understanding Sexual Addiction. Part 2, Helping the Sexual Addict.* Minneapolis, MN: CompCare, 1988.

Carter, Steven, and Julie Sokol. *Men Who Can't Love: When a Man's Fear Makes Him Run from Commitment.* New York: Evans, 1987.

Casey, Karen, and Martha Vanceburg. *The Promise of a New Day: A Book of Daily Meditations.* New York: Harper, 1983.

Celeni, David. *Leaving Home: The Art of Separating from Your Difficult Family.* New York: Columbia University Press, 2005.

Cermak, Timmen L. *A Primer for Adult Children of Alcoholics.* Pompano Beach, FL: Health Communications, 1985.

Cermak, Timmen L. *Diagnosing and Treating Codependency: A Guide for Professionals.* Minneapolis, MN: Johnson, 1986.

Cermak, Timmen L. *Evaluating and Treating ACAs [Adult Children of Alcoholics] A Guide for Professionals.* Minneapolis, MN: Johnson, 1988.

Cermak, Timmen L. *A Time to Heal: The Road to Recovery for Adult Children of Alcoholics.* Los Angeles: Tarcher, 1988.

Clausen, J. A., and C. L. Huffine. "The Impact of Parental Mental Illness on Children." *Research in Community and Mental Health* 1 (1979):183–214.

Cohen, Allen. *The Dragon Doesn't Live Here Anymore: Loving Fully and Living Freely.* Atlanta: New Leaf, 1981.

Cohler, B. J., D. H. Gallant, H. U. Grunebaum, and J. L. Weiss. "Child-Care Attitudes and Development of Young Children of Mentally Ill and Well Mothers." *Psychology Reports* 46 (1980):31–46.

Colazzi, R. R. "Psychological Research as the Phenomenologists View It." In R. S. Valle and M. King (eds.), *Existential-Phenomenological Alternative for Psychology.* New York: Oxford University Press, 1978.

Colgrove, Melba, Harold H. Bloomfield, and Peter McWilliams. *How to Survive the Loss of a Love.* New York: Bantam, 1976.

Combs, A. W., A. C. Richards, and F. Richards. *Perceptual Psychology.* New York: Harper, 1949.

Combs, A. W. (ed.). *Perceiving, Behaving, and Becoming.* Washington, D.C.: National Education Association, ASCD Yearbook, 1962.

Combs, A. W., D. L. Avila, and W. W. Parkey. *Helping Relationship: Basic Concepts for the Helping Profession.* Boston: Allyn, 1971.

Corke, Jean Illsley. *Self-Esteem: A Family Affair.* San Francisco: Harper, 1978.

Cousins, Norma. *Head First: The Biology of Hope.* New York: Dutton, 1989.

Covington, Stephanie, and Liana Beckett. *Leaving the Enchanted Forest.* San Francisco: Harper, 1988.

Cowan, Connell, and Melvyn Kinder. *Smart Women— Foolish Choices.* New York: Signet, 1986.

Crawford, C. *Mommie Dearest.* New York: Morrow, 1978.

Crum, Tom. *The Magic of Conflict.* New York: Simon, 1987.

Davis, Laura, and Ellen Bass. *The Courage to Heal: A Guide for Women Survivors of Child Sexual Abuse.* New York: Harper, 1988.

Davis, Laura. *The Courage to Heal Workbook: For Women and Men Survivors of Child Sexual Abuse.* New York: Harper, 1990.

Davis, Laura, and Laura Hough. *Allies in Healing: When a Person You Love Is a Survivor of Child Sexual Abuse.* New York: HarperCollins, 1991.

Davis, M., E. R. Eshelman, and M. McKay. *The Relaxation and Stress Reduction Workbook.* Oakland, CA: New Harbinger, 1982.

DeBecker, Gavin. *Gift of Fear.* New York: Dell Publishing, 1998.

Decker, Sunny. *An Empty Spoon.* New York: Scholastic, 1970.

Deutsch, C. *Broken Bottles, Broken Dreams: Understanding and Helping the Children of Alcoholics.* New York: Teachers College, 1982.

Diamond, Jed. *Looking for Love in All the Wrong Places.* New York: Putnam, 1988.

Dobson, Jane. *Hide and Seek: Self-Esteem for the Child.* Old Tappan, NJ: Revell, 1971.

Drever, J. *A Dictionary of Psychology.* Baltimore: Penguin, 1961.

Drews, Toby R. *Getting Them Sober* (Vol. 1). South Plainfield, NJ: Bridge, 1983.

Drews, Toby R. *Getting Them Sober* (Vol. 2). South Plainfield, NJ: Bridge, 1983.

Dwinell, Lorie. "Walking through Grief: The Essential Elements." *Focus on Family* (May–June 1985):18–19.

Dwinell, Lorie. "Working through Grief: The Pain That Heals Itself." *Focus on Family* (Jan–Feb. 1986):24–28.

Dwinell, Lorie, and Jane Middelton-Moz. *After the Tears.* Pompano Beach, FL: Health Communications, 1986.

Eastman, Philip D. *Are You My Mother?* New York: Random, 1960.

El-Gruebaly, N., and D. R. Offord. "The Competent Offspring of Psychiatrically Ill Parents." *Canadian Journal of Psychiatry* 25(6) (1980):457–460.

Elkind, David. *The Hurried Child: Growing Up Too Fast Too Soon.* Reading, MA: Addison, 1981.

Elliot, David. *Listen to the Silence.* New York: New America, 1969.

Emotions Anonymous International Services. *The Enormity of Emotional Illness.* St. Paul, MN: Emotions Anonymous International, 1973.

Fadiman, J., and R. Fragen. *Personality and Personal Growth.* New York: Harper, 1976.

Farmer, Steven. *Adult Children of Abusive Parents: A Healing Program for Those Who Have Been Physically, Sexually, or Emotionally Abused.* Chicago, IL: Contemporary, 1984.

Ferguson, M. *The Aquarian Conspiracy: Personal and Social Transformation in the 1980s.* Los Angeles: Tarcher, 1980.

Fishel, R. *The Journey Within: A Spiritual Path to Recovery.* Pompano Beach, FL: Health Communications, 1987.

Fisher, Bruce. *Rebuilding: When Your Relationship Ends.* San Luis Obispo, CA: Import, 1981.

Fisichella, A. *Metaphysics: Science and Life.* St. Paul, MN: Liewellyn, 1985.

Flaherty, F. *The Odyssey of a Film-Maker.* Urbana, IL: Beta Phi Mu, 1960.

Forward, Susan, and Craig Buck. *Betrayal of Innocence: Incest and its Devastation.* New York: Penguin, 1978.

Forward, Susan, and Craig Buck. *Toxic Parents.* New York: Bantam, 1989.

Forward, Susan, and Joan Torres. *Men Who Hate Women and the Women Who Love Them.* New York: Bantam, 1985.

Fossum, M. A., and M. J. Mason. *Facing Shame: Families in Recovery.* New York: Norton, 1986.

Frankl, V. E. *Man's Search for Meaning.* New York: Beacon, 1963.

Frankl, V. E. "Self-Transcendence as a Human Phenomenon." *Journal of Humanistic Psychology* (Fall 1966):97–106.

Frankl, V. E. *Psychotherapy and Existentialism: Selected Papers on Logotherapy.* New York: Simon & Schuster, 1967.

Fraser, Sylvia. *My Father's House: Memoir of Incest and of Healing.* New York: Harper & Row, 1987.

Freud, A. *The Ego and the Mechanisms of Defense.* (Rev. ed.). New York: International Universities, 1966.

Freud, S. *General Introduction to Psychoanalysis* (J. Riviera, Trans.). New York: Garden City, 1938.

Friel, John, and Linda Friel. *Adult Children: The Secrets of Dysfunctional Families.* Deerfield, FL: Health Communications, 1988.

Friends in Recovery. *The Twelve Steps, A Way Out: A Working Guide for Adult Children from Addictive and other Dysfunctional Families.* San Diego: Recovery, 1987.

Fromm, Erich. *Escape from Freedom.* New York: Avon, 1941.

Fromm, Erich. *Man for Himself: An Inquiry into the Psychology of Ethics.* Greenwich, CT: Fawcett, 1947.

Fromm, Erich. *Psychoanalysis and Religion.* New York: Bantam, 1950.

Fromm, Erich. *The Art of Loving.* New York: Harper, 1956.

Fromm, Erich. *You Shall Be as Gods: A Radical Interpretation of the Old Testament and Its Traditions.* Greenwich, CT: Fawcett, 1966.

Fromm, Erich. *The Revolution of Hope: Toward a Humanized Technology.* New York: Bantam, 1968.

Garfield, C. A. *Peak Performance.* New York: Warner, 1985.

Garmezy, N. "Competence and Adaptation in Adult Schizophrenic Patients and Children at Risk." In S. R. Dean (ed.), *Prize Lectures in Schizophrenia: The First Ten Dean Awards.* New York: MSS Information Center, 1973.

Garmezy, N. "Children at Risk: The Search for the Antecedents of Schizophrenia. Part II, Ongoing Research Programs, Issues, and Interventions." *Schizophrenia Bulletin* 6(4) (1974):96.

Garmezy, N. "The Study of Competence in Children at Risk for Severe Psychopathology." In E. J. Anthony and C. Koupernich (eds.), *The Child and His Family* (Vol. 3). New York: Wiley, 1974.

Garmezy, N. "Observations with Children at Risk for Child and Adult Psychopathology." In M. F. McMillan and S. Henao (eds), *Child Psychiatry: Treatment and Research.* New York: Brunner, 1977.

Garmezy, N. "Vulnerable and Invulnerable Children: Theory, Research, and Intervention." *Catalog of Selected Documents in Psychology* 6(4) (1976):96.

Garmezy, N., L. Nordstrom, A. Masten, and M. Ferrarese. "The Nature of Competence in Normal and Deviant Children." In M. W. Kent and J. E. Rolf (eds.) *Social Competence in Children.* Burlington, VT: University of Vermont, 1979.

Gawain, Shakti. *Creative Visualization: Use the Power of Your Imagination to Create What You Want in Your Life.* San Rafael, CA: New World, 1978.

Gawain, Shakti. *Creative Visualization Workbook.* San Rafael, CA: New World, 1982.

Gawain, Shakti. *Living in the Light: A Guide to Personal and Planetary Transformation.* San Rafael, CA: New World, 1986.

Gawain, Shakti. *Reflections on the Light: Daily Thoughts and Affirmations.* San Rafael, CA: New World, 1988.

Gawain, Shakti. *Return to the Garden.* San Rafael, CA: New World, 1989.

Gendlin, E. *Focusing.* New York: Everest, 1978.

Gerber, Richard. *Vibrational Medicine: New Choices for Healing Ourselves.* Sante Fe: Bean, 1988.

Gil, E. *Outgrowing the Pain: A Book for and about Adults Abused as Children.* San Francisco: Launch, 1984.

Gil, Eliana. *The Healing Power of Play.* New York: Guilford Press, 1991.

Ginott, Haim G. *Between Parent and Child.* New York: Avon, 1956.

Giorgi, A. "Phenomenology and Experimental Psychology." In A. Giorgi, W. Fischer, and W. R. Von Eckartsbery (eds.), *Duquesne Studies in*

Phenomenological Psychology (Vol. 1). Pittsburgh: Duquesne University Press, 1971.

Glatz, G. and Johnson, J. (eds.). *Resiliency and Development: Positive Life Adaptations.* New York: Kluwer, 1999.

Glenn, Stephen H. *Raising Self-Reliant Children in a Self-Indulgent World: Seven Building Blocks for Developing Capable Young People.* Rocklin, CA: Prime, 1989.

Goldberg, Herb. *The Hazards of Being Male: Surviving the Myth of Masculine Privilege.* New York: New American, 1976.

Goldberg, Herb. *The New Male-Female Relationship.* New York: Morrow, 1983.

Goldberg, Herb. *The Inner Male: Overcoming Roadblocks to Intimacy.* New York: New American, 1987.

Goleman, D. *Emotional Intelligence: Why It Can Matter More than I.Q.* New York: Bantam Books, 1995.

Gordon, R. *Your Healing Hands: The Polarity Experience.* Berkeley, CA: Wingkow, 1984.

Goulding, Robert, and Mary McClure Goulding. *Changing Lives through Redecision Therapy.* New York: Brunner, 1979.

Goulding, Robert, and Mary McClure Goulding. *The Power Is in the Patient.* San Francisco: TA Bookstore, 1987.

Gravitz, Herbert. *Children of Alcoholics Handbook.* South Laguna, CA: National Association for Children of Alcoholics, 1985.

Gravitz, Herbert L., and Julie D. Bowden. *Recovery: A Guide for Children of Alcoholics.* New York: Simon & Schuster, 1987.

Grosz, George. *Love above All.* New York: Shocken, 1985.

Harris, Sydney J. *The Authentic Person: Dealing with Dilemma.* Niles, IL: Argus, 1972.

Harris, Thomas A. *I'm Okay, You're Okay.* New York: Harper & Row, 1967.

Hay, Louise L. *Heal Your Body: The Mental Causes for Physical Illness and the Metaphysical Way to Overcome Them.* Santa Monica, CA: Hay, 1982.

Hay, Louise L. *You Can Heal Your Life.* Farmingdale, CA: Coleman, 1985.

Hayden, Torey. *One Child.* New York: Avon, 1980.

Hazelden Educational Materials. *Teen Drug Use: What Can Parents Do?* Center City, MN: Hazelden, 1970.

Hazelden Educational Materials. *No Substitute for Love: Ideas for Family Living.* Center City, MN: Hazelden, 1973.

Hazelden Educational Materials. *Step Four: Guide to Fourth Step Inventory for the Spouse.* Center City, MN: Hazeldon, 1976.

Hazelden Educational Materials. *Setting Boundaries.* Center City, MN: Hazelden, 1982.

Hazelden Educational Materials. *Learn about Families and Chemical Dependency.* Center City, MN: Hazeldon, 1985.

Hazelden Educational Series. *Shame.* Center City, MN: Hazelden, 1981.

Hazelden Meditational Series. *Each Day a New Beginning: Daily Meditations for Women.* San Francisco: Harper & Row, 1982.

Hazelden Meditational Series. *Twenty-Four Hours a Day.* San Francisco: Harper & Row, 1985.

Hazelden Meditational Series. *Day by Day.* San Francisco: Harper & Row, 1986.

Health Communications. *Codependency: An Emerging Issue.* Hollywood, FL: Health Communications, 1984.

Heiddegger, E. *Being and Time.* (J. Macquattie and E. Robinson, trans.) New York: Harper & Row, 1952.

Hendix, Harville. *Getting the Love You Want: A Guide for Couples.* New York: Harper & Row, 1988.

Hendricks, Gay. *Learning to Love Yourself: Workbook.* New York: Prentice-Hall, 1990.

Hendricks, Gay, and Russell Wills. *The Centering Book: Awareness Activities for Children, Parents, and Teachers.* New York: Prentice-Hall, 1975.

Herman, Judith. *Father-Daughter Incest.* Cambridge: Harvard University Press, 1981.

Hollis, Judi. *Fat Is a Family Affair.* San Francisco: Harper & Row, 1986.

Hollis, Judi. *Hope and Recovery: A Twelve-Step Guide for Healing from Compulsive Sexual Behavior.* Minneapolis, MN: CompCare, 1987.

Hora, T. "Transcendence and Healing." *Journal of Existential Psychiatry* 1 (1961):501–511.

Hornik-Beer, Edith Lynn. *A Teenager's Guide to Living with an Alcoholic Parent.* Center City, MN: Hazelden, 1984.

Howe, LeLand W., and Mary Martha Howe. *Personalizing Education.* New York: Hart, 1975.

Husserl, E. *Ideas.* New York: Collin Macmillon, 1962.

Ihde, E. *Experimental Phenomenology.* New York: Putnam, 1977.

Jacobson, E. *Progressive Relaxation.* Chicago: University of Chicago Press, 1974.

Jaffe, Dennis T. "Self Renewal: Personal Transformation Following Extreme Trauma." *Journal of Humanistic Psychology* 24(4) (1985):104–122.

James, W. *Talks to Teachers on Psychology and to Students on Some of Life's Ideals.* (1899). New York: Holt, 1962.

Jampolsky, Gerald. *Love Is Letting Go of Fear.* Berkeley, CA: Celestial, 1979.

Jampolsky, Gerald. *Teach Only Love.* New York: Bantam, 1983.

Jampolsky, Gerald. *Good-Bye to Guilt: Releasing Fear through Forgiveness.* New York: Bantam, 1985.

Jay, W. Brugh. *Joy's Way: Six Maps for the Transformational Journey.* New York: St. Martin's Press, 1979.

Jeffers, Susan. *Feel the Fear and Do It Anyway.* New York: Fawcett, 1987.

Johnson, Lois Walfrid. *Either Way, I Win: A Guide to Growth in the Power of Prayer.* Minneapolis, MN: Augsburg, 1979.

Johnson, Robert A. *He: Understanding Masculine Psychology.* New York: Harper & Row, 1989.

Johnson, Robert A. *She: Understanding Feminine Psychology.* New York: Harper & Row, 1989.

Jourard, Sidney M. *Disclosing Man to Himself.* New York: Van Nostrand, 1968.

Jourard, Sidney M. *The Transparent Self.* New York: Van Nostrand, 1971.

Joy, W. B. *Joy's Way.* Los Angeles: Tarcher, 1979.

Kauffman, C., H. Grunebaum, B. Cohler, and E. Gamer. "Superkids: Competent Children of Psychotic Mothers." *American Journal of Psychiatry* 136(11) (1979):1398–1402.

Keen, A. *A Primer in Phenomenological Psychology.* New York: Holt, 1975.

Keen, A. *Doing Psychology Phenomenologically.* Unpublished Manuscript.

Kelly, Dan. *The Peter Pan Syndrome: Men Who Have Never Grown Up.* New York: Dodd, 1983.

Kelly, Dan. *The Wendy Dilemma: When Women Stop Mothering Their Men.* New York: Arbor, 1984.

Kelly, E. C. *Urban Educator.* Detroit: Wayne State University, 1980.

Kierkegaard, S. *Concluding Unscientific Postscript.* (D. F. Swanson and W. Lowrie, trans.) Princeton: Princeton University Press, 1941.

Kimball, Bonnie-Jean. *The Alcoholic Woman's Mad, Mad World of Denial and Mind Games.* Center City, MN: Hazelden Educational Materials, 1978.

Kopp, Sheldon. *If You Meet the Buddha on the Road, Kill Him! The Pilgrimage of Psychotherapy Patients.* New York: Bantam, 1972.

Kopp, Sheldon. *Raise Your Right Hand against Fear: Extend the Other in Compassion.* New York: Ballantine, 1988.

Koupernik, C. "The Bled Discussion: A Review." In E. J.
Anthony (ed.), *The Child in His Family.* New York:
Wiley, 1974.

Kübler-Ross, Elisabeth. *On Death and Dying.* New York:
Macmillan, 1969.

Kübler-Ross, Elisabeth. *Death: The Final Stage of
Growth.* New York: Touchstone, 1988.

Kuenzli, A. E. (ed.). *The Phenomenological Problem.* New
York: Harper, 1959.

Kushner, Harold S. *When Bad Things Happen to Good
People.* New York: Avon, 1981.

Kushner, Harold S. *When All You've Ever Wanted Isn't
Enough: The Search for a Life that Matters.* New York:
Pocket Books, 1986.

Lane, Harlan. *The Wild Boy of Aveyron.* Cambridge:
Harvard University Press, 1976.

Lankton, Stephen, and Carol Lankton. *The Answer
Within: A Clinical Framework of Ericksonian
Hypnosis.* New York: Brunner/Mazel, 1983.

Larson, Earnie. *Stage II Recovery: Life Beyond Addiction.*
San Francisco: Harper & Row, 1985.

Larson, Earnie. *Old Patterns, New Truths: Beyond the
Adult Child Syndrome* (workbook). San Francisco:
Harper & Row, 1988.

LeDoux, Joseph. "Emotion Circuits in the Brain." *Annual
Review of Neuroscience* 23 (2000): 155–184.

Larsen, Earnie, and Carol Larson Hagarty. *Days of
Healing, Days of Joy: Meditations for Adult Children.*
New York: Harper & Row, 1987.

Leonard, Linda Schierse. *On the Way to the Wedding:
Transferring the Love Relationship.* Boston:
Lord, 1986.

Lerner, Rokelle. *Daily Affirmations.* Pompano Beach, FL:
Health Communications, 1985.

Lerner, Harriet. *The Dance of Anger: A Woman's Guide to
Changing the Patterns of Intimate Relationships.* New
York: Harper & Row, 1986.

Lerner, Harriet. *The Dance of Intimacy: A Woman's Guide to Courageous Acts of Change in Key Relationships.* New York: Harper & Row, 1989.

Leshan, L. *How to Meditate: A Guide to Self-Discovery.* New York: Bantam, 1984.

Lew, Mike. *Victims No Longer: Men Recovering from Incest.* New York: Nevraumont, 1988.

Lidell, Lucinda. *The Book of Massage: The Complete Step-By-Step Guide to Eastern and Western Techniques.* New York: Simon & Schuster, 1984.

Lindberg, Anne Morrow. *Gift from the Sea.* New York: Pantheon, 1975.

Lindquist, M. *Holding Back: Why We Hide the Truth about Ourselves.* New York: Harper & Row. 1988.

Lofland, J. *Analyzing Social Settings.* Belmont, CA: Wadsworth, 1971.

Luke, Catherine Ann. *Linking Up: How the People in Your Life are Road Signs to Self-Discovery.* West Chester, PA: Whitford, 1988.

MacClean, Charles. *The Wolf Children.* New York: Hill and Wang, 1977.

Marlow, Mary Elizabeth. *Handbook of the Emerging Woman: A Manual for Unleashing the Unlimited Power of the Feminine Spirit.* Norfolk, VA: Whitford, 1988.

Maslow, Abraham. *Toward a Psychology of Being.* New York: Van Nostrand, 1968.

Maslow, Abraham. *Motivation and Personality.* New York: Harper & Row, 1970.

Maslow, Abraham. *Farther Reaches of Human Nature.* New York: Viking, 1971.

May, Rollo. *Man's Search for Himself: Finding a Center of Strength within Ourselves to Face and Conquer the Insecurities of this Troubled Age.* New York: New America, 1953.

May, Rollo. *Psychology of the Human Dilemma.* New York: Norton, 1967.

May, Rollo. *Love and Will.* New York: Laurel-Dell, 1969.

May, Rollo. *Power and Innocence: The Search for the Sources of Violence.* New York: Norton, 1972.

May, Rollo. *The Meaning of Anxiety.* New York: Norton, 1977.

Mayo Clinic. *Child Abuse: How Does It Cause Borderline Personality Disorder.* Rochester, MN: Mayo Clinic Foundation Education and Research, 2005.

McConnell, Patty. *Adult Children of Alcoholics: A Workbook for Healing.* New York: Harper & Row, 1986.

McCourt, Frank. *Angela's Ashes.* New York: Scribner, 1996.

McCourt, Frank. *Angela's Ashes: A Memoir.* New York: Touchstone, 1996.

McGinnes, Kathleen, and James McGinnes. *Parenting for Peace and Justice.* New York: Orbis, 1983.

Mellody, Pia. *Facing Co-Dependency.* San Francisco: Harper & Row, 1989.

Mellody, Pia, and Andrea Wells. *Breaking Free: A Recovery Workbook of Facing Co-Dependency.* San Francisco: Harper & Row, 1989.

Middleton-Moz, Jane. *Children of Trauma: Rediscovering the Discarded Self.* Deerfield Beach, FL: Health Communications, 1989.

Miller, Alice. *The Drama of the Gifted Child.* New York: Basic Books, 1981.

Miller, Alice. *For Your Own Good.* New York: Farrar, Straus, & Giroux, 1984.

Miller, Alice. *Pictures of Childhood.* Toronto: Collins, 1986.

Miller, Alice. *Thou Shalt Not Be Aware: Society's Betrayal of the Child.* New York: New American, 1986.

Millonan, Dan. *Way of the Peaceful Warrior.* Tibieron, CA: Kramer, 1980.

Misiak, H., and V. Sexton. *Phenomenological, Existential, and Humanistic Psychologies: An Historical Survey.* New York: Grune & Stratton, 1973.

Morris, V. C. *Existentialism in Education.* New York: Harper & Row, 1966.

Moustakas, Clark E. *Psychotherapy with Children: The Living Relationship.* New York: Ballantine, 1954.

Moustakas, Clark E. *The Self: Exploration in Personal Growth.* New York: Harper & Row, 1956.

Moustakas, Clark E. *The Child's Discovery of Himself.* New York: Ballantine, 1966.

Moustakas, Clark E. *Creativity and Conformity.* New York: Van Nostrand, 1967.

Moustakas, Clark E. *Personal Growth: The Struggle for Identity and Human Values.* Cambridge, MA: Doyle, 1969.

Moustakas, Clark E. *Loneliness and Love.* Englewood Cliffs, NJ: Prentice-Hall, 1972.

Moustakas, Clark E. *Finding Yourself, Finding Others.* Englewood Cliffs, NJ: Prentice-Hall, 1974.

Moustakas, Clark E. *Individuality and Encounter: A Brief Journey into Loneliness and Sensitivity Groups.* Cambridge, MA: Doyle, 1974.

Moustakas, Clark E. *The Touch of Loneliness.* Englewood Cliffs, NJ: Prentice-Hall, 1975.

Moustakas, Clark E. *Who Will Listen?* New York: Ballantine, 1975.

Moustakas, Clark E. *Creative Life.* New York: Reinhold, 1977.

Moustakas, Clark E. *Turning Points.* Englewood Cliffs, NJ: Prentice-Hall, 1977.

Moustakas, Clark E. *Loneliness.* Englewood Cliffs, NJ: Prentice-Hall, 1981.

Moustakas, Clark E. *Rhythms, Rituals and Relationships.* Detroit: Harlow, 1981.

Moustakas, Clark E., and Cereta Perry. *Learning to be Free.* Englewood Cliffs, NJ: Prentice-Hall, 1973.

National Clearing House on Child Abuse and Neglect Information. *In Focus: Understanding the Effects of Maltreatment on Early Brain Development.* Washington, D.C.: National Clearing House, 2001.

Newman, M., and Berkowitz, B. *How to Be Your Own Best Friend.* New York: Ballantine, 1987.

Norwood, Robin. *Women Who Love Too Much: When You Keep Wishing and Hoping He'll Change.* New York: Tarcher, 1985.

O'Gorman, P., and P. Oliver-Diaz. *Breaking the Cycle of Addiction: A Parent's Guide to Raising Healthy Kids.* Pompano Beach, FL: Health Communications, 1987.

Oliver-Diaz, Phillip, and Patricia A. O'Gorman. *Twelve Steps to Self-Parenting: For Adult Children of Alcoholics.* Deerfield Beach, FL: Health Communications, 1988.

Otto, H., and J. Mann. *Ways of Growth.* New York: Grossman, 1968.

Paul, Jordon, and Margaret Paul. *Free to Love.* Los Angeles: Evolving, 1983.

Paul, Jordon, and Margaret. *Do I Have to Give Up Me to Be Loved by You?* Minneapolis, MN: CompCare, 1984.

Paul, Jordon, and Margaret. *If You Really Loved Me.* Minneapolis, MN: CompCare, 1987.

Paul, Jordon, and Margaret. *From Conflict to Caring.* Minneapolis, MN: CompCare, 1988.

Paulus, Trina. *Hope for the Flowers.* New York: Newman, 1972.

Peck, M. Scott. *The Road Less Traveled.* New York: Simon & Schuster, 1978.

Peck, M. Scott. *People of the Lie: The Hope for Healing Human Evil.* New York: Simon & Schuster, 1983.

Peele, Stanton. *Love and Addiction.* New York: Taplinger, 1975.

Peele, Stanton, and Archie Brodsky. *Love and Addiction.* New York: New American, 1976.

Perls, Fredrick S. *Gestalt Therapy Verbatim.* New York: Bantam, 1969.

Perry, Bruce, Duane Runyan, and Carrie Sturges. *How Abuse and Neglect in Childhood Impact Social and*

Emotional Development. Child Trauma Academy, Parent and Caregiver Education Series l(5) (1998):1–11.

Phillips, L. *Human Adaptation and Its Failures.* New York: Academic Press, 1968.

Pietsch, William V. *Human Be-Ing: How to Have a Creative Relationship Instead of a Power Struggle.* New York: Signet, 1974.

Pogrebin, Letty Cottin. *Growing Up Free: Raising Your Child in the 1980s.* New York: Bantam, 1980.

Polansky, Norman. *Damaged Parents: An Anatomy of Child Neglect.* Chicago: University of Chicago Press, 1981.

Polanyi, M. *Personal Knowledge.* Chicago: University of Chicago Press, 1958.

Polanyi, M. *Science, Faith, and Society.* Chicago: University of Chicago Press, 1964.

Powell, John. *Why Am I Afraid to Tell You Who I Am? Insight into Personal Growth.* Chicago: Argus, 1969.

Powell, John. *Why Am I Afraid to Love?* Valencia, CA: Taber, 1972.

Powell, John. *The Secret of Staying in Love.* Valencia, CA: Taber, 1974.

Powell, John. *Fully Human and Fully Alive: A New Life through a New Vision.* Valencia, CA: Taber, 1976.

Powell, John. *Unconditional Love: Love Without Limits.* Valencia, CA: Taber, 1978.

Powell, John. *Will the Real Me Please Stand Up?* Valencia, CA: Taber, 1985.

Powell, John. *Happiness Is an Inside Job.* Valencia, CA: Taber, 1989.

Prather, Hugh. *Notes to Myself: My Struggle to Become a Person.* Moab, UT: Real People, 1970.

Privette, G. "Transcendent Functioning: The Use of Potential." In H. Otto and J. Mann (eds.), *Ways of Growth.* New York: Grossman, 1968.

Provence, S. "Some Relationships between Activity and Vulnerability in the Early Years." In E. J.

318 If Marie Did It, So Can I!

Anthony (ed.), *The Child and His Family.* New York: Wiley, 1974.

Rainier, T. *The New Diary: How to Use a Journal for Self-Guidance Expanded Creativity.* Los Angeles: Tarcher, 1979.

Rank, O. *Will Therapy and Truth and Reality.* New York: Knopf, 1950.

Ray, Sandra. *Loving Relationships.* Berkeley, CA: Celestial, 1980.

Robin, Lillian. *Intimate Strangers: Men and Women Together.* New York: Harper & Row, 1983.

Rogers, Carl R. *On Becoming a Person: A Therapist's View of Psychotherapy.* Boston: Houghton Mifflin, 1961.

Rogers, Carl. R. "Toward a Science of the Person." *Journal of Humanistic Psychology* Fall (1963):72–92.

Rogers, Carl R. "Some Thoughts Regarding the Current Philosophy of the Behavioral Science." *Journal of Humanistic Psychology* 5 (1965):182–194.

Rogers, C., and W. R. Coulson. *Man and the Science of Man.* Columbus: Merrill, 1968.

Rogers, John, and Pete McWilliams. *You Can't Afford the Luxury of a Negative Thought.* Los Angeles: Prelude, 1988.

Rosellini, Gayle, and Mark Worden. *Of Course You're Angry.* San Francisco: Harper & Row, 1986.

Rosellini, Gayle, and Mark Worden. *Here Comes the Sun: Dealing with Depression.* San Francisco: Harper & Row, 1988.

Rothman, Esther. *The Angel inside Went Sour.* New York: Bantam, 1970.

Rubin, Theodore I. *The Angry Book.* New York: Macmillan, 1969.

Rubin, Theodore I. *Reconciliations: Inner Peace in an Age of Anxiety.* New York: The Viking Press, 1980.

Rush, Florence. *The Best Kept Secret: Sexual Abuse of Children.* Englewood Cliffs, NJ: Prentice, 1980.

Russianoff, Penelope. *Why Do I Think I Am Nothing without a Man?* New York: Bantam, 1982.

Rutter, M. "Sex Differences in Children's Responses to Family Stress." In E. J. Anthony and C. Koupernik (eds.), *The Child and His Family* (Vol. 1). New York: Wiley, 1970.

Rutter, M. "Protective Factors in Children's Responses to Stress and Disadvantage." In M. W. Kent and J. E. Rolf (eds.), *The Primary Prevention of Psychopathology, Vol. 3: Promoting Social Competence and Coping with Children.* New Hampshire: University Press of New England, 1979.

Sanford, John A. *The Invisible Partners: How the Male and Female in Each of Us Affect Our Relationship.* New York: Paulist, 1980.

Sanford, Linda Tschirhart, and Mary Ellen Donovan. *Women and Self-Esteem: Understanding and Improving the Way We Think and Feel about Ourselves.* New York: Penguin, 1986.

Sarton, May. *Recovering.* New York: Norton, 1980.

Sartre, Jean-Paul. *Existentialism and Human Emotions.* New York: Philosophical Library, 1957.

Satir, Virginia. *People Making.* Palo Alto, CA: Science and Behavior, 1972.

Satir, Virginia. *Your Many Faces.* New Orleans: Celestial, 1978.

Satir, Virginia. *Conjoint Family Therapy: Your Many Faces.* Palo Alto, CA: Science and Behavior, 1982.

Satir, Virginia. *Meditations and Inspirations.* New Orleans: Celestial, 1985.

Scarf, Maggie. *Unfinished Business: Pressure Points in the Lives of Women.* New York: Ballantine, 1980.

Schaef, Anne Wilson. *Co-Dependence: Misunderstood–Mistreated.* San Francisco: Harper & Row, 1986.

Schaef, Anne Wilson. *Women's Reality: An Emerging Female System in a White Male Society.* San Francisco: Harper & Row, 1986.

Schaef, Anne Wilson. *When Society Becomes an Addict.* San Francisco: Harper & Row, 1987.

Schaef, Anne Wilson. *Escape from Intimacy: Untangling the "Love" Addiction: Sex, Romance, Relationships.* New York: Harper & Row, 1989.

Schaef, Anne Wilson, and Diane Fassel. *The Addictive Organization.* San Francisco: Harper & Row, 1988.

Schaeffer, Brenda. *Is It Love or Is It Addiction: Falling into Healthy Love.* New York: Harper & Row, 1987.

Schmitt, R. "Husserl's Transcendental Phenomenological Reduction." In J. J. Kockleknabd (ed.), *Phenomenology: The Philosophy of Edmund Husserl.* New York: Anchor, 1967.

Schreibner, Flora Rheta. *Sybil.* New York: Warren, 1974.

Schuller, Robert. *Be Happy: You Are Loved.* Nashville: Nelson, 1986.

Schwartz, S. R. *Visualization: Breaking through the Illusion of Problems.* New York: Riverrun, 1985.

Siebert, Al. *The Resiliency Advantage: Master Change, Thrive Under Pressure, and Bounce Back from Setbacks.* San Francisco: Berrett-Koehler Publishers, 2005.

Siegel, Bernie S. *Love, Medicine, and Miracles.* New York: Harper & Row, 1986.

Simon S. B., L. W. Howe, and H. Kirschenbaum. *Values Clarification: A Handbook of Practical Strategies for Teachers and Students.* New York: Hart, 1972.

Simonton, Carl O., Stephanie Mathews-Simonton, and James L. Creighton. *Getting Well Again: A Step-by-Step, Self-Help Guide to Overcoming Cancer for Patients and Their Families.* New York: Bantam, 1978.

Simos, Bertha. *A Time to Grieve.* New York: Family Service, 1976.

Sinetar, Marsha. *Elegant Choices, Healing Choices: Finding Grace and Wholeness in Everything We Do.* New York: Paulist, 1988.

Smith, Ann W. *Grandchildren of Alcoholics: Another Generation of Co-Dependency.* Deerfield Beach, FL: Health Communications, 1988.

Smith, Manuel J. *When I Say No I Feel Guilty.* New York: Bantam, 1975.

Spiegelberg, H. (ed.). *The Phenomenological Movement* (Vol. 2). The Hague: Martinus Nijhoff, 1965.

Steiner, Claude M. *Games Alcoholics Play: The Analysis of Life Scripts.* New York: Grove Press, 1971.

Steiner, Claude M. *What Do You Say after You Say Hello?* New York: Grove Press, 1972.

Steiner, Claude M. *Scripts People Live.* New York: Grove Press, 1974.

Steiner, Claude M. *Healing Alcoholism.* New York: Grove, 1979.

Stephanie, E. *Shame Faced.* Center City, MN: Hazelden Educational Series; Hazelden Educational Material, 1986.

Stevens, J. *Awareness.* Moab, UT: Bantam, 1971.

Stone, H. and Winkleman, S. *Embracing Ourselves.* San Rafael, CA: New World, 1989.

Strasser, S. *Phenomenology and the Human Sciences.* Atlantic Highlands, NJ: Humanistic Press, 1963.

Sturges, J. S. "Children's Reactions to Mental Illness in the Family." *Social Casework* 59(9) (1978):530–536.

Sutich, A. J., and M. A. Vich (eds.). *Readings in Humanistic Psychology.* New York: Free Press, 1969.

Thoele, Sue Patton. *The Courage to Be Yourself: A Woman's Guide to Growing beyond Emotional Dependence.* Nevada City: Pyramid, 1988.

Timmerman, Nancy G. *Step One for Family and Friends.* Center City, MN: Hazelden Educational Series; Hazelden Educational Materials, 1985.

Timmerman, Nancy G. *Step Two for Family and Friends.* Center City, MN: Hazelden Educational Series; Hazelden Educational Materials, 1985.

Vale Allen, Charlotte. *Daddy's Girl.* New York: Berkley, 1980.

VanKaam, K. *Existential Foundations of Psychology.*
    Garden City, NY: Doubleday, 1969.

VanKaam, K., and T. Wahl. *A Short History of
    Existentialism.* New York: Philosophic Library, 1949.

Viorst, Judith. *Necessary Losses.* New York: Fawcett, 1986.

Vitale, Barbara Meisten. *Free Flight: Celebrating Your
    Right Brain.* Rolling Hills, CA: Jalman, 1986.

Warch, William. *How to Use Your Twelve Gifts from God.*
    Marina del Ray, CA: DeVorss, 1976.

Wegscheider-Cruse, Sharon. *Another Chance: Hope and
    Health for the Alcoholic Family.* Palo Alto, CA: Science
    & Behavior, 1981.

Wegscheider-Cruse, Sharon. *Choicemaking: For Co-
    Dependents, Adult Children, and Spirituality Seekers.*
    Pompano Beach, FL: Health Communications, 1985.

Wegscheider-Cruse, Sharon. *Learning to Love Yourself.*
    Pompano Beach, FL: Health Communications, 1987.

White Eagle. *The Quiet Mind.* Hampshire, England:
    White Eagle Trust, 1972.

Whitfield, Charles. *Healing the Child Within.* Deerfield
    Beach, FL: Health Communications, 1987.

Whitfield, Charles. *Letting Go of Shame.* Deerfield Beach,
    FL: Health Communications, 1987.

Wholey, Dennis. *The Courage to Change.* Boston:
    Houghton Mifflin, 1984.

Wilde, Stuart. *Life Was Never Meant to Be a Struggle.*
    Taos, NM: White Dove, 1987.

Williams, Margery. *The Velveteen Rabbit.* New York:
    Doubleday, 1975.

Woititz, Janet. *Marriage on the Rocks.* Pompano Beach,
    FL: Health Communications, 1979.

Woititz, Janet. *Adult Children of Alcoholics.* Hollywood,
    FL: Health Communications, 1983.

Woititz, Janet. *Struggle for Intimacy.* Pompano Beach, FL:
    Health Communications, 1985.

Wood, Wendy, and Leslie Hutton. *Triumph over Darkness: Understanding and Healing the Trauma of Childhood Sexual Abuse.* Hillsboro, OR: Beyond Words, 1989.

York, Phillis, David York, and Ted Wachtel. *Toughlove.* Garden City, NY: Doubleday, 1982.

Ziglar, Zig. *Raising Positive Kids in a Negative World.* New York: Ballantine, 1989.

LIVING FARM PRESS
If Marie Did It, So Can I!
How to Survive, Heal and Transcend Abuse and Neglect
Donna F. LaMMar, PhD
(231) 924-2401
www.livingfarm.org

QUICK ORDER FORM

Fax Orders: 231-924-2407

Telephone Orders: Call 231-924-2401. Have your credit card ready.

E-mail Orders: books@livingfarm.org

Postal Orders: The Farm: Where Living Things Grow, Inc., Orders, Donna LaMar, P.O. Box 67, Fremont, MI 49412

Please send the following books, disks or reports.

_____

_____

_____

Please send me more free information on:
- The Farm and eco-psychology youth and family programs
- Consulting
- Speaking, workshops, and seminars
- Newsletter

Name: _____

Address: _____

City: _____ **State** _____ **Zip** _____

Telephone: _____

E-mail: _____

Sales Tax: Please add 6.0% for products shipped to a Michigan address.

Shipping and Handling: Call for rates or check our Website at www.livingfarm.org. There is a discount for two or more books ordered.

Thank you for your order

LIVING FARM PRESS
If Marie Did It, So Can I!
How to Survive, Heal and Transcend Abuse and Neglect
Donna F. LaMMar, PhD
(231) 924-2401
www.livingfarm.org

QUICK ORDER FORM

Fax Orders: 231-924-2407

Telephone Orders: Call 231-924-2401. Have your credit card ready.

E-mail Orders: books@livingfarm.org

Postal Orders: The Farm: Where Living Things Grow, Inc., Orders, Donna LaMar, P.O. Box 67, Fremont, MI 49412

Please send the following books, disks or reports.

_____

_____

_____

Please send me more free information on:
  • The Farm and eco-psychology youth and family programs
  • Consulting
  • Speaking, workshops, and seminars
  • Newsletter

Name: _____

Address: _____

City: _____ **State** _____ **Zip** _____

Telephone: _____

E-mail: _____

Sales Tax: Please add 6.0% for products shipped to a Michigan address.

Shipping and Handling: Call for rates or check our Website at www.livingfarm.org. There is a discount for two or more books ordered.

Thank you for your order

LIVING FARM PRESS
If Marie Did It, So Can I!
How to Survive, Heal and Transcend Abuse and Neglect
Donna F. LaMMar, PhD
(231) 924-2401
www.livingfarm.org

QUICK ORDER FORM

Fax Orders: 231-924-2407

Telephone Orders: Call 231-924-2401. Have your credit card ready.

E-mail Orders: books@livingfarm.org

Postal Orders: The Farm: Where Living Things Grow, Inc., Orders, Donna LaMar, P.O. Box 67, Fremont, MI 49412

Please send the following books, disks or reports.

_____

_____

_____

Please send me more free information on:
- The Farm and eco-psychology youth and family programs
- Consulting
- Speaking, workshops, and seminars
- Newsletter

Name: _____

Address: _____

City: _____ **State** _____ **Zip** _____

Telephone: _____

E-mail: _____

Sales Tax: Please add 6.0% for products shipped to a Michigan address.

Shipping and Handling: Call for rates or check our Website at www.livingfarm.org. There is a discount for two or more books ordered.

Thank you for your order

Index

Death, childhood loneliness as,
170-171
grieving of, 147-148
threat of, and suicidal
feelings, 166
See also Transcenders' stories,
Marie
Decisions, will and, 92-93, 178
See also Turning point
Denial, of dysfunctional problems, 21
grieving process and,
168-169
Discovery, in reclamation
process, 208-210
self–discovery, 98–99, 186
Distancing, as survival technique, 101-102
Dysfunctional behavior, development of, 18,
22, 109
See also False self
Dysfunctional days, 225-226
Dysfunctional family, 19-30
and authenticity, 118
defined, 2-5
family system characteristics,
2-3, 22-29, 140
interactional characteristics of,
19-22
power imbalance and, 29
roles within, 24, 26-28, 29-30,
71-73
understanding of, 139-140,
150-151, 198, 202-203,
226-227
See also Parents; Transcenders'
stories

E
Eco-psychology groups, 277
Educational therapy, 276
Emotional chaos. *See* Transcen-
ders' stories, Paul

Emotional games. *See* Transcenders' stories, Chris
Emotions. *See* Feelings
Energy, behavior changes and,
148, 152-153, 220
and non-growth decision,
118-119
See also Tiredness
Environmental resources, as survival techniques, 62-64
Escape. *See* Daydreaming; Denial; Environmental re-
sources; Fantasy; Getting
out; Play; Sanctuary
Existential loneliness, definition, 232
Experiences. *See* Life experience

F
Failure, feelings of, 169-170
False self, definition and creation
of, 112-113, 191-193
reclamation and, 222
Family, as environmental resource, 63
pretend family, story, 61
Family system, definition and dy-
namics of, 3
of dysfunctional family, 2-5,
22-30
Family therapy, 275
Family transcendence, 64–65
Fantasy, as a survival technique,
57-58, 60-62, 84
and dysfunctional family secrets, 27-28
Fear, description and role of,
166-167, 192-193, 206-207
healthy fear, 171-172
and reclamation process,
192-193
relaxing into fear, 204
Feedback and sharing, in dysfunctional family, 20

grieving and reclaiming
phases, 125-127
layers within, 109, 114,
122-125
leaving home, 127-132
resistance to, 113-114, 117-119
responsibility for, 119-120
and spirituality, 238-239
stories, 120-122
transition period, 132-133,
203-206
See also Therapy

I
Identity. *See* Authentic self; Self
Inner child, 188
Inner-personal resources, 54-60
Inpatient therapy, 273-274
Integrity, 237-238
Interactional systems, within
families, 19-23
Internal frame of reference,
95-100
choices and change, 99-100
and constancies, 96-97
definition and shift in, 33,
50-51
turning-point decision and,
48-51, 97-98
Interpersonal relationships
styles, 68-71
Intervention, from others, 65-66,
73-74
Into my shell, as coping skill,
57-58
Intuition, as inner resource,
56-57
Isolation, within dysfunctional
family, 20-21, 26-27

J
Jobs. *See* Workplace
Joy, grieving process and,
177-178

L
LaMar, Donna, biography, xix-xx
personal introduction to transcending, xxi-xxiii
spirituality, personal stories,
229-230, 231-232
as therapist, xxv, 231
Layers, definition, 205
in grieving process, 114,
178-179
reclamation and, 122-125
Learning, definition, 99, 112
as discovery and growth,
208-210
transfer of learning, 97
Leaving home, 48-49, 127-132
Leftovers, definition, xx
therapy and, 126, 133-134
Life experiences, control of, 98,
100-102
definition, 1-2
internal frame of reference
and, 95-96
processes of, 109
Limits. *See* Boundaries
Living Farm Press, order forms,
324-326
Loneliness, dysfunctional family
and, 20-21, 32-33
grieving process and, 170
stories of, 33-39
and turning point decision,
31-32
Love, as choice, 260-261
as directive in life, 1, 239,
255-256
as goal of transcendence, 106,
141-142
in reclamation process, 212

M
Male domination in dysfunctional
family. *See* Transcenders'
stories, Tiffany

Memories, memory block of
childhood abuse, 93-94, 168
prenatal and felt senses, 43,
171, 194
Milieu therapy, 274
Moods, and countermoods, 103
definition, 102-103
Mother, child's role as, 24, 26,
72-73
See also Transcenders' stories,
Marie; Transcenders' sto-
ries, Steve
Multiple personalities, as protection layer, 123
Music, 82, 86

N

Nature, eco-psychology, 277
use in transcending, 62-64, 68
See also The Farm: Where Liv-
ing Things Grow
Needs, reclamation and, 216-218
unmet needs, 22, 25-26
Neglect. *See* Abuse and neglect;
Transcenders' stories, Steve;
Transcenders' stories, Tim
Neurosis, definition, 152
Nurturance, nurturing to be
liked, 73
and survival, 1-2, 6, 53-54, 105
as therapy, 141-142

O

Observing, as transcending skill,
59
Old patterns, and dysfunctional
days, 225-226
in grieving and healing
process, 104, 111, 152, 162
purpose of, 148
reexamination of, 140, 186-187
and struggle, 112-113
workplace and, 209, 223
See also Tapes

Organizations, as support, 74-75
Original package, 1
See Authentic self
Others, and advice on therapy, 145
importance of, 73-74
outside of family, 74-78
relating style and, 68-71
stories, 66-67
as transference, in Therapy, 290
and transfer of dysfunctional
family roles, 210, 223
within the family, 76, 78-81,
216-218
Outpatient therapy, 273-274
Overachiever. *See* Transcenders'
stories, Paul

P

Pain and suffering, avoidance
of, 147
as catalyst for change, 32-33,
39, 139, 152
importance of pain, 145-146, 149
suffering vs. struggle, 113
turning point and, 41
Parenting, healthy, 5
Parents, acknowledged short-
comings of, 150-151, 165,
202-203, 226-227
confronting, 149, 175
later friendships with, stories,
149, 251
Past revisited, 112, 171,
186-188, 199
Patterns, codependency patterns, 207
See also Generational learning;
Old patterns
Peer support group therapy, 277
Perfectionism, definition, 4, 21
reclamation and, 212-214
See also Transcenders' stories,
Paul; Transcenders' sto-
ries, Tiffany

Suicide, thoughts of, 123,
165-167, 291
Support networks, failure in dys-
functional families, 25-26
reclamation and, 209-212
See also Others
Survival skills. *See* Transcen-
dence techniques
Survive, the decision to survive.
See Turning point decision
Survivors, as dysfunctional
people, 18, 22
See also Transcenders

T
Tapes, definition, 131, 198
examples of, 131, 159, 165,
167, 198
and flashbacks, 165, 167-168
transcender's response to-
wards, 196
See also Therapy, taped therapy sessions
Teachers, 70-71, 76
Tears, importance of, 149
therapy and, 139
The Farm: Where Living Things
Grow, vi, xix-xx, 60, 63
Therapists, children, advice for
working with, 259
emergencies and, 290-291
finding and effectiveness
of, 265-266, 269-270,
286-288
and mistakes, 221-222
relationship and trust with,
136-137
responsibilities of transcenders and, 160-161, 281
role of, 288-292
therapy orientations and therapeutic styles, 285
and transference, 290
types of therapists, 284, 288

Therapy, 136-144, 265-292
benefits of, 268-269
childhood and family, understanding of, 93, 137-140
completion of, 144-145
confidentiality and, 281
definition of psychotherapy,
136, 265, 267-268
and doubt, 203-204
fear and the grieving process,
138, 171-173
fees and payments, 283-285
modalities types, 273-278
need for, 270-273
other resources, 126, 278
seeking help, 132-134
starting therapy, 278-281
stories, 134-136
taped sessions, 159
teaching transcendence,
99-100
time away and return to, 139,
142-144
and transition period, 136,
203-204
tune-ups, 144
and what not allowed,
281-283
See also Therapists
Tiredness, in reclamation
process, 214-216
Torture *See* Transcenders' stories, Marie
Transcendence, helping others,
119, 257-261
Transcendence process, definition of transcending, xxiii,
xxv, 6, 104
survival and, 53-54
teaching of, 99-100, 237
transcending of self, 104-107
transcending the family, 64-65
See Transcendence techniques;
Transcenders' stories